Saul Kripke

Key Contemporary Thinkers
Published:

Saul Kripke
Puzzles and Mysteries

John P. Burgess

polity

First published in 2013 by Polity Press

Polity Press
65 Bridge Street
Cambridge CB2 1UR, UK

Polity Press
350 Main Street
Malden, MA 02148, USA

ISBN-13: 978-0-7456-5284-9 (hardback)
ISBN-13: 978-0-7456-5285-6 (paperback)

A catalogue record for this book is available from the British Library.

Typeset in 10.5 on 12 pt Palatino
by Toppan Best-set Premedia Limited
Printed and bound in Great Britain by the MPG Books Group

The publisher has used its best endeavors to ensure that the URLs for external websites referred to in this book are correct and active at the time of going to press. However, the publisher has no responsibility for the websites and can make no guarantee that a site will remain live or that the content is or will remain appropriate.

Every effort has been made to trace all copyright holders, but if any have been inadvertently overlooked the publisher will be pleased to include any necessary credits in any subsequent reprint or edition.

For further information on Polity, visit our website: www.politybooks.com

Contents

Preface

Saul Kripke has been for a half-century and more a major influence in philosophy and allied fields, despite the fact that only a fraction of his work has ever seen print. Recently the pace of publication has picked up a bit, and commentaries based on authorized access to parts of the extensive archives of unpublished Kripkeana have also begun to appear. I have nevertheless thought it best, in an introductory survey, to concentrate on a handful of works, beginning with his major classic *Naming and Necessity* and his minor classic 'A Puzzle about Belief,' that have been before the public for decades, and have by now already long proved immensely influential. Coverage is pretty strictly confined to work in philosophy proper as contrasted with history of philosophy. The famous or notorious *Wittgenstein on Rules and Private Language* is therefore examined only for what it tells us about Kripke's own views, to the exclusion of all controversial issues of Wittgenstein exegesis. I take into account lesser works, from the long-published 'Speaker's Reference and Semantic Reference' to the just recently released 'Vacuous Names and Fictional Entities,' to the extent that they in one way or another illuminate or amplify the views developed in the Kripke's best-known philosophical works.

Kripke has been as important a contributor to logic as to philosophy, or very nearly so. Moreover, his influence in fields outside philosophy, notably theoretical computer science and linguistics, has to a considerable degree been through his work in logic. An account of Kripke's thought omitting his technical contributions to logic can give only a partial indication of why he ranks as high as he does among key contemporary thinkers. But a volume in the present series is simply not the appropriate place for a survey of Kripke's technical papers. I do discuss – not in the body of the text, but in two appendices, the only places in the book where logical symbols appear – the two items among Kripke's logical works that are most directly relevant to philosophy, his 'Semantical Considerations on Modal Logic' and his 'Outline of a Theory of Truth.' Those papers are themselves only semitechnical, and my account is semipopular.

At the beginning of each chapter I give a list of the works of Kripke most relevant thereto; ideally these should be read immediately after the chapter itself. Unpublished works of Kripke, to which most readers would have no access, are not discussed in detail, but only mentioned in notes at points where they would be relevant, with citations of publications where one can read second-hand accounts by reliable commentators. Though it is ideally to be read together with Kripke's works, this book is not a crib going through those works section by section. Kripke does not really need that kind of commentary, since his style is clear, and difficulties for the reader are very much more likely to lie in seeing the woods as a whole than in seeing the trees one by one. That is why I have adopted an expository procedure more or less the reverse of Kripke's own. Kripke characteristically moves back and forth among several subjects, enlarging our understanding of a given issue a bit more each time he returns to it, and weaving the different topics together. My approach is to try to separate the strands of argument that Kripke intertwines, expounding one line of thought more or less completely before taking up another.

When it comes to providing context, I have given more of my limited space to the historical background to Kripke's works than to their critical reception. Given the frequency of allusions to his predecessors in Kripke, there is clearly some need for capsule summaries of the views of some of the earlier major philosophers he cites, but another kind of background seemed to me even more needful: an account of the climate of opinion on the topics Kripke addresses as it was a half-century or so ago, before Kripke's intervention. Kripke's work has had so much impact that without such background it may be difficult for newcomers to appreciate how very differently the issues struck philosophers before Kripke came on the scene, and hence to appreciate just what Kripke contributed. As to critical responses, there can be no question, in a book of modest size, of attempting to survey the vast secondary literature.

My citations are selective, concentrating on works I believe will enlarge rather than distort the reader's understanding of Kripke's thought. When I discuss criticisms, I generally limit my discussion to those that in my judgment are based on a good understanding of Kripke's views, and point to real gaps or tensions in them. There have been a great many objections based on misreadings, and some of these have unfortunately become rather influential, and I issue explicit warnings against a few of the worst; but only a few. Mostly I proceed in the hope and belief that the most effective way to immunize readers against being misled by misrepresentations of Kripke's work is simply by providing an accurate representation of it.

Acknowledgments

My first debt is, I hardly need say, to Saul Kripke, for providing me with my topic. Since it is well known that he and I were colleagues for many years, I should at once add a disclaimer to the effect that, though we had many discussions on matters of intellectual interest over those years, the topic of discussion was virtually never the interpretation of Kripke's philosophical works. Nor have I sought to involve Kripke in any way in the production of the present volume. So I am in no way his authorized spokesman.

The philosopher who has most influenced my understanding of Kripke's philosophical works has been Scott Soames. He is the commentator and critic most often cited in the pages to follow, and those scattered citations hardly begin to express the extent of my debt. Nonetheless, he had no direct involvement in the present project, and he has no direct responsibility for the views I express.

Two experts on Kripke, Mario Gomez-Torrente and Mark Steiner, were good enough to provide comments on an earlier draft, and I have made use of their information and advice in several places, especially in connection with the tricky issues and contentious questions addressed in the middle chapters of this book. Arudra Burra also carefully reviewed the manuscript, and his comments on matters of presentation, from the perspective of an avowed non-expert – his specialty is philosophy of law, a topic rather far from any Kripke has treated, unless there is some real surprise waiting for the philosophical public among Kripke's unpublished papers – have been most useful, persuading me to undertake any number of revisions of my original organizational plans.

The publisher's external reviewers also provided useful reports, one full of cogent criticisms, and the other of welcome encouragement. The former moved me to revise many details of presentation, the latter confirmed my decision to stick to my chosen overall approach. Susan Beer, Neil de Cort, Emma Hutchinson, and David Winters of Polity were efficient and helpful throughout.

Introduction

Saul Kripke's most celebrated work, *Naming and Necessity*, culminates in a discussion of the mind–body problem, as will the present book. This central issue in modern philosophy goes right back to its origins with René Descartes, who, while not claiming to be able to prove that the mind or soul actually *does* survive death of the body, claimed to be able to prove at least that it possibly *could*. His materialist or physicalist opponents generally deny this possibility, maintaining that a living body, with a functioning brain, is necessary for conscious thought and feeling. When the issue is put this way, it is seen to be not just about mind and body, but also about possibility and necessity. Kripke's greatest contribution to contemporary analytic philosophy is widely held to lie in his clarification of the nature of *modality*, the category to which the notions of possibility and necessity belong.

Above all, Kripke has striven to disentangle the notion of necessity from two other notions with which, over the course of two hundred years or so of philosophizing, it had tended to become conflated: the notions of the a priori, and of analyticity.[1] The notion of the necessary, which contrasts with the contingent, is the notion of *what is and could not have failed to be*; its home is metaphysics or the general theory of being. The notion of the a priori, which contrasts with the a posteriori, is the notion of *what is known or knowable independently of sense-experience*; its home is epistemology or the general theory of knowledge. The notion of the analytic, which contrasts with the synthetic, is the notion of *what is true by virtue of meaning*; its home is semantics or the general theory of meaning. It was Kripke's achievement to convince many of the importance of carefully distinguishing these three notions.

It is not that before Kripke it had been wholly forgotten that the trio are at least conceptually distinct, but rather that the three notions generally tended to be assumed to be *coextensive*, exemplified by exactly the same cases, and accordingly the three labels generally tended to be treated as more or less freely interchangeable. It is not that no one ever mentioned in passing cases where one of these notions might seem to come apart from another, but rather that no one systematically explored the gaps between them in a way that made such gaps impossible for subsequent philosophers to ignore. That is what Kripke accomplished in *Naming and Necessity*.

That work was not written as a book. Rather, it consists of an edited transcript of an audiotape of a series of three lectures given at Princeton in January 1970, with the addition of footnotes and a section of addenda for publication in an anthology two years later as Kripke (1972), and of a further preface for republication in less expensive book form as Kripke (1980). Henceforth 'N&N' will refer indifferently to either version. The first lecture introduces the themes that will be developed in the others. Early on, Kripke has some preliminary remarks on the necessary, the a priori, and the analytic. It will be well to begin here also with a preliminary discussion of the three notions, familiarity with which will be presupposed in most subsequent chapters of this book. A preview of what is in those chapters will follow.

Background

The preliminary account of the necessary, the a priori, and the analytic to be presented here will have a different purpose from the preliminary discussion in Kripke. Kripke's main aim is simply to remind his audience that the three notions are at least conceptually distinct, and that one should not just thoughtlessly use the three labels interchangeably. My aim is in large part to convey how high the stakes were when Kripke stepped up to deliver his three-lecture series, by presenting the issue in historical terms, as Kripke does not. This will involve indulging in broad-brush historical writing, of the kind in which virtually every assertion can be no more than a first approximation to some more complicated truth, a genre of writing that Kripke himself avoids.

One way to view the history of the dwindling of the necessary, in the thinking of many philosophers, first to the a priori and then to the analytic, is as a history of two centuries of attempts at demystification. The mystery of modality is how we can have knowledge of it. It is often hard enough to understand how we are able to know what is and what isn't; but how can we, beyond that, know that some but not others of the things there are *had to* have been, or that some but not others of the things there aren't *might* have been? The eventual conflation of necessity with analyticity can be viewed as in large part the result of attempts to solve or resolve or dissolve this mystery. I will briefly trace the relevant history from this point of view through three key eighteenth, nineteenth, and twentieth-century thinkers: Immanuel Kant, Gottlob Frege, and Rudolf Carnap.

Kant, whose Inaugural Dissertation came exactly two centuries before Kripke's lectures, and whose famous *Critique of Pure Reason* followed in the next decade, takes the necessary, the a priori, and the analytic to be distinct classifications. All analytic judgments are known a priori and everything known a priori is necessary, but there are necessities that are not known a priori, and a priori knowledge going beyond analytic judgments: In effect, the necessary properly includes the a priori, which in turn properly includes the analytic. Let me illustrate how these distinctions work for Kant.

The existence of God, a stock example considered a necessary truth by Kant's 'rationalist' predecessors such as Descartes or Leibniz, is still believed to be one by Kant, but for Kant it is supposed to be an example of a necessary truth that is *unknowable*. Kant thought it important for morality – never mind why, for this is not the place to go into Kant's moral philosophy, nor am I the person to do so – that there should be such unknowable truths. He famously wrote, 'I have had to deny knowledge in order to leave room for belief' (Kant 1929, B3). Of course, for necessary truths that are unknowable, there is no mystery about how they are known: They aren't. For Kant, the existence of God is a necessary truth that is not a priori, and not a posteriori, either, for that matter, since the distinction between a priori and a posteriori, or 'pure' and 'empirical,' is for Kant a distinction between two kinds of knowledge.[2]

That seven plus five makes twelve is, by contrast, for Kant an example of a *known* necessity: We know not only that seven plus five is twelve, but also that it couldn't have been anything else. Kant, indeed, counts all of mathematical science, both arithmetical and geometrical, as a body of known necessary truths. Kant observes that experience, our greatest source of knowledge, seems unable to give us knowledge that mathematical truths hold of necessity. He gives the canonical formulation of the mystery of modality in a line that Kripke quotes in the addenda to N&N: 'Experience teaches us that a thing is thus and so, but not that it cannot be otherwise' (Kant 1929, B3). Kant concludes that knowledge of necessity must be pure or a priori, as opposed to empirical or a posteriori, and indeed he virtually identifies the two classifications of known necessities and a priori truths (apart from the purely verbal point that it is our knowledge that is called a priori and what it is knowledge of that is called necessary). So for him the mystery of modality takes the form of the question: How is a priori knowledge possible?

Well, in one special case he thinks the question not so hard to answer. The special case in question is that of knowledge of certain trivial truths of the form 'All As are Bs,' where being a B is simply part of the *concept* of being an A. That is Kant's definition of analyticity. Later philosophers, preferring linguistic-sounding talk to psychological-sounding talk, prefer to put it slightly differently: Being a B is simply part of the *meaning* of being an A. Kant's examples of analytic judgments are notoriously very bad,[3] and it is customary to substitute for them the example 'All bachelors are unmarried.' To know this we need not know anything about objects outside us, but only the content of our own concepts, or the meanings of our own words, and that is why examples like this one are for Kant easy cases. Arithmetic, and Euclidean geometry, and even some principles of Newtonian physics, Kant by contrast supposes to be equally known a priori, but synthetic. So his final formulation of the mystery of modality, excluding the trivial case where he thinks there is no serious problem, is just this: How is synthetic a priori knowledge possible? This is the central question of Kant's theoretical philosophy. Fortunately, for present purposes there is no need to go into his very complicated answer.

Let us instead move forward a century or so to Frege. Frege was the author of the work that founded modern logic, the *Begriffsschrift* or *Concept-Writing*, and was besides the grandfather of the analytic tradition in philosophy, the style of philosophizing that prevails in academic departments of philosophy in the English-speaking world today. Early on in the book he explains in the following words why he will have no symbols for necessity or possibility in his conceptual notation: 'By saying that a proposition is necessary, I give a hint about the grounds for my judgment. But...this does *not affect the conceptual content of the judgment'* (Frege 1967, §4). Thus the classification as necessary or otherwise is for Frege a classification pertaining to how something is known, and in this he is typical of much of later analytic philosophy. By a hundred years after Kant, Kant's supposed unknowable necessities have generally dropped out of the discussion, and the necessary, if not forgotten altogether, as it effectively is by Frege, is identified with what is known or knowable a priori.[4] Frege does still distinguish the a priori from the analytic, since he accepts Kant's claim that geometry is synthetic a priori, but we are at this stage down from three notions to two.

Frege has a new conception of analyticity. For Frege, even in a simple example like 'All bachelors are unmarried' there are two components to be distinguished. Pure formal logic teaches us that all unmarried men are unmarried, while our knowledge of the definition or meaning of 'bachelor' tells us that we may substitute it as a synonym for 'unmarried man.'[5] So for Frege, the analytic is what follows by logic from definitions, or what reduces to logic on substituting synonyms for synonyms. Because his logic is vastly richer than anything available in Kant's day or indeed in the whole previous history of the subject, his concept of analyticity is vastly broader than Kant's. In consequence, he is prepared to reject one of Kant's examples of the synthetic a priori by reclassifying arithmetic, after a searching examination of its foundations and basic laws, as analytic. Fortunately, for present purposes there is no need to go into Frege's very complicated arguments on this point, or the even more complicated revised arguments offered by Bertrand Russell after he found a flaw in Frege's work.

Let us instead move forward a half-century or so to Frege's one-time student Carnap. Carnap was the most influential representative of the logical positivist or logical empiricist school of the nineteen twenties through forties, but his views on issues relevant to the present discussion were shared well beyond that school. For Carnap, as for other positivists, Kant's whole classification *synthetic a priori* has been rejected: Every supposed example has been reclassified either as analytic or else as a posteriori. In particular, in the wake of Frege and Russell, arithmetic is taken to be analytic; while in the wake of Einstein, the question whether the geometry of the physical space in which we live and move is Euclidean or non-Euclidean is agreed to be empirical or a posteriori. So the necessary, having first dwindled to the a priori, now dwindles to the analytic, and we are down from three notions to one.

In Carnap (1947), among other writings going back to the nineteen thirties and with roots even earlier, 'the Leibnizian concept of
necessity' and 'the Kantian concept of analyticity,' as he calls them,
are explicitly assimilated to each other. A common 'rational recon-
struction' or 'explication' is offered for both: in effect, a new analysis of analyticity. With Frege's notion it is really not so very clear
why we should be able to have analytic knowledge. The problem
is not with knowledge of definitions or synonymy or meaning,
which presumably we acquire as we learn our language. The
problem is with knowledge of logic, given that logic has been
vastly expanded. For Carnap, however, our knowledge of logic,
too, is ultimately a matter of knowledge of meaning: of the meanings of the logical particles 'not' and 'and' and 'or' and 'all' and
'some' and so on. Given this linguistic doctrine of logical truth,
analyticity becomes simply 'truth by virtue of meaning.'

And the mystery of modality seems to be solved: We are able to
know, for instance, that seven plus five is *necessarily* twelve, that in
no circumstances could seven plus five turn out to be anything
other than twelve, simply because we recognize that the rules and
conventions of our language, which we have implicitly learned in
learning to speak, *do not allow any circumstances to be described* as
ones in which seven plus five has turned out to be something other
than twelve. While this sort of view, and the identification of necessity with analyticity, is especially explicit and prominent in the
positivist Carnap, it is not limited to Carnap or the positivists, but
is found throughout much of analytic philosophy – down to the
time of Kripke.[6]

Kripke's achievement has been to reverse the whole development I have just roughly sketched, thus reinstating the mystery of
modality, previously erroneously thought to have been dissolved.
(He also offers some hints toward a new solution.) According to
Kripke, the whole line of thought from Kant to Frege to Carnap
went wrong at its very first step. Kant's claim that experience does
not teach us that something could not have been otherwise may be
plausible if what is meant is that sense-experience by itself is not
sufficient to teach us that something is necessary, that some additional a priori element is required. But in classifying knowledge of
necessity as a priori, Kant has in effect assumed experience is never
required, in addition to any a priori element, to teach us that something is necessary. This is definitely a mistake, according to Kripke.
Most philosophers *circa* 1970 found it difficult to conceive of cases
where experience would be required to establish necessity, but

Kripke in N&N presents many plausible examples of such a posteriori necessities.

Kripke also holds that there are, besides a posteriori truths that are necessary, also a priori truths that are contingent. In the end, the only connection among the three notions that Kripke accepts is that whatever is analytic is also a priori and necessary. Thus an a posteriori necessity or an a priori contingency will be synthetic. So will be the disjunction of two unrelated examples of these types, though such a disjunction is both a priori and necessary. And so the analytic is properly contained in the overlap of the a priori and the necessary, giving a Kripkean picture sharply contrasting with the Kantian or Fregean or Carnapian.

Plan

Let me now describe the plan of this book: the topics and texts to be discussed and the order in which they will be taken. N&N consists of three lectures, and three chapters, constituting the first half of this book, will be devoted to it here, interspersed with some discussion of pertinent lesser works of Kripke's.[7] Kripke opens his lectures by saying, 'I hope that some people see some connection between the two topics of my title.' Perhaps some did; surely many did not. That there should turn out to be a connection between the question of the meaning of proper names and the question of the nature of necessity was for many one of the great surprises of the lecture series. Kripke was not, however, the first to see a connection between the seemingly arcane linguistic topic of naming and a resonant philosophical topic like necessity. On the contrary, several of his philosophical predecessors, seeing some such connection or other, had already involved themselves with the linguistic issue. Notable among these predecessors were John Stuart Mill (otherwise best known for his work as political theorist and reformer) and Frege (otherwise best known for his work on the foundations of logic and arithmetic, already alluded to above). Their views on naming Kripke takes as foils to his own.

The first two chapters in this book will both be concerned with what Kripke has to say about Mill, Frege, and naming in the first two lectures of N&N. Rather than dealing with the first lecture in Chapter 1 and the second lecture in Chapter 2, I will deal in Chapter 1 with the parts of both lectures that do *not* involve modality, and in Chapter 2 with the parts of both that *do*. This way of proceeding

involves a deliberate unraveling, in hopes of making logical relationships clearer, of two strands of argument that in Kripke are
tightly intertwined.

The first two lectures taken together offer both Kripke's new
picture of how naming works (with criticism of the older pictures
it seeks to replace), and what arise therefrom, Kripke's first examples of a posteriori necessities. Chapter 3 will take up Kripke's third
lecture, in which he vastly expands the range of examples of a
posteriori necessities. The same chapter will take briefer note of the
addenda to the lectures, in which Kripke offers a hint toward a new
solution to the mystery of how we are able to acquire knowledge
of necessity and possibility, even after recognizing that the route of
reducing the necessary to the a priori and the a priori to the analytic
is closed. It is in these parts of his work that Kripke's most intriguing discussions of the nature of necessity are to be found.

The contents of the second half of this book will be more mixed.
Philosophers in the analytic tradition give a good deal of attention
to what they frankly call 'puzzles' of one sort or another. Generally
there is some deeper purpose, some wider moral to be drawn from
the puzzling example, though it would be idle to pretend that
philosophers only ever engage with puzzles because they have
some deeper purpose clearly in view, and never for the sheer challenge of the puzzle itself. Kripke in particular is a philosopher who
has never hesitated to digress from work on deep mysteries to
work on well-known puzzles, or new ones of his own creation.
Chapter 4 will deal with the best known, most-discussed of Kripke's
puzzles, the 'Puzzle about Belief' from the paper of that title (Kripke
1979).[8] There is indeed a 'deeper purpose and wider moral' connected with this puzzle, for it is connected with certain questions
about naming left hanging in N&N, and so there will be in this
chapter a final discussion of naming.

Returning to more direct confrontation with the issue of the
nature of necessity, at the moment when the mystery of modality
erroneously seemed to have been solved, it appeared that the
source of necessity lay in ourselves, and was traceable back to the
rules of our language. But the notion of 'rule' itself conceals mysteries. It was supposed by many philosophers that the necessity of,
say, the laws of arithmetic could be explained by saying that those
laws simply follow from linguistic rules. But what sort of a fact is
it that they thus follow? Embarrassingly, it would seem to be a
necessary fact, and one the source of whose necessity cannot lie in
ourselves. Kripke's subtle thinking about such elusive problems,

insofar as it available to us in print, takes the form of a commentary, *Wittgenstein on Rules and Private Language* (Kripke 1982), on key sections of Ludwig Wittgenstein's *Philosophical Investigations*. That Kripke should present his own views only in the context of discussion of another thinker is from one point of view rather unfortunate, because in the literature the examination of Kripke's views has all too often been neglected in favor of debates over purely exegetical issues, over whether Kripke has got Wittgenstein right. Chapter 5 offers a summary or outline of Kripke's views on rules that leaves entirely to one side all exegetical questions about Wittgenstein, a summary or outline that it is hoped will help make it clearer that Kripke's views on this topic are by no means as disconnected from his views on necessity and related issues as they may at first appear.

Chapter 6 takes up Kripke's contributions to the philosophy of mind, his criticisms of the currently fashionable views known as physicalism and functionalism, criticisms based on considerations developed in part in the course of his study of naming and necessity and in part in the course of his reading of Wittgenstein. Kripke has so far published only fragments of his work on these topics: a compressed, rushed discussion of physicalism at the very end of N&N, a single long footnote on functionalism in the Wittgenstein book that amounts to a little more than one full page of small type, and a remark or two in some very recently published work. What Kripke has to say about the mystery of the relation of mind and body is suggestive, but it cannot become compelling without the release of more currently unpublished material; and so the discussion of Kripke's work in philosophy ends with hopes for the future, but a question mark for the present. Two optional appendices on Kripke's work in logic then follow.

Appendix A will offer a semipopular account of the nature of Kripke's technical work on modal logic. If by the time Kripke stepped down after delivering the third of his Princeton lectures on naming and necessity he had become a very prominent figure indeed in analytic metaphysics and epistemology, even before he stepped up to deliver the first lecture he was already a very prominent figure in logic. He was famous most of all, and from well before he presented any philosophical work on the substantive nature of modality, for his technical work on the formal logic of modality. It is this early work that repopularized Leibniz's old talk, never perhaps entirely forgotten, but no longer very often echoed before Kripke, of necessity as 'truth in all possible worlds.' This

usage has since, for good or ill, become ubiquitous among philosophers, even those with next to no interest in the technical side of
modal logic, and the appendix will, among other things, show
where it first came from.[9]

Appendix B will show Kripke's grappling with one of the oldest
and thorniest puzzles in philosophy and logic, the notorious liar
paradox: If I say that I am speaking falsely, is what I say true or
false? If the traditional attribution to the semi-legendary Cretan
sage Epimenides can be believed, this paradox goes back to before
the beginnings of logic itself. At the very least it goes back to Eubu-
lides, a contemporary of logic's founder Aristotle. Kripke's work
on this problem, as made available in his 'Outline of a Theory of
Truth' (Kripke 1975), another transcript of an audiotape of a lecture,
has again generated a large literature. I have tried to keep everything as nontechnical as possible, and for that reason have confined
myself to no more than an outline of an outline of the 'Outline,'
though it is hardly feasible to avoid *all* technicalities while still
giving a genuine idea of the nature of Kripke's contribution.[10]

1

Naming

Let us now begin our examination of Kripke's *magnum opus*, N&N. In this chapter we will be concerned mainly with the first two lectures, and specifically with the parts thereof that do *not* involve modality. The follow-up paper (Kripke 1977) will be briefly noted in the last section.

The plan will be to begin, as Kripke does, with a discussion of the opposing views on naming of his predecessors Mill and Frege. Next we will turn to Kripke's intervention on the pro-Mill, anti-Frege side. Then we will pause to mention a third alternative, neither Millian nor Fregean. After that we will examine Kripke's attempt to provide what anyone who rejects Frege will need and what Mill fails to supply: an account of what links a given name to its bearer, along with another loose end.

Mill *vs* Frege

Kripke's discussion moves gradually, as will this book, from seemingly rather specialized linguistic issues toward questions of more obvious philosophical significance, and ultimately the mind–body problem. The central linguistic issue for Kripke concerns the relationship between two classes of expressions – names and descriptions.[1]

With descriptions, there is a distinction to be made between what the expression *designates*, and what the expression *means*. For instance, the descriptions 'the most famous student of Socrates'

and 'the most famous teacher of Aristotle' both designate the same
person, Plato, but the two are quite different in meaning: Each
describes Plato in a way that uniquely identifies him, but the two
ways are by no means the same. The central linguistic issue for
Kripke is whether when we turn from descriptions to names there
is still such a distinction between meaning and designation to be
drawn. Does Plato's name, for instance, have any meaning that
identifies its bearer, or describes him in some way?

Kripke was by no means the first philosopher to take up the
question of the meaning of names, which indeed can be traced back
to Plato's own time, and he discusses fairly extensively the views
of two of his nineteenth-century predecessors, Mill and Frege, who
both, like Kripke, saw a connection between the problem of the
meaning of names and larger philosophical issues. Now one complication for the reader is that each of Mill and Frege had his own
preferred terminology for discussing these matters, and when
Kripke is discussing one of them, following scholarly custom he
will generally use the peculiar terminology of the one he is discussing. For Mill the meaning/designation distinction becomes the
connotation/denotation distinction, and Mill also has a term 'signification' for the whole package of denotation plus connotation.
For Frege the meaning/designation distinction becomes the *Sinn/
Bedeutung* distinction, usually translated sense/reference.

If we wish to state Frege's view in ordinary, everyday terms, it
would be roughly this: that every name has the same meaning as,
or is synonymous with, some uniquely identifying description. The
description might serve as something like a definition of the name,
and the name might serve as something like an abbreviation for
the description. All this is not something Frege says in so many
words, but rather is a view that is attributed to him on the strength
of two facts: first, that he does say that every name has a sense as
well as a reference; second, that when he gives examples of what
the sense of a name might be, he gives a description. (For instance,
he tells us the sense of 'Aristotle' may be 'the teacher of Alexander.') Frege allows that the same name may have different senses
for different speakers. (Perhaps 'Plato' could mean 'the most
famous student of Socrates' for some, and 'the most famous teacher
of Aristotle' for others.) That the name should have a single sense,
the same for all speakers, is for Frege not a fact about actual natural
languages, but a norm for an ideal scientific language. There is
some reason to believe that for Frege the norm for an ideal scientific
language would go further, and require that each name be synony-

mous with some description *not itself involving names* (a description like 'the most famous student of the philosopher who drank hemlock' rather than 'the most famous student of Socrates'). Only in this way could we be sure of avoiding circularities of the kind that would arise if one defined Plato in terms of his relationship to Socrates, and Socrates in terms of his relationship to Plato. But this stronger requirement is not something Frege states explicitly.

If we wish to state Mill's view using the ordinary, everyday term 'meaning,' we face a choice. Mill's view, stated in his own terms, was that a name has no connotation, so that its signification is just its denotation. Align 'meaning' with the technical term 'connotation,' and this comes out as saying that names have no meaning. Align it instead with the technical term 'signification,' and it comes out as saying that the meaning of a name is just the individual it designates, the individual who bears the name. Both formulations can be found in discussions of Mill in the literature. A minimal, least-common-denominator formulation would be that a name has no descriptive meaning. It should be noted that Mill, despite this denial of descriptive *meaning*, does allow a name to have a descriptive *etymology*. (Etymology, unlike meaning, is something a speaker of the present-day language does *not* need to know anything about in order to speak correctly.) Thus 'Dartmouth' derives from 'town at the mouth of the river Dart.' What Mill insists is that the name is not *synonymous* with this description: If an earthquake changed the course of the river, there would be no need to change the name of the town.

Russell, another predecessor whom Kripke discusses, introduced considerable terminological confusion by often writing as if he agreed with Mill, whereas he really agreed more, though not entirely, with Frege. Russell defined a name as a simple symbol designating an object, which object is its meaning. This, we have just seen, is what Mill's view becomes if we use the everyday term 'meaning' in place of his technical term 'signification' (rather than his technical term 'connotation'). But then, as Kripke remarks, Russell turns around and says that few if any of what are commonly called names are genuinely names in this sense. Ordinary names are for Russell abbreviated or 'truncated' descriptions, much as Frege maintained. When reading writers influenced by Russell in the later literature, it is often unclear whether by 'names' they mean names in the ordinary sense, what traditional grammar calls 'proper nouns,' or names in Russell's idiosyncratic sense, often distinctively called 'logically proper names.'

When Russell offers an example of what the description associated with a name in the ordinary sense might be, what he offers is sometimes quite similar to what Frege would have offered; but sometimes it is interestingly different. Where Frege might have taken the name 'Sir Walter Scott' to abbreviate some such description as 'the author of *Waverley*,' Russell by contrast suggests that the name is a truncation of the description 'the individual *called* "Sir Walter Scott."' Where the description Frege would associate with a name generally involves the 'famous deeds' of the bearer of the name, the description Russell here mentions involves nothing more than *being* the bearer of the name. So where Frege gives a description that uniquely identifies the bearer of the name, Russell here gives a description that does nothing at all toward identifying that bearer. For to say 'Sir Walter Scott' designates the individual called 'Sir Walter Scott' is no help at all in identifying who that is.

As already remarked, both Mill and Frege saw a connection between issues about naming and larger philosophical questions; this is true of Russell as well. The larger project with which Mill connects his view on naming is the critique of certain intellectual holdovers from medieval scholastic metaphysics. The scholastics maintained that some of an individual's properties are *essential* and others *accidental*. With the former, possession of the property by the individual is necessary if the individual is to exist at all; with the latter, it is contingent. A typical scholastic view would be that it is essential to Socrates that he be capable of thinking, but accidental that he be capable of walking. This for Mill is pure medieval superstition: There are no individual essences.

And how does his view about names come in? Well, Mill was an early and forceful advocate of the demystifying identification of necessity with analyticity, though he expressed this view by the slogan that *all necessity is verbal necessity*, rather than using the Kantian terminology. For Mill, an example in subject–predicate form can be necessary only if the predicate is part of the connotation of the subject. Mill thus would have been willing to grant that 'All philosophers are rational' is necessary, because 'rational' is arguably part of the connotation of 'philosopher.' But Mill would *not* have been willing to grant 'Socrates (if he exists) is rational' is necessary. For on his view of names, 'Socrates' has no connotation for 'rational' to be part of.

Mill is best remembered today as a political thinker, and what the connection if any is supposed to be between his stout denial of individual essences and his forceful advocacy of press freedom or female suffrage is less than obvious. I do get the impression that in his own mind at least the metaphysical issue and the political issues were battles on different fronts in the same war, a general campaign against reactionary obscurantism of all kinds. It is perhaps more than a mere coincidence that the best-known philosopher to advocate a no-descriptive-meaning view of proper names before Mill's time was John Locke, another British philosopher who is best remembered today as a libertarian political theorist.

By contrast, the larger projects with which Frege and Russell connect their views on naming are quite apolitical, and the fact that the two philosophers stood at opposite ends of the political spectrum did not prevent their sharing very similar views on naming. Those views were closely connected with the ambition, alluded to earlier, of showing, in opposition to Kant, that arithmetic is analytic. It would take us too far afield into technicalities to try to spell out the connection here in detail, and knowledge of the details is not needed to follow Kripke's discussion, so I will at this point bring my sketch of historical background to a close.[2]

We may identify three ideal types of theory about the meaning of names, to which the views of various historical figures approximate. A minimal *Millianism* holds that a name has no descriptive meaning or connotation or sense. The remaining two types of theory are *descriptivist*. They both hold that every proper name has a meaning, and indeed the same meaning as some description. The two differ from each other over the nature of the descriptions involved. *Fregeanism* is the type of descriptivism holding that each name has the same meaning as some uniquely identifying description, ideally one that is name-free. The *metalinguistic* type of descriptivism holds that a name '____' is synonymous with 'the individual called by the name "____"' or 'the individual bearing the name "____"' or something of the sort. Kripke finds hints toward such a view in the remarks of several writers from Russell (in the Scott example mentioned earlier) onwards, and offers some critical remarks about it, but the metalinguistic view was only really developed into a full-fledged theory in the period *after* N&N, and in reaction to it.[3] Since the view was not very influential in 1970, Kripke in N&N gives it less attention than Fregeanism or Millianism. Treatment of it will be deferred here to the section after next of this chapter.

Circa 1970, the dominant view was that some version of or variation on Fregeanism must be right, and Kripke's anti-descriptivist arguments are directed mainly against the Fregean and kindred

positions. But Kripke, before arguing at length against the Fregean
view, first emphasizes that it has several advantages or attractions.
The first two advantages are just the ability to solve two puzzles,
one stressed by Frege, the other by Russell.

Co-designative Names: Hesperus and Phosphorus. One feature of
names is that two of them may be *co-designative*, designating the
same individual. Moreover, an identity statement linking two co-
designative names can be informative. The full background to the
stock example, one used and reused again and again in philosophical discussions to illustrate this point, is as follows.

The Greeks of the time of Homer called the second planet from
the sun 'Hesperus' (etymologically 'Evening One') when they saw
it in the evening, and 'Phosphorus' or 'Eosphorus' (etymologically
'Light-bringer' or 'Dawn-bringer') when they saw it in the morning.
They took themselves to be seeing two different 'wandering stars'
or planets, and their mythology associated two different minor
godlings with them. The pair of terms corresponding to 'Hesperus'
and 'Phosphorus' is 'Vesper' and 'Lucifer' in Latin, 'Abendstern'
and 'Morgenstern' in German, and 'Evening Star' and 'Morning
Star' in English, though 'Hesperus' and 'Phosphorus' themselves
survive in English as minor, poetic alternatives. Mesopotamian
astronomers of the period already recognized that it was the same
heavenly body being seen, sometimes in the west in the evening,
sometimes in the east in the morning. They associated the planet
with their goddess Ishtar. By classical times the Greeks had adopted
the same view, associating the planet with their corresponding
goddess, Aphrodite. The Romans, in turn, associated it with their
corresponding goddess, Venus, and 'Venus' remains the primary
name for the planet in English.

The point to note in all this is that an identity statement linking
distinct names, such as

(1)   Hesperus is Phosphorus.

can be news to someone, as it would have been to Homer, whereas
any identity statement linking to copies of the same name, such as

(2)   Hesperus is Hesperus.

would be news to no one.

Fregeanism easily accommodates this phenomenon, explaining
how it is possible. On a Fregean view, each of 'Hesperus' and
'Phosphorus' has the same meaning as some description, perhaps
'the brightest heavenly body regularly seen near the western

horizon just after sunset' for the former, and 'the brightest heavenly body regularly seen near the eastern horizon just before sunrise' for the latter. Then (1) and (2) amount to

(3)   The brightest heavenly body regularly seen near the western horizon just after sunset is the same as the brightest heavenly body regularly seen near the eastern horizon just before sunrise.

(4)   The brightest heavenly body regularly seen near the western horizon just after sunset is the same as the brightest heavenly body regularly seen near the western horizon just after sunset.

and there is no difficulty in seeing how (3) can be informative while (4) cannot. Frege used the Hesperus *vs* Phosophorus (or Abendstern *vs* Morgenstern) example to motivate his sense/reference distinction.

Empty Names: Pegasus. Another feature of names is that some of them are *empty*, and do not have bearers, and that for such a name, for instance 'Pegasus,' the *singular negative existential* statement

(5)   Pegasus does not exist.

is both meaningful and true. This may be puzzling, because the statement looks as if it were picking out an individual by name, and then saying something about that individual, that it is non-existent; and how can we thus speak about something that isn't there to be spoken of?

Fregeanism needs some help in solving the problem here. Merely taking 'Pegasus' to have the same meaning as some description, perhaps 'Bellerophon's winged horse,' reduces (5) to

(6)   Bellerophon's winged horse does not exist.

but this does not by itself solve the problem. For (6) still appears to be mentioning something, Bellerophon's winged horse, and then saying something about it, that it is non-existent. The move from (5) to (6) does, however, pave the way for a solution. For Russell has a famous theory of descriptions that, not to put too fine a point on it at this stage, allows something like (5) to be paraphrased as something more like

(7)   Bellerophon had no winged horse.

With this rephrasing, the appearance that we are in some way saying something 'about' a nonentity evaporates. Russell used such examples (involving the Golden Mountain among other non-existents) to motivate his theory of descriptions.

Another feature for which Fregeanism can easily account is the existence of *shared* names. For instance, as Kripke himself reminds us in the preface to (Kripke 1980), 'Aristotle' is the name of not one but two famous Greeks, an ancient philosopher and a modern shipowner. Fregeanism accommodates this feature by assimilating it to the familiar phenomenon of homonyms, distinct words with distinct meanings but identical pronunciation and spelling, such as 'bank' for riverbank and 'bank' for moneybank. According to Fregeanism, the meaning of a name has enough descriptive content to identify its bearer; hence names borne by two different individuals must have different descriptive meanings, and so be distinct words, even if they sound and look alike. Kripke acknowledges that any theory of names must eventually give some account of sharing, but commits himself to neither to the homonym nor any other specific account.

Yet another feature for which Fregeanism can easily account is the apparent existence of *at least* enough meaning to a name to indicate whether its bearer is a male person, female person, place, or thing. There is reason to suppose such information would be part of the meaning of a name, because it is needed in order to use the name in a grammatically correct way. Without it, one does not know what pronouns to use with the name. The meaning Fregeanism attributes to a name is supposed to be sufficient to identify its bearer uniquely, and it can therefore be expected to suffice to tell us whether that bearer is a who or a where or a what, a he or a she or an it. Kripke does not discuss the grammatical phenomenon, and is rather cool to the suggestion of Peter Geach (1957, chapter 16) that names have 'sortal' information as part of their meanings, insisting that, if so, the 'sortals' must be very broad ones; but he does not absolutely deny that there is some very broad sortal meaning to a name, though neither does he affirm as much or offer any theoretical account of the alleged phenomenon.

For Kripke, the central attraction of the Fregean view lies less in its ability to account for co-designative names or empty names, let alone the other two phenomena I have just mentioned, than in its providing a straightforward account of what links a name to its bearer: The name has a meaning, this meaning is a description uniquely identifying some individual, and whatever individual it is that fits said description is the bearer of the name. If 'Socrates' just *means* 'the philosopher who drank hemlock,' then we understand who Socrates, the bearer of the name, is just as well as we understand what it is for someone to be a philosopher, for someone to drink something, and for something to be hemlock. By contrast, what the Millian thesis that names have no descriptive meaning tells us about who bears the name 'Socrates' is precisely nothing. It is a non-negotiable demand that theory of names must provide an account of some kind of the linkage of a name to its bearer. It would be very nice if we could meet this demand by adopting the Fregean view, but the fact that it would be *nice* if some theory were true is no evidence that it *is* true, and certainly no answer to objections. And Kripke has some objections against Fregeanism that are quite serious.

Error and Ignorance

In the simplest terms, Kripke's objection against Fregeanism is that if, say, 'Socrates' just means 'the philosopher who drank hemlock,' then the assertion 'Socrates is the philosopher who drank hemlock' would be analytic, and as such both a priori and necessary. But, Kripke would say, it is neither.[4] Leaving to the next chapter 'metaphysical' objections to the effect that the assertion is contingent, let us turn here to the 'epistemological' objection that it is a posteriori, and more generally to 'epistemic' problems with the Fregean view.

According to the preface in Kripke (1980), the central ideas of N&N date from 1963–1964. The clearest internal evidence of a 1963–1964 date is that N&N is thick with citations and discussion of the literature on naming from the five years or so just prior, and much thinner with citations and discussions of the subsequent literature. Kripke quotes quite a few writers from the late nineteen fifties and early sixties, and his own positive view very largely emerges from his criticism of these writers. As Kripke's discussion recalls, a number of his immediate predecessors had already noted epistemic problems with the ideal Fregean theory.

The problem given the most attention by Kripke's predecessors was the problem of *error*: The first description that comes to mind in connection with a name may simply be false, yet this doesn't prevent the name from designating its bearer. Perhaps it wasn't hemlock Socrates drank, but some other poison. In the worst case, perhaps some *other* philosopher *did* drink hemlock – maybe Diogenes the Cynic, since the traditional story given out about his death, that he killed himself by holding his breath, is not credible

– while Socrates didn't. Even so, 'Socrates' still designates Socrates and not Diogenes, or no one.

This point matters even if classical scholars have carefully surveyed the available evidence and found that it overwhelmingly supports the traditional view that Socrates drank hemlock and Diogenes did not. For if it is on account of a careful survey of the available evidence by classical scholars that one believes 'Socrates is the philosopher who drank hemlock,' then it is on an a posteriori and not an a priori basis that one believes it; whereas if the description gave the *meaning* of the name 'Socrates,' mere armchair reflection on the meanings of words would suffice to establish, without the need for any substantive historical investigation, that if there was any such person as Socrates at all, that person drank hemlock.

In any case, Kripke notes that, in addition to hypothetical cases such as 'Socrates,' there are actual cases where the only description that in fact comes to many, perhaps most, people's minds is a false one. According to Kripke, many people can tell you nothing about Einstein except that he invented the atom bomb. According to Kripke, these people are still speaking about Einstein, not Oppenheimer or Satan or whoever it was that was the true inventor of the atom bomb, if it may be said to have had a single principal inventor. They are speaking about Einstein and expressing a widely held false belief about him: Their error about what Einstein's real claim to fame consists in does not prevent their uttering misinformation *about Einstein*.

Given the attractions of the Fregean view, it is perhaps not surprising that theorists attempted to deal with the error problem by amending the view rather than abandoning it. Kripke considers in varying degrees of detail a considerable range of amended Fregean views, attacking them partly with epistemic, partly with modal arguments. In the case of some variations on Fregeanism he directly argues that they are wrong; with others, his first complaint is that amended version loses Fregeanism's chief advantage, that of giving clear account of the relationship of a name to its bearer.

One variation of which Kripke takes note is that some advocates of Fregean-like views take the line that the description associated with a name does not really 'give the meaning' of the name – names don't really *have* meanings in the way other words do – but merely 'determine the reference' of the name. If I say something about Socrates, I am merely saying something about a certain man. Which man? That is where the descriptions come in. On this view 'Socrates is the philosopher who drank hemlock' is not supposed to be analytic, because 'Socrates' is not supposed to *mean* 'the philosopher who drank hemlock.' And so the argument from error as I formulated it above does not directly apply. But the Einstein example, for instance, still creates trouble for this view. The description 'the inventor of the atom bomb' simply does *not* 'determine the reference' of 'Einstein': if it did, 'Einstein' would denote Oppenheimer or whoever, whereas it designates Einstein and no one else.

The most popular variation is a different one, known as the *cluster* theory. According to this view, there is not just a single description but a cluster of descriptions associated with a name. Kripke cites, as the *locus classicus* for the cluster theory, the paper Searle (1958), where we read the following:

> Suppose, for example, that we teach the name 'Aristotle' by explaining that it refers to a Greek philosopher born in Stagira, and suppose that our student continues to use the name correctly, that he gathers more information about Aristotle, and so on. Let us suppose it is discovered later that Aristotle was not born at Stagira at all, but in Thebes. We will not now say that the meaning of the name has changed, or that Aristotle did not really exist at all. (Searle 1958, 168)

On Searle's picture, multiple descriptions get associated with the name 'Aristotle,' and if one or several get knocked out of the cluster, no matter; we can go on with the rest. Similarly one imagines multiple descriptions being associated with 'Socrates,' mentioning not only drinking hemlock, but having a snub nose, being the teacher of Plato, and so on. If any one of these is knocked out, say by the discovery that it wasn't hemlock but deadly nightshade that Socrates drank, the rest will keep us going.

That in the nineteen sixties the cluster variation on the Fregean view achieved the status of something like the received view or conventional wisdom is suggested by Searle's having been chosen as the expert to write the article on proper names in the first edition (1967) of the *Encyclopedia of Philosophy*.[5]

The cluster view comes in many variant versions. On a simple formulation, the bearer of the name is the unique individual if any of whom most of the descriptions in the cluster are true; if there is no single individual of whom most of the descriptions in the cluster are true, then the name has no bearer. Among other departures from this simple version, variants allow some of the descriptions in the cluster to count as more important than others.[6] Kripke examines a number of variant versions of the cluster theory and finds similar problems with all of them.

Basically, the difficulty is that *all* the descriptions in the cluster may be false of the bearer of the name. Perhaps the Athenians ran out of hemlock and gave Socrates deadly nightshade. Perhaps Plato never studied with Socrates but only pretended to, having heard about him second hand from relatives such as Charmides who really were among Socrates' students. Perhaps Socrates really had a long, sharp, pointy nose, and ancient mentions of him as snub-nosed were originally an inside joke (like calling Robin Hood's huge companion 'Little John') which later writers mistook. Perhaps every element of the tradition about Socrates is off in one way or another. In the worst case, not only may all the descriptions be false of Socrates; they may even all be true of someone else. This is conceivable, if improbable, and it cannot be established by a priori armchair reflection not to be so; and this is enough to show that 'Socrates' is not synonymous with, cannot be defined as, and does not abbreviate 'Whoever it is of whom most (or most of the most important) of the following are true...' followed by the cluster of descriptions.

In any case, as the Einstein example already suggests, many people may be able to come up with no more than one description, and it a false one, so the cluster idea never gets off the ground. Worse than this, Kripke notes that in some cases many people may not be able to think of *any* suitable description – not any *definite* description as the one-and-only something-or-other, as opposed to an *indefinite* description as one of several something-or-others. No uniquely identifying description, such as would distinguish the bearer of the name from all other individuals, may be known to a speaker. For a possible instance, many Americans may know nothing about Disraeli and Gladstone, except that they were nineteenth-century British prime ministers. So the only description such speakers can come up with for either name is something like 'a nineteenth-century British prime minister,' which does not distinguish the two party-leaders from each other.[7]

Thus there is a problem of *ignorance* in addition to the problem of error. One reason this is worth noting is that in an attempt to neutralize the problem of error, it may be suggested that one should replace descriptions like 'the philosopher who drank hemlock' or 'the scientist who invented the atom bomb' by something like 'the person *thought to be* the philosopher who drank hemlock' and 'the person *thought to be* the scientist who invented the atom bomb.' If, owing to ignorance, we haven't even one definite description to begin with, this idea won't get off the ground.[8]

Kripke cites Strawson (1959) for one suggested way of escaping the problem of ignorance: For X the uniquely identifying description associated with the name 'Socrates' may simply be 'The person Y calls "Socrates."' Supposing Y's use of 'Socrates' is in order, backed by a suitable cluster of descriptions, X's usage can, in Strawson's phrase, 'borrow its credentials' from Y's usage. Or if Y's usage is not backed by a suitable cluster of descriptions, Y's usage can 'borrow its credentials' from some Z's, and so on, so long as the chain does not come round in a circle, but eventually leads back to someone whose usage is backed by a suitable cluster of descriptions. It will emerge that on Kripke's view Strawson's focus on the history of the name (X's getting it from Y) is on the right track; what is wrong, according to Kripke, is that Strawson's view still involves *descriptions*,[9] even if these are descriptions of the history of the name ('The person Y called "Socrates"'). Kripke notes several difficulties with the Strawsonian escape route, but perhaps the most basic is that X simply may not *remember* any specific Y he has heard using the name 'Socrates.'

Kripke considers many attempts to save the Fregean view through additions and amendments to meet the error, ignorance, and other problems, and his discussion contains many memorable examples: The prophet Jonah, the logician Kurt Gödel, and more join the physicists Einstein and Feynman and Newton in the cast, and Christopher Columbus puts in a cameo appearance. In the end, Kripke concludes that Fregeanism is unsalvageable. Indeed, Kripke rejects descriptivism in *all* its forms, which is to say, he rejects both Fregeanism and all its variants while equally rejecting all versions of the metalinguistic view, though he gives the latter less attention.

Citations of the literature, as I have said, become much thinner in N&N once one gets past the period of the works of Searle and Strawson mentioned above. For the period from the mid-nineteen sixties onward, Kripke's citations often consist just of brief footnote acknowledgments of work of which Kripke has become aware since developing his own view that is presumably independent of his, and leads to overlapping conclusions. But one of these items is worthy of special mention in the present context: (Donnellan 1970), which came out between the time Kripke lectured and the time his lectures were first published. Where Kripke's discussion moves back and forth between modal and nonmodal considerations, Donnellan's covers almost exactly the same topic – naming without necessity – as the present chapter. Donnellan's work appears to have been largely independent of Kripke's (except that he acknowledges that one of his examples may have come to him third hand from Kripke).

Kripke and Donnellan agree that the error and ignorance problems that motivated additions and amendments to the Fregean theory can be pushed further, and should motivate its abandonment. (Kripke differs from Donnellan by having in addition to the error and ignorance arguments a modal argument; but that must wait for the next chapter.) They agree that the reason a name designates the bearer that it does has to do with the history of the name, rather than any associated description or descriptions – not even a description or descriptions of its history, which may be and usually is unknown to or misunderstood by the speaker. They agree that it is difficult to formulate any precise theory about just *how* the history determines what the name designates. Kripke differs from Donnellan in that he so far overcomes his reluctance to propose a theory as to offer at least a 'picture.' For many, it is really only by offering this alternative picture of what determines which object a name designates that Kripke makes his case against Fregeanism compelling.

Metalinguistic Theories

Before presenting Kripke's picture there is another question worth going into, that of the status of metalinguistic theories. Kripke's discussion of these in N&N is addressed to versions, such as the one to be found in Kneale (1962), that are quite crude compared to versions developed in the years since 1970, especially after linguists joined in the discussion.

Linguists cite, as favoring descriptivism in general and metalinguisticism in particular, a number of factors that have hardly figured in philosophical discussion. One consideration is simply the fact that some names come with definite articles: 'the Amazon,' 'the Nile,' 'the Atlantic,' 'the Pacific.' There are even languages such as modern Greek where *all* names come with such articles. If 'Socrates' abbreviates some kind of description 'the such-and-such,' it is not surprising that the description should be in some languages abbreviated to 'Socrates' and in others to what amounts to 'the Socrates.' It is harder to see where the 'the' could be coming from if 'Socrates' or 'Amazon' or 'Nile' is not an abbreviation. Another consideration is simply the fact that most actual names, at least of persons, are complex, with multiple independently significant components, typically one that is purely personal and one that indicates family connections. This fact would have become conspicuous earlier if our examples had been the names, not of Socrates, Plato, and Aristotle, but of, say, Rodrigo Borgia, Ceasare Borgia, and Lucrezia Borgia. The fact is easily accommodated by metalinguistic views: Obviously the person called 'Lucrezia Borgia' is called both 'Lucrezia' and 'Borgia.'

Of the factors that, unlike the two just mentioned, had figured in philosophical discussions at least back to Kripke if not earlier, the most conspicuous advantage of the metalinguistic view seems to be with the problem of ignorance. What user of 'Socrates' is unaware that Socrates bears the name 'Socrates'?

Metalinguisticism may, however, seem to be in trouble over the problem of error. If we understood 'the person called by the name "Socrates"' to mean 'the person *commonly* called "Socrates"' and 'the bearer of the name "Socrates"' to mean 'the bearer of "Socrates" *as commonly used*,' then indeed there will be room for error, and Kripke reverts to points like this several times in N&N. A speaker might, through mishearing or misreading a commonly used name, come to have an idiosyncratic variant thereof in his or her idiolect, in the mistaken belief that this is the form in general use. A child, for instance, among the crowds that greeted the current US President on his visit to Ireland, may have gotten the misimpression that the man is commonly called 'Barry O'Bama,' and may have come to use that name for him. (I have seen in print a case like this involving 'Jackie O'Nassis.') If a name like 'Barry O'Bama' had to mean 'the person *commonly* called "Barry O'Bama"' then the name as used by the child would designate no one, whereas surely that name, in the child's usage, designates Barack Obama. Thus it seems that if the metalinguistic theory is to be tenable, we must understand 'the one called "Socrates"' to mean for each user 'the one called "Socrates" by me, in my present, actual circumstances,' or something of the sort.

Metalinguisticism may also seem to be in trouble over the problem of shared names. For it seems to imply that in the case of 'Aristotle,' the name of the philosopher and the name of the shipowner both have the *same* meaning, 'the bearer of the name "Aristotle."' However, it is a commonplace that we often use a description 'the such-and-such' when there is in fact more than one such-and-such. If I tell a student visiting my office, 'Please sit in the chair,' I do not mean to suggest that there is only one chair in the whole wide world, but just that there is only one chair that is pertinent in the context. If visibly there is only one vacant chair in my office, I will be understood to intend that one. Similarly when I say, 'Mary is quite capable of taking care of it,' context may make clear which of the millions of persons named 'Mary' is the pertinent one, the one intended. If two of the many people named 'Mary' are equally pertinent, or if none is, then indeed my utterance will be defective; but likewise 'Please sit in the chair' is defective if there are two equally pertinent chairs, or none. In short, the metalinguistic theory makes the phenomenon of shared names just another case of a familiar linguistic phenomenon. Moreover, the metalinguistic theory actually has an easier time of it than the Fregean in explaining such usages as 'the other Mary' or 'the two Aristotles.' But it does seem that if the metalinguistic theory is to be tenable, we must understand 'the one called "Socrates"' to mean something like 'the contextually pertinent one called "Socrates."'

Metalinguisticism may also seem in trouble if we grant that names have at least some sort of broad sortal, classificatory meaning. The very purest form of metalinguistic view will have to be modified, so that the meaning of 'Athens' is not 'the bearer of the name "Athens,"' but 'the *place* that bears the name "Athens,"' while the meaning of 'Socrates' is not 'the bearer of the name "Socrates,"' but 'the *male person* who bears the name "Socrates."'

In the light of the points we have been examining recently, we may have to reopen the question of the ignorance objection. We have arrived at the conclusion that if the metalinguistic theory is to be tenable, 'Socrates' must more specifically mean for each speaker something like 'the contextually pertinent male person who in my own actual, present usage is called "Socrates,"' or something of the sort. And one may very well question whether speakers really have in mind, associated with the name, anything so complicated or sophisticated as this very long phrase. After all, young children learn names for their siblings and playmates long before they get expressions like 'in my own usage' or 'male person' or 'contextually pertinent' into their vocabularies. Even speaking to adults, the long phrase can hardly be substituted for 'Socrates' in a simple sentence without producing bizarreness reactions.

Kripke's occasional critical remarks on the metalinguistic view do not develop this objection, but we may wonder how it could be answered. Evidently, the relationship between the name and its metalinguistic analysis can't be taken to be a case of synonymy of expressions of the kind that makes for free interchangeability in everyday usage. This would not be troubling for linguists, who are in the forefront of advocacy for metalinguisticism today. For while the analyses linguists offer of the structure of phrases and clauses may be generally assumed to be psychologically real in the sense of being represented somehow in speakers' brains, they are at the same time generally taken to be subconscious in the sense of being something of which speakers are not directly aware.[10] Often this is quite obvious, because the analyses are written out using not only specialist jargon, but also special symbols. If the metalinguistic theory of proper names is to be tenable, the metalinguistic analysis of names must be regarded as resembling other analyses in linguistics in this respect.

There remain yet other objections to the metalinguistic view that arise in connection with modality (treated in the next chapter) and belief attribution (treated still later). In the meantime, for Kripke, perhaps the objection he finds most compelling is simply the oddity of treating names in a way so very different from all other expressions in the language. Who would want to define 'horse' as 'animal of the kind called "horse"' or 'yellow' as 'of the color called "yellow"'? (Well, perhaps after reading Kripke's third lecture some would; but that is not an issue we are ready to take up.)

Kripke's occasional critical remarks on the metalinguistic view also stress a great difference between the two kinds of descriptivist theory, metalinguistic and Fregean: the difference that with the former view, in sharp contrast to the latter, what we are told about who or what the bearer of a name is – that the bearer of 'Socrates' is the bearer of 'Socrates,' for instance – is completely circular and trivial and useless. Kripke in N&N, not having before him the versions of the metalinguistic theory that are under discussion today, tends to belabor this point, as if someone were trying to conceal or deny it. The metalinguistic theory admittedly does stand in need of some non-circular account of what connects a name with its bearer quite as much as a Millian theory would. But there is no reason why a metalinguistic theorist should not just appropriate – with suitable acknowledgments to Kripke – the account, to be discussed in the next section, that Kripke offers the Millian.

The Historical Chain Picture

One point Kripke emphasizes is that in offering his picture he is
not attempting to give any general reductive analysis of the name-
to-bearer relation in other terms. As you read the account of his
picture below, you will see that it simply presupposes from the
beginning the *general* notion of using or intending to use an expression as a name for a person or place or thing. What is being
explained is, rather, what connects a *particular* name to the *particular* person or place or thing bearing that name.

Kripke's picture comes in two parts, an account of the *introduction* of a name, and an account of the *transmission* of a name from
one speaker to another. To begin with introduction, suppose I have
in mind an object and want to give it a name for use in the language
I share with you and others. Then I must first of all draw to your
attention the object in question; I must pick it out for naming
somehow. Kripke says this may be done by ostension (literally,
'showing' or 'exhibiting' the object) or by description, but then
immediately adds in a footnote that the case of ostension may be
subsumable under the case of description, and that the main application of the descriptive theory is to the initial introduction of a
new name. Let us try to unpack this.

Pure ostension, showing simply by holding up an object or
pointing at a person, unaccompanied by words except for the name
itself – or accompanied only by the imperative 'Look!' – is rather
uncommon. Perhaps I may unveil a work of art and simply say,
'Behold! *The Oath of the Handball Court!*' or 'Lo! *Nude Descending
Escalator!*' But it is surely more usual to use some words in picking
out the item to be named, even if only a single demonstrative
pronoun 'that [pointing]' or a short demonstrative phrase 'that star
[pointing].' Longer phrases still requiring supplementation by
gesture may be used, as with 'that bright star over there [pointing],'
or expressions requiring no such supplementation, as with 'the
brightest star you see just above the eastern horizon.' All these,
from the simple 'that' onward may be construed or classified as a
description of sorts.

The description used obviously cannot be of the kind contemplated by the metalinguistic theory: I cannot pick out the person I
want to give the nickname 'Caligula' by describing him as the
person nicknamed 'Caligula' – for he isn't *yet* nicknamed 'Caligula.' What Kripke emphasizes is that the description need not be,

and usually is not, of the kind that tends to be cited by proponents
of the Fregean view, its cluster-theory variant, or similar proposals,
either. It cannot in general be a description in terms of 'famous
deeds' (teaching Plato, drinking hemlock, and so on). Most often,
even if it does not contain a demonstrative pronoun and require
supplementation by gesture, it will be a description applicable only
for the nonce, such as 'the infant before you.' The infant won't
always be before you, and the person I am naming won't always
be an infant.

More importantly, even if the description is one of long-term
applicability, as when I pick out a star not by pointing and saying
'that one!' but by citing celestial coordinates, the name need not
retain any long-term association with the description. We may all
soon forget just how the name was introduced. Thus name and
description are in no way synonyms, even in the less common case
where the description remains true of the bearer even long after
the occasion of naming.

But, indeed, the description need not even have been true originally. That is to say, 'So-and-so is the such-and-such' need not even
be *true*, even at the time the name 'so-and-so' is assigned to its
bearer, even if that bearer is picked out by the description 'the such-
and-such.' This is because my use of the description 'the such-and-
such' may succeed in getting *you* to bring to mind the object that *I*
have in mind and want to name 'so-and-so' even though the
description is not in fact true of or applicable to that object. I may
succeed in getting you to consider the object I *think* is the such-and-
such even if it is not; I may succeed in doing so either because you
share my error, or because, though you recognize my error, you
also recognize my intention. For this general phenomenon of attention getting directed to the right object though the wrong thing is
said about it, Kripke cites the *locus classicus*, Donnellan (1966).
Kripke, however, disagrees with Donnellan's theoretical account of
the phenomenon. That issue will be taken up in the next section;
what matters at this point is simply the occurrence of the
phenomenon.

For the phenomenon does occur, and is not even especially rare.
There is perhaps no serious chance of mistake with 'this baby':
Only in Wonderland might the supposed baby turn out to be a
piglet. But there is a serious chance of mistake with 'that star,' since
the putative star may in fact be some other kind of celestial object.
And indeed any number of star-names ('Alpha Centauri' and 'Cor
Caroli' and 'Procyon' among them) have in fact turned out to des-

ignate, not individual stars, but binary systems whose two components are not resolvable by the naked eye.

What does seem to be very rare is for the introducer of a name to have pure intention to assign it to the item fitting a certain description *whatever it may be*, regardless of or in the absence of any conjectures about what item that is. It is far more common to have the intention to assign the name to some item with which the introducer of the name is acquainted and *thinks* fits the description. Of course, in many case there will be no serious chance of error, and the distinction will be of no moment.[11]

The role of the description in picking out the item to be named Kripke calls 'fixing the reference.' This is to be distinguished from 'determining the reference,' the notion mentioned earlier as found in some variants of the cluster theory. On these variants, the cluster of descriptions does not give the meaning of a name, but only determines what the name designates. But with 'determining the reference' in this sense, the association of the cluster with the name is supposed to be long term, whereas with 'fixing the reference' in Kripke's sense, the connection may be ephemeral: The description used to pick out the item for naming may then be almost immediately forgotten, and in any case is most typically only true of the item being named for a very short time if at all. Thus though for Kripke descriptions may play a role in the introduction of a name, their role is not the same, and generally the descriptions themselves are not of the same kind, as contemplated by the Fregean theory and variations on it.[12]

So much for the first introduction of the name, or 'initial baptism.' Kripke himself offers no substantial account of *maintenance* to go along with his accounts of introduction and transmission. Beyond a passing remark in the short follow-up note (Kripke 1986), he tells us next to nothing about subsequent uses of the name by its original introducer and members of the audience at the original introduction. He takes it for granted that if I have introduced a name to you, then we may both go on using it on subsequent occasions, and we will still be using it as a name for the thing it was originally introduced to be a name for. Of course, we must not have a conscious intention, in our later uses, to *change* what it designates to something other than what it originally designated, as is done when a child is 'named after' some living or deceased relative. But Kripke does not say that we need to have even a semiconscious intention to *leave unchanged* what the name designates. Certainly we need not remember our *most recent* previous use of the name, any more than we need to remember its *first* use or original introduction.

Kripke's account of speaker-to-speaker transmission remains to be discussed. In some cases, indeed, subsequent transmission may work very much like a typical case initial introduction, in that the bearer of the name is present and is made the object of attention. Such is the case with social introductions. With 'I'd like you to meet Ms Wutzerneym,' name and bearer are presented simultaneously, and the description 'the person I'm introducing you to' will naturally be associated with the name, even if not said aloud.

In other cases, though the bearer of the name is not present, descriptions may still be used. So it is with historical figures. Thus an American teacher may tell the class, 'Today we will learn about George Washington, our first president.' As with the first introduction of a name, the description may be erroneous. The teacher may tell the class, 'Today we will learn about Albert Einstein, the inventor of the atom bomb.' This is one sort of way in which speakers may acquire a name with only a false description attached.

In yet other cases, there may be no role played by descriptions at all. The second speaker may simply overhear the first speaker using a certain expression, infer from the way it is being used that it is being used as a *name*, and begin using that same name to designate whatever it is that the first speaker is using it to designate. This is one way among others in which we can end up with a speaker who uses a name without having *any* non-circular uniquely identifying description associated with it. Kripke imagines the case of a male mathematician overheard by a suspicious spouse muttering the name 'Nancy.' The wife may go on to use the name, saying perhaps, 'Why is my husband so obsessed with this Nancy, whoever or whatever she or it may be?' while remaining ignorant as to whether Nancy is a woman or a Lie group.[13]

There is at transmission the possibility of a sort of slippage mentioned but not extensively discussed by Kripke. In a silly TV sitcom, the wife would leap to the conclusion that Nancy is the attractive young new staff member at her husband's department, and start using 'Nancy' as a name for that person, called 'Francine' by everyone else, with all sorts of ridiculous misunderstandings following, especially since there *is* a person generally called 'Nancy' in the office, a sixty-something cleaning lady noted for her no-nonsense disposition – all this when in fact the mathematician has been muttering in a bad accent about the French city of Nancy, site of a famous center of mathematical research to which he is hoping to wangle an invitation.

Thus one must distinguish, on the part of the second speaker, an intention to use a name for *what she supposes*, perhaps wrongly, the first speaker has been using it for, from a pure intention to use the name for what the first speaker has been using it for, *whatever that may be*, regardless of or in the absence of any conjectures about what it is. For the general phenomenon of the name getting attached by a second speaker to what that speaker erroneously thinks it is attached to by the first speaker, Kripke cites Gareth Evans. The *locus classicus* is a work a little later than N&N, Evans (1973). Kripke disagrees with Evans's theoretical account of the phenomenon, but does not doubt that the phenomenon occurs. Of course, in many cases there will be no serious chance of error, and the distinction will be of no moment.

Slippage in transmission of a different kind can also occur. For there may be inadvertent distortion of the pronunciation or spelling of the name as it passes from one user to another, as well as deliberate informal clipping or shortening of a long name. Cases of a single item with two names do not all resemble the case of Hesperus and Phosphorus, where the chains of transmission go back to two initial baptisms. There are also cases like Cicero and Tully, where there is only one initial baptism, assignment of the name 'Marcus Tullius Cicero' to a Roman baby eventually to grow up to become a famous orator, but there are different routes of transmission, involving different distortions or truncations of the name.

Kripke gives some attention to slippage, for instance from a real fourth-century bishop Saint Nicholas to a mythical immortal elf Santa Claus. He does so in particular when emphasizing that a mere chain of causal connections is not enough to explain why *this* name refers to *that* object. It would be very difficult, he thinks, to formulate any precise theory about which causal connections count and which don't. He gives no sign of expecting that this could be done in a way that would produce a general reductive analysis of the name-bearer relation in non-semantic, causal or physicalistic, terms.[14] It is somewhat ironic, therefore, that the label 'causal theory of reference' has been attached in some of the literature to Kripke's picture. Kripke's picture does not even, it should be noted, require a causal connection leading back to the bearer of the name: One *could* perfectly well introduce 'Nancy' as a name for a Lie group or other mathematical object – Kripke seems to count 'π' as a proper name of a certain real number, for instance – and there are no causal connections with mathematical objects.

Kripke himself sometimes uses 'chain-of-communication picture' for his account; the best label, however, is perhaps the one that stands at the head of this section, except that some subsequent writers have suggested that 'web' may be better than 'chain,' to allow for a name coming to a new speaker through multiple mutually reinforcing contacts with old speakers using it.[15]

Reference *vs* Attribution

N&N is peppered with digressions and footnotes mentioning side topics that Kripke has not time to pursue at length. Little of his work on such topics has been published, but there is a paper (Kripke 1977) that came out between the anthology and book versions of N&N, and that constitutes the earliest follow-up publication to N&N, which may be mentioned here because it is closely connected to the topics we have just been examining, and because it has generated a fair amount of discussion in the later literature, perhaps as much for its interesting methodology (which is what Kripke stresses) as for its results. The issue is one alluded to in passing in the preceding section, Donnellan's theoretical explanation of the phenomenon of descriptions that draw attention to the intended item even though that item does not fit them.

Donnellan's starting point is the difference between (i) saying 'the perpetrator of this outrage,' having no idea who that may be, so that for emphasis one might have said 'the perpetrator of this outrage, *no matter who that may be*,' and (ii) saying 'the perpetrator of this outrage,' having in mind a specific person that one rightly or wrongly thinks is the perpetrator of the recent outrage, so that by way of acknowledgment of human fallibility one might have said '*the individual I rightly or wrongly think is* the perpetrator of this outrage.' The expressions 'the perpetrator of this outrage, no matter who that may be' and 'the individual I rightly or wrongly think is the perpetrator of this outrage' differ in meaning and may designate different individuals, and substituting one expression for the other in a sentence might change it from true to false or vice versa.

Donnellan's claim is that the description 'the perpetrator of this outrage' by itself, without italicized additions, though not ambiguous as between two meanings, is at least capable of being used in two conventionally distinguished ways, which he calls *referential* and *attributive*. He also claims that Russell's famous theory of descriptions, which I have mentioned but not yet expounded, works only for attributively used and not for referentially used descriptions; but this is an aspect of the issue that I will not go into in the present brief discussion.

Though Donnellan (1966) is the *locus classicus* for the ideas in question, even before Donnellan the gist of the relevant thought had been stated in passing, though not developed, by Arthur Prior:

> [L]et us say that *a name in Russell's strict sense* is a simple identifier of an object... [T]here is no reason why the same expression, whether it be a single word like 'This' or 'Tully,' or a phrase like 'The man who lives next door' or 'The man at whom I am pointing,' should not be used sometimes as a name in Russell's strict sense and sometimes not. If 'The man who lives next door' is being so used, and successfully identifies a subject of discourse, then 'The man who lives next door is a heavy smoker' would be true if and only if the subject thus identified *is* a heavy smoker, even if this subject is in a fact a women and doesn't live next door but only works there. (Prior 1963, 195–196)

Prior's 'use as a name in Russell's strict sense' is much the same as what is called by Donnellan 'referential as opposed to attributive use.' What application Prior wanted to make of this view will appear in the next chapter.

Note the commitment in the quoted passage to the view that using an expression as 'a name in Russell's strict sense' or 'referentially rather than attributively' may make a difference to truth value. On this way of judging truth, when I say 'The man who lives next door is a heavy smoker,' using the description in a 'referential' or 'Russellian' way, it is as if I said in the imperative 'Consider the man who lives next door' and then added in the declarative 'The individual I want you to consider is a heavy smoker.' The truth value, true or false, of my utterance is on this view just the truth value of the declarative. The mistake in the imperative, that the individual I want you to consider does not fit the description I provide, doesn't count against the truth of the utterance on this view.

In N&N Kripke imagines such a doctrine being invoked in defense of Fregeanism. It would allow 'Einstein played the violin' to count as true even if taken to mean 'The inventor of the atom bomb played the violin,' and even if the true inventor of the atom bomb did *not* play the violin. Kripke argues that even one who favors Donnellan's theory should not accept this application of it (as of course Donnellan himself, whom I have already cited for his anti-descriptivist views, did not). The view so used is little more than a fancier version of the form of Fregeanism that would take the meaning of 'Einstein' to be, not 'the inventor of the atom bomb,' but 'the person thought to be the inventor of the atom bomb.'

For Kripke, one sign of a difference between 'Einstein played the violin' and 'The inventor of the atom bomb played the violin' is that, if the historical error is explained, the former statement will not be withdrawn, while the latter will be taken back. The speaker will not say, 'I still insist, the inventor of the atom bomb played the violin; you must understand that I am using "the inventor of the atom bomb" referentially, not attributively.'

Kripke agrees with what Prior's formulation (in contrast here to Donnellan's formulations) seems to suggest, that however exactly the phenomenon illustrated by the heavy smoker is to be explained theoretically, it is not a phenomenon limited to descriptions ('the man who lives next door') but can arise also with proper names ('Tully') and demonstratives ('this'). Kripke gives an example involving a proper name, where I say 'Jones is raking leaves,' intending the person I see in the foggy distance, who happens to be Smith rather than Jones. One can give an example involving a demonstrative also, where I point and say 'That guy is a famous philosopher,' intending the man who was standing where I am pointing until just a moment ago when, unnoticed by me, he slipped away and was replaced by another man.

But how should the phenomenon be explained? Kripke believes that there is no distinction here between two conventionally recognized ways of using a description or other expression, and certainly not one that would make a difference to truth value. The phenomenon exhibited is, for him, simply that of a speaker saying something literally false, but being charitably interpreted by those addressed as in some sense intending something true.[16]

The most interesting point about the paper is the way in which Kripke argues for his picture as opposed to Donnellan's. Kripke employs the methodology of imagining a language otherwise like English but in which there *is* such a distinction as Donnellan posits, one openly marked in speech somehow (perhaps by speaking the description with a rising tone when intended referentially and with a falling tone when intended attributively). Even so, speakers using the attributive form would sometimes make mistakes, and say something false. Their hearers would charitably interpret them as intending something true, and would behave toward them just as they would toward those using the referential form, and saying something true. If this is so, then positing two uses, not marked in speech, in actual English is superfluous. Or so Kripke claims. As with N&N itself, (Kripke 1977) is peppered with asides mentioning topics that Kripke did not have time to pursue, and that we have not space to pursue here.

2

Identity

Let us next, as promised in the preceding chapter, re-examine the first two lectures of N&N, now with an eye to how issues about naming interact with issues about necessity. Another pertinent reading would be (Kripke 1971), a single lecture given between the delivery and the publication of the three lectures that became N&N, going over much of the same ground as the parts of N&N relevant to the present chapter and the next.

The plan will be to begin with a review of a conflict over the status of the logic of modality that began when Kripke was a toddler, reached a climax when he was an undergraduate, and is mentioned by Kripke both in N&N and in Kripke (1971). Then we will introduce Kripke's key notion regarding the behavior of proper names in modal contexts, called 'rigidity,' and after that the key consequence Kripke takes to follow therefrom, the 'necessity of identity,' which provides him both with his modal argument against descriptivist views of naming, and with his first examples of a posteriori necessities. After that we will turn to various attempts to resist Kripke's conclusions, before finally taking brief note of a less important companion to the phenomenon of a posteriori necessity, the phenomenon of alleged a priori contingency.

Modal Logic and its Archenemy

One need not go deeply into the technicalities of modal logic to understand the bulk of N&N, but some background is needed to appreciate what is going on in certain paragraphs thereof. Where ordinary logic is concerned with the twofold distinction between *is* and *is not*, modal logic is concerned with a fourfold distinction among

(1a)   *what is and could not have not been*
(1b)   *what is but could have not been*
(1c)   *what is not but could have been*
(1d)   *what is not and could not have been*

Its main categories are

(2a)	*necessity*:	case (1a)
(2b)	*actuality*:	cases (1a) and (1b)
(2c)	*possibility*:	cases (1a) and (1b) and (1c)
(2d)	*contingency*:	cases (1b) and (1c)

with the complementary categories of *non-necessity, non-actuality, impossibility,* and *non-contingency* understood in the obvious way.

From these terminological specifications it is clear that necessity implies actuality, which in turn implies possibility, that the necessary is what is not possibly not and the possible what is not necessarily not, and so on. Such observations are the first baby steps in the formal logic of modality, and go right back to the beginning of logic with Aristotle. Modal logic was extensively developed in the ancient and medieval periods, only to be almost wholly forgotten in modern times. A few scraps survived in the days of Kant. Frege, refounding logic in its modern form, discarded even these: Recall that I quoted him explaining why he would admit no symbols for necessity or possibility in his concept-writing.

The subject of modal logic was reinvented from scratch in the twentieth century by the Harvard philosopher C. I. Lewis, and the first book on the topic did not appear until the nineteen thirties (Lewis and Langford 1932), and the standardization of the symbols used by logicians for necessity and possibility occurred even later. But already by the nineteen thirties, as we have seen, necessity had dwindled in the minds of many philosophers to analyticity. In particular, Lewis understood necessity as analyticity.

First to be developed was modal sentential logic, concerned with the interaction of necessity and possibility with the logical notions of negation, conjunction, disjunction, conditional ('not,' 'and,' 'or,' 'if'), and so forth. The 'first baby steps' mentioned above are principles of modal sentential logic, as is for instance the law

> If it is necessary that p and it is possible that q,
> then it is possible that both q and p.

In the nineteen forties there followed the work of Marcus (1946) and Carnap (1947) – the latter a work I have already cited for its explicit and emphatic identification of necessity with analyticity, which is reflected even in its title, *Meaning and Necessity* – on modal predicate logic, also called quantified modal logic (QML), which brings in the logical notions of universal and existential quantification ('all' and 'some'). Among its laws is

> If it is possible that all *Gs* are *Hs* and it is necessary that some *Gs* are *Fs*, then it is possible that some *Fs* are *Hs*.

Kripke made major contributions (to be discussed in this book in Appendix A) to the formal, technical, mathematical side of sentential and predicate modal logic while still a high-school student. When he came as an undergraduate to Harvard at the end of the nineteen fifties, the leading philosopher there was W. V. Quine. Quine had by that time long been notorious for a series of critical articles attacking the project of modal predicate logic, beginning in the early nineteen forties before there were even any systems of modal predicate logic in the literature, and culminating in Quine (1953). If Quine's doubts had been about the formal consistency of modal logic, Kripke's technical, mathematical results might have allayed them. But Quine's doubts were about the intuitive intelligibility of modal predicate logic.

To indicate the nature of Quine's concern, consider the following:

(3)   For every heavenly body x there is a heavenly body y such that $y = x$.

This is true, simply taking y to be x itself, and (3) is a law of classical, non-modal logic. As such, it is presumably necessary, and indeed the following is a recognized law of modal logic:

(4)   Necessarily, for every heavenly body x there is a heavenly body y such that $y = x$.

So far, so good. But modal logic, whether or not it recognizes the following variation on (4) as a law, at least recognizes it as something meaningful:

(5)   For every heavenly body x there is a heavenly body y such that necessarily $y = x$.

To give one instance, consider the following:

(6)   There is a heavenly body y such that necessarily y is identical with the Morning Star.

What we see in (6), where the 'necessarily' comes between the first occurrence of y and the second occurrence of y, is in jargon called 'quantifying into a modal context,' or 'quantifying in' for short. Quine's worry is not over whether (6) is true, but over whether it is *even meaningful to say that* (6) is true, or whether 'quantifying in' is simply meaningless.

For (6) to be true, there would have to be some heavenly body such that the following condition would be true of it:

(7)   Necessarily, y is identical with the Morning Star.

But Quine's worry is that it may not even be meaningful to say, of a given heavenly body, that (7) is true of it. A revived medieval terminology is much used in discussions of the issue here, the contrast between necessity *de dicto* ('of the saying') and necessity *de re* ('of the thing'). What we see in (4) is *de dicto* necessity, because in (4), a saying that can stand alone as expressing a complete thought, namely (3), is considered and claimed to be necessarily true. What we see in (7) is by contrast necessity *de re*. In (7), applied to a given thing y, it is said that a certain condition is necessarily true *of that thing*. Quine questions the meaningfulness of such *de re* as opposed to *de dicto* modality.

One might hope to make sense of *de re* modality by 'reducing *de re* to *de dicto*,' that is to say, one might hope explain what it means to say that the condition (7) is true of some heavenly body, in terms of the necessary truth of some statement or statements that can stand alone as expressing a complete thought or complete thoughts. The obvious strategy to follow in attempting to accomplish this would be to say that (7) counts as true of a given heavenly body just in case, if one substitutes a term or expression designating that heavenly body for the variable 'y' in (7), then the result is true. Let's see what happens if we try this.

At first it seems that there is one heavenly body such that (7) is true of it by this criterion, to wit, the Morning Star. For what we get when we put in 'The Morning Star' for 'y' in (7), to wit

(8)   Necessarily, the Morning Star is identical with the Morning Star.

is surely analytic, or necessary, isn't it?[1] It also seems that there are many heavenly bodies such that (7) is *not* true of them, and that among these is the Evening Star. For what we get when we put in 'The Evening Star' for '*y*' in (7), to wit

(9)   Necessarily, the Evening Star is identical with the Morning Star.

is surely synthetic, or contingent. But now incoherence threatens. We have said that (7) is true of one heavenly body, and false of another heavenly body, *but it is the same heavenly body both times!* For the Morning Star and the Evening Star are both just the planet Venus.

Quine has other examples of true–false pairs illustrating the phenomenon of 'substitutivity failure,' such as

(10)   Necessarily, if there is life on the Morning Star, then there is life on the Morning Star.
(11)   Necessarily, if there is life on the Morning Star, then there is life on the Evening Star.

In view of such examples, Quine considers it meaningless to ask whether the planet Venus – the very heavenly body itself, which is both Morning Star and Evening Star, and not more one than the other – is such that *it* is necessarily identical with the Morning Star, or is such that necessarily, if there is life on the Morning Star, there is life on *it*. If Quine is right about this, then *de re* modality is meaningless, 'quantifying in' is meaningless, and modal predicate logic is meaningless, despite Kripke's brilliant work on the *mathematics* of formal systems of modal logic.

Arthur Smullyan (1947) replied that Quine's example (8) and (9) is ambiguous, since 'the Morning Star' and 'the Evening Star' might be interpreted either as descriptions or alternatively as names. If they are taken as descriptions, there is a long story to be told, but if they are taken as names, then Smullyan claims that (9) is just as true as (8), and indeed obviously so. We find such claims in two works (both with credits to Smullyan) of Frederic Fitch (1949, 1950), and two works (the first with a credit to Fitch, the second with a remark that the point is familiar) of Fitch's former student Marcus (1960, 1961), who as a pioneer of modal predicate logic was particularly concerned to defend its philosophical coherence. Similar ideas recurred at a famous 1962 Helsinki conference on modal logic in the presentations of both Marcus and Prior, published as Marcus (1963) and Prior (1963). I have quoted from the latter paper already toward the end of the preceding chapter.

Smullyan is clearly rejecting Fregeanism, since on a Fregean view there would be no important difference between names and descriptions. The main difficulty in interpreting his brief remarks is over whether he means by 'names' names in the ordinary sense, what traditional grammar called 'proper nouns,' or names in the extraordinary sense, Russellian 'logically proper names.' Church (1950) challenged defenders of Smullyan's point to identify a class of expressions in English that function as 'names' in the relevant sense, expressions such that 'Necessarily $a = b$' is *obviously* true on the assumption that a and b are co-designative 'names' of this kind. The view quoted from Prior (1963) in the preceding chapter is in effect an answer to Church's challenge: There is no fixed class of expressions that *always* function as 'names in Russell's strict sense,' but expressions of different classes *sometimes* do.

But it is hard to see how positing either that names in the ordinary sense are Millian, or that various classes of expressions can be used as Millian names can help. For if names have no descriptive meanings, as Millianism maintains, then never mind problems about *de re* necessity, because even *de dicto* necessity is already going to be hard to interpret, as applied to sentences involving names, so long as we continue to identify necessity with analyticity or truth by virtue of meaning. Just as Mill's view that all necessity is verbal amounts to an identification of necessity with analyticity, so Mill's view that there are no individual essences amounts to a rejection of *de re* modality. Quine himself gave an example very much in the spirit of Mill. It is arguably analytic that mathematicians are rational but synthetic that cyclists are rational, and analytic that cyclists are bipeds but synthetic that mathematicians are bipeds. What then can we say, Quine asks, of a man who is at once a mathematician and a cyclist? Is it necessary or contingent that *he* is rational or a biped?

There is a play here on the ancient dispute between Plato, who defined 'human being' as 'featherless biped,'[2] and Aristotle, who defined 'human being' as 'rational animal.' For Aristotle and his medieval scholastic followers, being rational was an 'essential' property of a human being, one a human being could not exist without, one necessary for his or her existence, while being a biped was an 'accidental' property of a human being, one a human being could have failed to have without failing to exist, one he or she only possesses contingently. Quine maintains that one would have to go back to such 'Aristotelian essentialism' to make sense of modal predicate logic. And this is something the writers he was primarily interested in criticizing, Lewis and Carnap, were definitely unwilling to do. It would, after all, represent the undoing of two hundred years of progress in demystification, wouldn't it?

(Marcus 1961), the most elaborate restatement of Smullyan's reply to Quine, is actually (despite the 1961 date on the cover of the journal in which it appeared) the text of a talk given in early 1962 at the Boston Colloquium for the Philosophy of Science. Quine was commentator, and in his comments (Quine 1961) he took the opportunity to cut through any supposed ambiguity about descriptions *vs* names by substituting 'Phosphorus' and 'Hesperus,' which are unambiguously proper nouns, for 'the Morning Star' and 'the Evening Star.' He also took the opportunity to repudiate any suggestion that his example depended on a descriptivist theory of names:

> I think I see trouble anyway in the contrast between proper names and descriptions as Professor Marcus draws it. Her paradigm of the assigning of proper names is tagging. We may tag the planet Venus, some fine evening, with the proper name 'Hesperus'. We may tag the same planet again, some day before sunrise, with the proper name 'Phosphorus'. When at last we discover that we have tagged the same planet twice, our discovery is empirical. And not because the proper names were descriptions. (Quine 1961, 327)

Dagfinn Føllesdal, at the time a graduate student at Harvard, relates in the preface to (Føllesdal 2004) that on his way to the session he ran into Kripke, then a Harvard undergraduate, and persuaded him to come along. The discussion after the talk and commentary was audiotaped and transcribed and edited and published as (Marcus et al. 1962). Kripke was an important participant, and what he is shown as saying in Marcus et al. (1962) represents the first published record of his taking a step beyond formal, technical, mathematical work in modal logic, to grappling with questions of philosophical interpretations and foundations. It was not yet a very big step.

To Kripke, with his deep understanding of the formal logic of the situation, it was obvious that if we want to pursue the attempt to make sense of *de re* modality by explaining it in terms of *de dicto* modality, what we want is a class of distinguished terms meeting certain key requirements, of which the most basic is that if t_1 and t_2 are two distinguished terms designating the same object, then $t_1 = t_2$ is necessary.[3] Kripke spends more or less the whole of the discussion period seeking confirmation on two points from the speaker and commentator. From Marcus he just wants confirmation that she is making the assumption he indicates for her 'tags.' From Quine he wants confirmation that for him positing such a class of distinguished terms already constitutes an objectionable 'essentialism.' All this would at least sharpen the issue. Though it is like pulling teeth, Kripke does eventually extract confirmation on both points, first from Marcus, then from Quine – whereupon the moderator promptly calls a halt to the discussion, so we never do find out what Kripke would have done with his characterization of the dispute once having it confirmed.

Marcus takes the occasion of Kripke's asking for confirmation to reply to the remark of Quine quoted above. Kripke asked whether, when an object has two 'tags' a and b, the identity '$a = b$' was analytic, or necessary.[4] Marcus replies that for her 'tags' – or 'names in the ideal sense' as she now also calls them – she is assuming there would be a dictionary, so finding out that 'Hesperus' and 'Phosphorus' were two tags for the same object would only require going to a dictionary. Someone as 'flexible' as Quine might want to call even looking something up in a dictionary an 'empirical' procedure, but this is misleading, since it is not an empirical procedure in the same sense that astronomical observation is:

> [W]e can and do attach more than one name to a single object. We are here talking of proper names in the ideal sense, as tags and not descriptions. Presumably, if a single object had more than one tag, there would be a way of finding out such as having recourse to a dictionary or some analogous mode of inquiry, which would resolve the question as to whether the two tags denote the same thing. If 'Evening Star' and 'Morning Star' are considered to be two proper names for Venus, then finding out that they name the same thing as 'Venus' names is different from finding out what is Venus' mass or its orbit. It is perhaps admirably flexible, but also very confusing to obliterate the distinction between such linguistic and properly empirical procedures. (Marcus et al. 1962, 142)

Kripke took this for an affirmative answer to his question of whether she was assuming $t_1 = t_2$ is necessary, or analytic, whenever we have two 'tags' for the same thing. In the 1962 discussion he was prepared, at least for the sake of argument, to allow Marcus her assumption, and turned at once to ask Quine whether such an assumption does not for him constitute 'essentialism.' But when Kripke alludes to the Boston colloquium in N&N, he notes the obvious point that the assumption about a dictionary is very implausible, at least if one is speaking about names in the ordinary sense, what traditional grammar called 'proper nouns,' and not, say, hypothetical Russellian 'logically proper names.' So Quine is right as against Marcus in the two contrasting quotations.[5]

In Kripke (1971) it is said, however, that overall Quine and Marcus were both partly right and partly wrong: 'Hesperus = Phosphorus' is indeed synthetic and not analytic, a posteriori and not a priori, as Quine asserted, but it is also necessary and not contingent, as Marcus asserted; the mistake both of them were making was that of using 'analytic' and 'necessary' interchangeably. But the importance of distinguishing necessity from analyticity is *not* a point Kripke himself was insisting upon in the 1962 discussion. It was perhaps another year or so before Kripke took the giant step of reversing the conflation of necessity with analyticity. For recall that according to the preface in Kripke (1980), the central ideas of N&N, of which the crucial importance of maintaining the distinction between necessity and analyticity is surely one, date from 1963–1964.

Rigidity

Kripke, by the time he delivered his Princeton lectures, had long since revolted against the prevailing assumption that necessity is to be identified with analyticity, and gone back to the notion of necessity as *what is and couldn't have failed to be.* Henceforth I will always understand necessity in that sense, sometimes called 'metaphysical' necessity, after a remark of Kripke's to the effect that necessity is a 'metaphysical' rather than an epistemological notion. (Kripke uses scare-quotes just as I have done.)

Linguists use a different terminology. Palmer (1986) distinguishes three varieties of modality. The kind of concern to us, called by philosophers 'metaphysical,' is closest to the kind called by him 'dynamic.'[6] Modalities of this kind are contrasted with 'deontic' and 'epistemic' modalities. The former are exemplified when we say, 'He must stay, but she may go,' meaning 'He is obligated to stay, but she is permitted to go.' The latter are exemplified when we say, 'She must have gone, but he may have stayed,' meaning 'Given what we know, she must have gone, but for all we know, he may have stayed.' Though the same modal auxiliaries 'must' and 'may' are usable in English to express all three flavors of modality, the linguistics literature abundantly demonstrates that there are many languages in which the three flavors are expressed in quite distinct ways, so the conceptual distinction cannot be in doubt.

Kripke is prepared to assume provisionally that our ordinary judgments or 'intuitions' about 'metaphysical' modality can largely be trusted. (The methodological issue of how far they may be trusted will be discussed in a little more detail at the beginning of the next chapter.) Almost the first thing that Kripke does under this head is to draw out an intuition about the behavior of proper names in modal contexts. Now in natural language, modal distinctions and temporal distinctions are often expressed by similar means, either modifications of the verb (to distinguish past and present and future tense, and indicative and subjunctive mood), or by special auxiliary verbs (in English, 'will' and 'would,' 'shall' and 'should,' 'may' and 'might,' 'can' and 'could'). Since temporal notions are generally much clearer than modal notions, it may be well, before considering what Kripke claims about the behavior of names in modal contexts, to consider first their behavior in temporal contexts.

Let me do so, taking as an example the name of the first Roman emperor, whose nomenclature had a rather complex history. He was born on 23 September, 63 BCE. Romans did not name their infants until eight or nine days after birth. He then received the name 'Gaius Octavius Thurinus,' the first element being personal, the second and third family names. After his great-uncle Julius Caesar was assassinated in 44 BCE, it was given out that he had been posthumously adopted in Caesar's will. By the ordinary Roman rules his name would then have become 'Gaius Julius Caesar Octavianus,' where the fourth element is derived from but not identical to his original family name before the adoption. It seems, however, that only his political opponents, not his supporters, used 'Octavianus,' a reminder of his original comparatively undistinguished birth. He defeated the chief of these opponents, Mark Antony, at the battle of Actium in 31 BCE, and by 27 BCE he had become undisputed master of the Roman world. He was then voted an additional honorific by the Senate, making his full name 'Gaius Julius Caesar Augustus.'

Modern historians, for clarity, will sometimes make a point of calling him 'Octavius' when referring to events prior to 44, and 'Octavian' when referring to events from then until 27, and 'Augustus' thereafter;[7] but they have no hesitation in writing also 'Augus-

tus was born in 63,' even though it would be forty-six years from
that date before he acquired the name. For non-historians, if they
think about him at all, he is generally just 'Augustus.' The name
'Augustus' designates, when speaking about *any* period, the same
individual that it designates when speaking about the present, as
when we say 'In *I, Claudius,* Augustus is portrayed by Brian
Blessed.' More generally, *a proper name designates the same individual
when speaking about how things were in past or will be in the future that
it designates when speaking about how things are in the present.*

Kripke's main intuition in this area is that, analogously, *a proper
name designates the same individual when speaking of how things potentially might have been that it designates when speaking of how things
actually were or are or will be.* Thus when we say, 'Augustus might
have been defeated by Antony at Actium,' we are speaking of the
same person as when we say, 'Augustus defeated Antony at
Actium.' This is so even though if Augustus had been defeated by
Antony at Actium he would never have been named 'Augustus,'
and Antony might well have been named 'Augustus' instead.
(Being voted the honorific name 'Augustus' was in effect a sort of
victory prize.)

One type of putative counterexample may be mentioned. In a
long novel of counterfactual history about Cleopatra, the author
may depict Antony as defeating Octavian, and Antony and Cleopatra becoming emperor and empress and receiving the names or
titles 'Augustus' and 'Augusta.' In the later chapters of such a
novel, the other characters would certainly address Antony as
'Augustus' in dialogue, and very likely the author would slip into
calling him 'Augustus' in narrative passages as well. Similarly, in
a very long counterfactual conditional beginning 'If Antony had
defeated Octavian at Actium, then...' a speaker might well slip into
using 'Augustus' for Antony as well, if there has been explicit
mention of the Senate's counterfactually awarding Antony that
honorific. So perhaps in some cases, where naming has been explicitly mentioned, one might in discussing a counterfactual situation
use a name for the person who would have borne it in that counterfactual situation rather than the person who does bear it in
the actual situation. Though he does not discuss this particular
example specifically, Kripke would presumably regard it as concerning some kind of quasi-literary departure from the normal
pattern of language, not to be given serious weight in theorizing.
It is of a piece with the linguists' example, 'If parents named their
children Bambi and Thumper, Thumper would not thank them,'

where 'Thumper' is not (one hopes) the actual name of any actual child.

The feature of proper names Kripke cites, that what they designate does not vary between actual and counterfactual circumstances, he calls *rigidity*. It contrasts with the non-rigidity or flexibility of typical definite descriptions, such as 'the first Roman emperor,' which when speaking of actual history designates Augustus, but when speaking of counterfactual history might designate Antony. In atypical cases, definite descriptions may be rigid, too. For instance, 'the square of three' rigidly designates nine. This is because, though the battle of Actium could have gone either way, there are no two ways about what you get when you multiply three by itself.

There are two differences between Kripke's official account of rigidity and that given so far. For one thing, Kripke's official definition of rigidity includes specifications about the case of a counterfactual situation in which the individual in question would not have existed. This is a subtlety and complication that Kripke himself often ignores in N&N, and that will be ignored here. For another thing, Kripke's official definition uses a bit of jargon that he repopularized in his early technical work on modal logic, the jargon of 'possible worlds.'

As Kripke somewhat ruefully admits in N&N, the jargon of possible worlds may have had the effect of making some of his doctrines seem more controversial than they ought. A usage safer from misconstrual, Kripke now recognizes, would be to speak of possible *states* of the world, or ways the world might have been, or counterfactual situations (the terminology I have been using so far). Expressed in terms of possible worlds, rigidity is the property of designating the same item regardless of what possible world we are speaking of. Kripke emphasizes that what matters is how *we* speak *of* a 'possible world,' not how its residents speak *in* that 'possible world,' supposing any of its residents are capable of speech. We are concerned with what is designated by a word of our actual language, *with the meaning or use it has in our actual language*, not with a mere string of letters or phonemes that might, with a very different meaning or use, be a word of some hypothetical language in some hypothetical situation.

Kripke's own usage, however, remains somewhat sloppy, moving back and forth between speaking of how things *would have been* if the world at been in a different state from the one it is in, and speaking of how things *are* in a non-actual world. In some respects it is perhaps not so much speaking of 'worlds' rather than 'states' that invites misunderstanding, but this dropping of ordinary distinctions of grammatical mood, expressed in English using modal auxiliary verbs ('would have been' *vs* 'are'), in favor of a 'moodless' use of the indicative ('are'). We all engage every day in talk of what we would have done if the world *had been* in a different state, just as much as of talk of what we used to do when the world *was* in a different state, or are planning to do when the world *comes to be* in a different state. Change all this to talk of what I *am* doing in some non-actual possible world, or what I *am* doing in some non-present past or future world, and immediately the objection suggests itself that I *am* in this actual, present world and no other.[8]

The respect in which Kripke recognizes that 'possible world' talk may be misleading is a different one. It is that such talk has encouraged thinking of counterfactual situations, ways the world isn't but might have been, as if they were 'other worlds' in the sense of remote planets. Thinking of 'possible worlds' as remote planets means thinking of them as things or places seen through some sort of telescope. Thinking of them as seen through a telescope means thinking of them as given only by properties of a kind that could be seen through such an instrument, and describable in 'purely qualitative' terms. And when we think of things *that* way, a pseudoproblem arises about 'cross-world identification.' I see through the telescope various humanoid creatures moving around doing things. How can I tell whether in seeing a given individual through the telescope, or in reading someone's description of a given individual purely in terms of the sort of qualitative properties that can be seen through a telescope, I am seeing or reading about the *Socrates* – or the *me* – of the other world?

That is the problem, how to trace identity of individuals across possible worlds, as many in effect perceived it.[9] But ordinarily, Kripke emphasizes, when we speak of counterfactual situations, or ways the world might have been, we don't restrict ourselves to descriptions in 'purely qualitative' terms, mentioning only features such as would be visible through a telescope looking at a remote planet. We mention people *by name*, and consider what *they* might have done. There may be an epistemological problem about how we know that what we are imagining a certain person doing or suffering is genuinely possible, but there is no epistemological problem about who it is we are imagining doing or suffering whatever it is.

In mentioning people, and considering what *they* might have done, we are making judgments of *de re* possibility. So long as we tried to identify necessity with analyticity, it was profoundly obscure what a judgment of *de re* possibility could mean; now that we are identifying the possible with what could have been, we see that we make intuitive judgments of *de re* possibility every day. Of course, to say the notion is intuitively familiar is not to say that it couldn't do with some critical analysis; but it means that we start the critical analysis with a presumption in favor of this established way of speaking, rather than with a suspicion about it.

The Necessity of Identity

Closely connected with the notion of rigidity is the notion of the necessity of identity. Here a different kind of clarification about terminology is needed. As Kripke notes, 'necessity of identity' is used in the literature as a label for (at least) three different principles. The first is the trivial-seeming, and comparatively uncontroversial principle that anything is necessarily identical with itself:

(1)   For every thing x, necessarily $x = x$.

The second is a theorem found in formal systems of modal predicate logic, of which versions appear in various sources from Marcus (1947) onwards. It reads as follows:

(2)   For every thing x and every thing y, if $x = y$, then necessarily $x = y$.

The easy though not quite trivial proof is given at the beginning of (Kripke 1971). Kripke thinks (2) should be no more controversial than (1), and even Quine held that *if 'quantifying in' makes any sense*, we must have (2) as well as (1).[10]

The third is the principle saying that whatever names we write in the blanks we have:

(3)   If ____ = ..., then necessarily ____ = ...

In (Marcus 1961) it seems to be asserted that this somehow follows from (2), but, as Kripke emphasizes, it does not. For (2) only says that two objects that are identical are necessarily so, and thus (2) in and of itself implies nothing whatsoever about terms such as proper names or definite descriptions. It implies that if the thing designated by one term and the thing designated by another term are actually the same, then those things, the things the terms actually designate, couldn't have been different; but it by no means implies that if two terms actually are co-designative, they couldn't have failed to be co-designative.

To get to (3), which is the version of 'necessity of identity' pertinent in the present context, we need rigidity, and a further assumption that lurks almost invisibly in the background in Kripke's discussion, and which may be stated thus:

(4)   ____ would have been identical to .... in a given counterfactual situation just in case '____' and '............' designate the same individual when used by us in speaking about the given counterfactual situation.

Suppose, for instance, we are speaking of a counterfactual situation in which the battle of Actium went the other way. Then (4) tells us that Augustus would have been identical to Octavian in that situation just in case 'Augustus' and 'Octavian' designate the same individual when we are speaking of that situation.

That they indeed do so follows from rigidity, thus:

the individual 'Augustus' designates
when speaking of the specified counterfactual situation

= (by rigidity)

the individual 'Augustus' designates
when speaking of the actual situation

= (as a matter of actual, historical fact)

the individual 'Octavian' designates
when speaking of the actual situation

= (by rigidity)

the individual 'Octavian' designates
when speaking of the specified counterfactual situation

Thus Augustus indeed *would* have been identical with Octavian in the counterfactual situation – and this no matter what counterfactual situation is in question, since all our considerations have been perfectly general. Thus Augustus would have been identical with Octavian no matter what; Augustus could not have failed to be identical with Octavian; Augustus is necessarily identical with Octavian – and similarly in any other case of co-designative proper names, as per (3). The necessity of *non*-identity, of Augustus's not being Antony, for instance, is established by a very similar argument.

I have given the derivation that I take to be implicit in Kripke somewhat more explicitly than he does, isolating the role of assumption (4), in order to be able to bring out the following point. If we tried to prove by parallel reasoning that

(5)   According to Homer's beliefs, Hesperus is identical with Phosphorus.

we would need *both* an analogue of rigidity, as follows:

(6)   What 'Hesperus' and 'Phosphorus' designate when we are speaking of how Homer believes things to be, are the same as what they designate when we are speaking of how things really are.

and a principle analogous to (4), as follows:

(7)   Hesperus and Phosphorus are identical according to Homer's beliefs just in case 'Hesperus' and 'Phosphorus' designate the same object when used in speaking about Homer's beliefs.

Of course, Kripke, who has expressed agreement with Quine about the a posteriori status of 'Hesperus = Phosphorus,' does *not* want to prove (5), and he does *not* endorse anything like (6) or (7), neither of which is an especially compelling intuition.

The point is that the intuitions to which Kripke explicitly or implicitly appeals in arguing for the necessity of identity are specific to modal contexts as contrasted with various other kinds of contexts, including belief contexts. Kripke does not invoke any *general* claim about the interchangeability of co-designative names in *all* contexts, and obviously he cannot think that 'Hesperus' and 'Phosphorus' are interchangeable in all contexts. 'It is a priori that _____ is the same as Phosphorus' and 'It is analytic that _____ is the same as Phosphorus' and 'Homer believed that _____ is the same as Phosphorus' would presumably all three be counter-examples, for Kripke.[11]

There is, however, one class of contexts to which Kripke's rigidity intuitions do seem to extend. For presumably the modal intuitions or principles Kripke endorses have *temporal* analogues. Though Kripke does not discuss the analogous temporal case explicitly, he undoubtedly would adopt a similar view, and maintain the *permanence of identity*: Augustus has been and will be Octavian no matter when; he never has failed and is never going to fail to be Octavian; he is *permanently* identical with Octavian (and permanently *non*-identical to Antony).

Resistance

The modal argument against descriptivist theories of names is basically just this: that the kinds of descriptions proponents of such theories cite cannot be synonymous with the names, because they generally involve what are rather obviously *contingent* properties of the individual bearing the name. The argument bears equally against Fregean and metalinguistic versions of descriptivism.

If 'Socrates' were synonymous with 'the philosopher who drank hemlock,' then 'Socrates is the philosopher who drank hemlock' would be synonymous with 'Socrates is Socrates,' and 'Socrates is the philosopher who drank hemlock', being synonymous, would be just as necessary as 'Socrates is Socrates.' But surely it is contingent. For Socrates need not have been the philosopher who drank the hemlock, since he might have taken the opportunity to escape into exile, or the Athenians might have adopted a different mode of execution, or he might have behaved less provocatively at his trial and been acquitted – and he need not have gone in for philosophizing at all, of course. Nor need Socrates have been the most famous teacher of Plato, or Plato the most famous student of Socrates. If Socrates had not gone into philosophy, neither of these things would have come about.

And surely Socrates need not have borne the name 'Socrates,' and Plato need not have been called by the name 'Plato.' Indeed, according to some sources, Plato's name was originally 'Aristocles,' and he was given the name 'Plato' only by his teacher, Socrates; so if he hadn't become a student of Socrates, he wouldn't have been called by the name 'Plato' either. But in all the counterfactual circumstances being postulated, Socrates would still have been Socrates, and Plato Plato. Since 'Socrates = Socrates' and 'Plato = Plato' are necessary, while 'Socrates = the philosopher who drank hemlock' and 'Plato = the bearer of the name "Plato"' are contingent, the names cannot be abbreviations of the descriptions, or the descriptions definitions of the names.

Any number of descriptivists have attempted to counter or circumvent this simple but compelling line of thought. Generally they grudgingly concede or anyhow do not strenuously challenge Kripke's points about the distinction between the necessary and the a priori, the rigidity of proper names, the necessary truth of identity statements linking proper names with the same bearer, and our ability to say *de re* of a thing that *it* necessarily has a certain property (independently of how or whether it is named or described) just by saying of the individual under any one of its proper names that it necessarily has the property in question. Though letting all this pass, some still seek to preserve a role for descriptions in connection with proper names.

There have been two main strategies, each of which comes in variant versions.[12] Their common feature is that they in one way or another require the description associated with a name to be understood as it applies to the *actual* world, or *actual* state of the world, even when the name appears deeply embedded in some modal or other context. Exactly what this means should become clearer as we review the strategies.

The 'Actually' Operator. One strategy would insert into a description such as 'the philosopher who drank the hemlock' the adverb *actually*, understood in a 'regimented' way as meaning 'in the actual world,' or less misleadingly, 'in the actual state of the world.' Thus 'Socrates need not have drunk the hemlock' may become 'There is a possible world in which the individual who in the actual world was a philosopher and drank hemlock did not drink hemlock,' or 'There is a state the world could have been in such that, had the world been in that state, the individual who in the actual state of the world was a philosopher and drank hemlock would not have drunk the hemlock.' Similarly, 'Plato need not have been named "Plato"' may become 'There is a possible world in which the individual who in the actual world bore the name "Plato" did not bear the name "Plato"' or 'There is a state the world could have been in such that, had the world been in that state, the individual who in the actual state of the world bore the name "Plato" would not have borne the name "Plato."'[13]

Scope Distinctions. Another strategy turns on Russell's theory of descriptions. According to Russell, 'The present king of France is bald' amounts to something like 'There exists a unique present king of France, and any present king of France is bald.' What of 'The present king of France is *not* bald'? Here Russell sees an ambiguity between what is called the *wide-scope* reading,

(1)   There exists a unique present king of France, and any present king of France is *not* bald.

which is false, and what is called the *narrow-scope* reading,

(2)   It is *not* the case both that there exists a unique present
       king of France and that any present king of France is
       bald.

which is true. With the *double* negation 'the present king of France
is not not bald' there would be *three* readings. The widest and nar-
rowest would be just like (1) and (3) except for having 'not not' in
place of 'not'; they would be false. But there would also be an
intermediate reading that is true: 'It is not the case both that there
exists a unique present king of France and that any present king of
France is not bald.' In general, the deeper a description is embedded inside other constructions, the more scope distinctions can be
made, and the more readings will be available.

The defense of descriptivism based on these ideas is simply this:
that a name is taken to be equivalent to a description *but* with the
convention that one is always to take *widest* scope. So 'Socrates
need not have drunk the hemlock' might amount to 'There is a
unique man who was a philosopher and drank hemlock, and of
any man who was a philosopher and drank hemlock it is true that
he need not have drunk it.' Similarly, 'Plato need not have been
named "Plato"' might amount to 'There is a unique man named
"Plato," and of any man named "Plato" it is true that *he* need not
have been named "Plato." ' The question, 'In such-and-such a counterfactual situation, would it have been true that Aristotle taught
Alexander?' similarly is to be understood as something like 'There
is a unique individual who taught Alexander. In such-and-such a
counterfactual situation, would it still have been true that *he* taught
Alexander?'[14]

The descriptivist still has the error and ignorance objections to
confront; or at least, the Fregean still has these objections to confront; we have seen that a sufficiently carefully formulated version
of the metalinguistic theory may be able to avoid them. Both types
of descriptivism face difficulties over belief attribution, as in 'Homer
believed that Hesperus and Phosphorus are distinct,' as well.
Meanwhile, Kripke's defense of Millianism remains incomplete
insofar as he has given no solution to the Hesperus *vs* Phosphorus
and the Pegasus puzzles. But let us for the moment (in fact, until
the chapter after next) leave these issues pertaining to naming
hanging, with several loose ends dangling, just as Kripke himself
did in N&N, and press on with the topic of modality. We can begin
by taking up the companion phenomenon to the a posteriori necessities, to wit, a priori contingencies.

The Contingent a Priori

Kripke seems recently, in Kripke (2011d), to have accepted an old suggestion he attributes to Harry Frankfurt, to the effect that the simplest example of a statement at once contingent and a priori is one going back to Descartes, who said that 'I am, I exist' is true each time one thinks it. The example is certainly highly contingent, for any one of us can truly say that it was only through the confluence of many contingencies that we were ever born, let alone that we managed to live to our present age. The example is a priori in the sense that if I think 'I exist' I need no further empirical evidence beyond the experience of thinking it to conclude that I must exist, since only what exists can think (or do anything else, for that matter).

Of course, the Cartesian example is private, and only a priori for one thinker: My thought that I exist and your thought that you exist are not the same thought; I only know a priori that my thought is true, and you only know a priori that your thought is true; that I exist is for you an empirical claim, and that you exist is an empirical claim for me. The Cartesian example is ephemeral, as well, or so it seems. For though, as Descartes says, 'I exist' is true each time I think it, still each time I think it, is it not a different thought that I think: the thought that I exist at *that* time? No one thought remains for longer than the duration of the specious present.

N&N contains two main examples of the contingent a priori, both superficially looking rather different from the Cartesian example. The more straightforward of the two runs as follows. I have said that it seems to be very rare for the introducer of a name to have pure intention to assign it to the item fitting a certain description *whatever it may be*, regardless of or in the absence of any conjectures about what item that is. Kripke imagines a case. He imagines Urbain Le Verrier conjecturing that the observed perturbations of the orbit of Uranus are caused by some further planet beyond, and adopting 'Neptune' as the name of this as-yet-undiscovered planet. In this case, Kripke allows, Le Verrier does when introducing the name know a priori that if Neptune exists, then it is the cause of the observed perturbations of the orbit of Uranus. But it is contingent that Neptune thus perturbs Uranus, since a cataclysm in the early history of the solar system might have knocked Neptune so far out as to make its perturbing influence on Uranus negligible.

Identity   57

If one considers the Neptune example closely, it seems to me to share the privacy and ephemerality of the Cartesian example, though this is not something Kripke acknowledges in N&N, or elsewhere either, so far as I know. As to privacy, if Le Verrier introduces the name 'Neptune,' with the reference-fixing description indicated, at a public lecture, those in the back of the auditorium, or whose hearing is poor, or who are distracted by whispering going on around them, may only take away that Neptune is some kind of new heavenly body, not catching the part about the link to Uranus. Some, perhaps, having dimly heard something about Uranus, may even leap to the conclusion that it is a new-discovered moon of Uranus that is being discussed. Such ignorance and error are commonplace and almost inevitable with genuine proper names, as we have seen Kripke argue. For those with good hearing and a seat in the front row, practically speaking there is no serious chance of error, but even a remote theoretical chance of error seems enough to disqualify 'Neptune, if it exists, is responsible for the perturbations of the orbit of Uranus' as a priori for anyone but Le Verrier himself, the introducer of the name.

Writing his memoirs twenty years later, Le Verrier may have difficulty recalling which of several scenarios actually occurred: (a) he decided months or years before the thought occurred to him that the perturbations of the orbit of Uranus were evidence of the existence of another planet, that if ever there was reason to suppose there was another planet in the solar system beyond Uranus, it should be named 'Neptune'; (b) after the thought about Uranus occurred to him, he decided to name the as-yet-undiscovered perturbing planet 'Neptune' (the case we have been assuming in the discussion so far); (c) at the time he had the thought about Uranus he considered several candidate names for the new planet, only settling on 'Neptune' after the planet had been sighted and he was able to see it through a telescope and noticed its sea-blue color. In short, Le Verrier may not *remember* twenty years later what the reference-fixing description used in introducing the name 'Neptune' was, being undecided among several candidates: (a) 'the next planet beyond Uranus, if there is one'; (b) 'the planet perturbing Uranus' (the case we have been assuming in the discussion so far); (c) 'that bluish planet that I see over there [while looking through a telescope].' Once he has forgotten what the reference-fixing description was, it can no longer be a priori for him that Neptune fits it; and needless to say, it may take him a lot less than twenty years to forget. Moreover, even if he remembers, his knowledge seems to depend on the assumption of the reliability of his memory, and hence on an empirical assumption. So the a priori knowledge may not survive longer than the duration of the specious present, as with the Cartesian example.[15]

In Kripke's primary example, 'meter' or 'metre' is held to designate rigidly a certain length, the reference-fixing specification being that it is to be the length a certain bar had at a certain time t_0. According to Kripke, it is a priori that the bar was one meter long at time t_0, though it is also contingent, since the temperature and therefore the length of the bar might easily have been different from what they actually were at time t_0. There are a number of distracting features to this example, which it would take us too far afield to discuss in detail.[16]

From the clearer Cartesian and Neptune examples, the existence of a priori contingencies appears to be something in the nature of a curiosity, whose main importance lies simply in underscoring the conceptual distinctness of the categories of the necessary and the a priori. Some commentators have tried to deny the phenomenon altogether, insisting that one cannot fix the reference of a new name by the pure thought that *whatever it may be* that fits a certain description is to be the bearer of the name, that one must somehow be *acquainted* with the object getting the name. Others have tried to claim that by stipulating that 'so-and-so' is to rigidly designate the such-and-such, one can easily introduce into the permanent, public language an amphibious 'descriptive name,' and in this way generate a large class of a priori contingencies. All I will say about this is that the incompatible anti-Kripkean assumptions being made here are quite unobvious.[17] But the contingent a priori remains a minor side-issue compared with the necessary a posteriori.

3

Necessity

We now come to the core of Kripke's philosophical work on the nature of modality. In Kripke's first and second lectures in N&N, naming was the lead actor, with necessity in a supporting part; in the third lecture, the main topic of this chapter, the roles are reversed. The same is true of the later parts of (Kripke 1971) also, and to a degree of the addenda to N&N.

The plan will be to consider first additional modal intuitions Kripke elicits in these writings, about what is essential and what accidental for individuals such as Hesperus or Socrates. Then we will turn to analogous modal intuitions that Kripke elicits, not about individuals, but about natural substances such as gold or water, then natural kinds such as tigers or cats, and then natural phenomena such as heat or light. Having all these examples before us, we will turn briefly to consider how to account for our ability to reach the kinds of judgments about necessity and contingency that figure in Kripke's discussion, without positing an occult faculty, unknown to orthodox psychology, allowing us to detect metaphysical essence.

Imagination and the Necessary a Posteriori

Already in connection with the modal argument against Fregeanism, Kripke has elicited any number of intuitions concerning what could have been the case – for instance, that Aristotle need not have taught Alexander, or that Socrates need not have taught Plato. Now

he will be eliciting many more. Various methods are used throughout the third lecture of N&N to draw out intuitions, and to argue,
in varying degrees of detail, that in a great many examples certain
facts are necessary though only knowable a posteriori, and certain
properties essential to their possessors but only knowable a posteriori to be possessed by them. It will be well to begin with some
methodological discussion.

Two imaginative techniques especially are employed by Kripke
in his third chapter. With the method of *backtracking*, we imagine
running the engine of history in reverse back to a certain time, and
then running it forward again along a different track. As Kripke
says (N&N, footnote 57):

> Ordinarily when we ask intuitively whether something might have
> happened to a given object, we ask whether the universe could have
> gone on as it actually did up to a certain time, but diverge in its
> history from that point forward so that the vicissitudes of the object
> would have been different from that time forth.

This is the method employed in concluding that Aristotle need not
have taught Alexander: We backtrack to some time early in Aristotle's career before he had decided go into teaching, and go forward
from there to imagine him deciding instead to follow his father's
profession of medicine. Kripke adds that in some cases

> the time at which the divergence from actual history occurs may be
> sometime before the object itself is actually created.

To establish that Aristotle might have had hemophilia, for instance,
we may have to backtrack to before his birth and even to before
his conception, before the coming together of the egg and sperm
cells from whose fusion he was to develop, and imagine a cosmic
ray striking the egg and causing a mutation to a gene on its
X-chromosome.

With the method of *duplication*, we imagine a counterfactual situation or 'possible world' in superficial, outward, qualitative respects
indistinguishable from our own so far as it had been observed up
to the time of certain scientific investigations, but where subsequent scientific investigation discloses features very different from
those of the actual situation or world. We will see applications of
this method shortly.

But while our main guide to what is possible is such techniques of imagination, the techniques must be used with caution. For what we seem to be able to imagine may nonetheless be impossible, and this for either of two reasons. First, once we have acknowledged the necessary a posteriori, we must distinguish being *genuinely possible* (not necessarily false) from merely being *coherently conceivable* (not knowable a priori to be false). For instance, ancient historians tell us that someone named 'Petronius' was appointed by Nero to be the 'arbiter of elegancy' at his court, while medieval manuscripts indicate that someone named 'Petronius' was the author of the comic novel *Satiricon*. Scholars are divided over whether the one Petronius and the other Petronius are the same person. No a priori reasoning can settle the question: Both the identity and the non-identity of the two Petronii are coherently conceivable and epistemically possible. But whichever holds, holds necessarily according to Kripke's doctrine of the necessity of identity and non-identity, and its opposite is not genuinely 'metaphysically' possible.

Second, what seems *superficially* imaginable may not be *coherently* conceivable: More careful thought may produce an a priori demonstration that something cannot be the case even though it was not immediately obvious that it could not be the case. Thus Ellen White seemed to herself to be able to imagine – indeed, claimed to have had an actual vision of – 144,000 saints arranged in a perfect square. But it is a priori that, saints or sinners, 144,000 people cannot be arranged in a perfect square. For calculation shows this to be contrary to the laws of arithmetic.

The potential for this second kind error, which seems to pertain mainly to examples involving mathematics, has not played any great role in subsequent discussions. By contrast, the potential for the first kind of error has been important both for Kripke and for his critics. To begin with, the possibility of being misled by imagination and the need for caution in using imaginative techniques (along with the importance of distinguishing 'metaphysical' possibility from epistemic possibility) is stressed by Kripke in attempts to explain away apparent intuitions *against* his doctrine of the necessity of identity.

For it may be objected, 'It has turned out that Hesperus and Phosphorus are identical, but couldn't it have turned out that they were distinct?' A Kripkean will answer that though in one idiomatic, *epistemic* sense we may, colloquially speaking, say that 'it could have turned out' that they were distinct, this means no more than '*for all anyone knew at the time*, it might have been going to turn out that they were distinct.' In another important sense, it could *not* have turned out – it could not have been *discovered* – that they were distinct. Hesperus and Phosphorus could not have been discovered to be distinct, because one can only discover what is there to be discovered, and that goes for facts about which things are identical or and which things are distinct as much as it goes for anything else. And yet, unsatisfied with this answer, the objector may protest, 'But surely we can *imagine* them being distinct!' To this Kripke would reply that we must, when using imaginative techniques, be very careful to avoid *misdescribing* what we are imagining. What the objector is *really* imagining in the Hesperus *vs* Phosphorus case, according to Kripke, only *seems* to be a situation in which Hesperus and Phosphorus are distinct.

Perhaps what one is really doing may be more accurately described in back-tracking terms as imagining the early evolution of the solar system being disrupted, perhaps by a Velikovskian giant comet, so that instead of the planet Venus being formed, two smaller bodies sharing roughly the same orbit were produced. Or perhaps it may more accurately be described in duplication terms as imagining a world to superficial, outward, qualitative appearances indistinguishable from ours so far as it had been observed down to the time of Homer, but which subsequent scientific investigation proves to have two different planets tied for second closest to the central star. Though in either case there are two planets that get *called* 'Hesperus' and 'Phosphorus,' these are not our Hesperus and Phosphorus – not what *we* call 'Hesperus' and 'Phosphorus' – since those are both just Venus.

In the Socratic examples considered so far, the results produced by the imaginative exercise of backtracking have been negative: It has been concluded that certain traits of Socrates are merely accidental, and therefore cannot be part of the very meaning of his name. Can we produce any positive results? Can we find anything essential to Socrates, other than his being himself, Socrates, and not being anyone else, such as Confucius? Kripke would say we can. He holds in particular that the (biological) *origin* or *parentage* of any person is essential to him or her. Picking up on an example in one of the authors he quotes and criticizes, Kripke says the Queen could not have been the daughter of Harry Truman. He would equally say that Socrates could not have been the child of Pericles, even though the dates are right. (Pericles was 26 at the time Socrates was born.)

We can imagine Pericles, dismayed at the discovery that some less famous predecessor of Aspasia has borne him an ugly, snub-nosed son, persuading the childless mason Sophroniscus and midwife Phaenarete to adopt the infant secretly and give out that it is their own. They name him 'Socrates,' he grows up and pursues philosophy, teaches Plato, and in the end drinks hemlock. This for Kripke would be a typical case where one must be careful in describing what one is imagining. What has actually been imagined, on the Kripkean view, is *someone other than Socrates* having a career like that of Socrates, in counterfactual circumstances in which *Socrates* never would have been born.

If that is not clear, try the following exercise. First imagine back-tracking to the day of Socrates' birth, and going forward along the following lines: Infant morality being very high in those days, to his parents' distress but to no one's very great surprise the newborn dies a few days after birth; some weeks later, Pericles appears with an offer to the bereaved parents, and so on. Now imagine back-tracking a little further, so that Socrates is stillborn; or a little further still, so that there is a miscarriage at an early stage in the pregnancy; a little further still, to the moment of Socrates' conception, when something happens so that implantation never occurs and preg-nancy never results; or a little further still, to just before the egg-cell and sperm-cell come together, so that this is somehow prevented and no conception occurs; or a little further still, so that Sophronis-cus is called away from Athens for a month or more, including the whole pertinent ovular cycle of Phaenarete. Clearly in the first case the son of Pericles is not Socrates, since Socrates has already been born, lived his too-short life, and died before the substitute is brought on the scene. But continuity from case to case suggests that the son of Pericles is still not Socrates even where there is no child of Sophroniscus and Phaenarete present as a rival claimant for that identity.

Though Socrates, it is thus argued, is necessarily the child of Sophroniscus and Phaenarete, it is hardly needful to say that it is not a necessary truth that if someone is a child of that pair, then he or she is Socrates: Even if Socrates was in actual fact an only child, he *could have* had siblings. Is it a necessary truth that anyone who grew from the fusion of the very egg and the very sperm that produced Socrates would be Socrates, even if that egg and that sperm had come together at a slightly different time or place? Kripke seems to think so, but the question is not one he discusses in detail.

Note that Kripke's view now implies that we have a substantial class of rigid descriptions quite unlike the mathematical example 'the square root of nine' cited earlier. These include such descriptions as 'the father of Socrates' and 'the mother of Socrates.' Further examples of rigid descriptions are associated with the further examples of a posteriori necessity to be discussed in the remainder of this chapter.

It was not always clear to the earliest readers of N&N, and perhaps not *fully* clear to anyone before the appearance of Salmon (1981), how far the claims of necessity that were being made were supposed to be consequences simply of various intuitions about *reference* (those appealed to in arguing for anti-descriptivism and rigidity) and how far they were dependent on further intuitions. I hope it has been evident from the foregoing exposition that the intuition about parentage is *not* to be taken to be anything like an immediate consequence of rigidity, in the way the necessity of identity and non-identity are, but is something over and above all that. The same seems to be so with many of further claims of necessity or essence to be considered in this chapter, though there will not be space to go into cases.

These further claims begin with some additional assertions about what features are essential to, or necessary for the existence of, individual persons or things. For apart from his discussion of ancestry of living beings, Kripke argues that an artifact's material composition may be essential to it. For instance, the Parthenon, in whose shadow Socrates taught, could not have been from the beginning made of concrete rather than marble, like the replica in Nashville.[1] The treatment of such cases, however, is largely relegated to footnotes and is partly qualified, not to say retracted, in the face of objections from Nathan Salmon and others, in the preface to (Kripke 1980). So I will leave these cases aside, being eager, as was Kripke, to press on to examples beyond those pertaining to individuals.

Natural Substances

Kripke considers three types of nouns, beyond proper names, all supposed to give rise to examples of posteriori necessities. They comprise certain simple terms designating natural substances (such as 'water'), certain simple terms designating natural kinds (such as 'whale'), and certain simple terms designating natural phenomena (such as 'heat'). The supposed a posteriori necessities at issue include 'water is H_2O' and 'whales are mammals' and 'heat is random molecular motion.' All three of these are scientific conclusions that clearly were not and could not have been arrived at without appeal to sense-experience; but all three express facts that Kripke is prepared to argue could not have been otherwise. For his discussion elicits intuitions to the effect that a substance having a composition other than H_2O wouldn't be water, that a kind of creature that was not mammalian wouldn't be a whale, and that a phenomenon that did not involve random molecular motion wouldn't be heat.

It should be admitted at the outset that Kripke's highly suggestive discussion is short on details in a couple of important respects. First, as regards the scope of his claims, he never gives an exact specification of the class or classes of terms to which his claims are intended to apply. In his first two lectures, Kripke was discussing more or less the same class of expressions that grammarians traditionally classed as 'proper nouns' or 'proper names.' Traditional grammar classed all other nouns as 'common nouns' or 'common names,' and recognized one important subdivision of these: The fact that one speaks of one waiter, two waiters, a few waiters, many waiters, but of some water, more water, a little water, much water, marks 'waiter' as a *count* noun and 'water' as a *mass* noun. Many of the terms Kripke considers in his third lecture (among them 'water' and 'heat') belong to the class of mass nouns, but there is no sign that Kripke's claims are intended to apply to *all* mass nouns (a class that includes, for instance, 'furniture' and 'gossip'), and some of his examples involve count nouns (among them 'tiger'). Thus the class of terms to which he intends his claims to apply does not coincide with any class recognized by traditional grammar. Nor does Kripke offer any non-grammatical characterization. He merely gives examples.

Second, while Kripke indicates that in his view those terms to which he intends his claims to apply resemble proper names in that what connects them to what they designate is an historical communicative chain rather than a defining qualitative description, and in that they enjoy a property somehow analogous to rigidity, he provides little detail about the nature of the analogy, or about how far his claims are supposed to follow from rigidity considerations alone, and how far they depend on further, supplementary intuitions. The exact nature of the rigidity-like property or properties supposed to be enjoyed by his examples, and its precise connection with the various claims about necessity and essence that he makes, have therefore become the topic of considerable discussion and disagreement in the ensuing secondary literature.[2] Doubtless the eventual release of previously unpublished Krip-keana will enlighten us on a number of points, but doubtless also Kripke has left a good deal of work for his successors in the way of developing his suggestions into full-blown theoretical accounts.

With the understanding that we should not look for any such full-blown theoretical account in N&N itself, let us turn now to the first of three types of term to which Kripke addresses himself in his third lecture. These are simple terms for natural kinds of sub-stances. His chief examples are terms for chemical elements and compounds such as 'gold' and 'water' and the like. His discussion *may* apply also to mixtures or alloys such as brass and pewter, and to physical phases of chemical substances, such as graphite and diamond, but Kripke does not commit himself.

One respect in which Kripke takes it that the natural substance terms under discussion resemble proper names is their lacking of any descriptive sense or connotation. Under this head Kripke actu-ally makes a pair of claims: (1a) It is not analytic or a priori that the substance designated by the term fits the description one might find given as a definition for the term, say in a dictionary or ency-clopedia. (1b) It is not analytic or a priori that the term would be correctly applicable to any substance that did fit such a description. Kripke also makes, as already hinted, another claim: (2) What con-nects a user of the term to the substance it designates is not an associated description, but rather a chain of communication leading back to an initial baptism event, generally involving exposure to specific samples of the substance. Kripke argues these points taking sometimes gold, sometimes water as his example.[3]

As to point (1a), Kripke considers, perhaps making things rather easy for himself, the case of the notoriously bad Kantian example of a supposedly analytic judgment, the definition of gold as 'a yellow metal.' He argues that it is not a priori that gold fits this definition by being yellow: He maintains that it is coherently con-ceivable that gold is blue, with its apparent yellowness being an illusion produced by special features either of the atmosphere in gold-rich environments, or of the brains of those who gaze at the costly material.[4] (He hints also that it is not analytic or a priori that gold fits the definition by being a metal, but begs off defending this claim, on the grounds that the question involves too much chem-istry.) As to point (1b), Kripke seems to take it to be obvious that not every yellow metal is gold, though he mentions no specific counterexample.[5]

As to point (2), Kripke sketches a modified version of the 'chain of communication' picture he developed for proper names, a version intended to apply to simple natural substance terms like 'water' or 'gold.' The chain begins with an initial introduction of the term, where its reference may be fixed by citing a range of samples, and indicating that the term is to apply to the substance of which they, or the bulk of them, are samples. There is one significant difference concerning initial baptism between proper names and substance terms. In the case of names for individuals, especially where ostension is involved, it is comparatively rare for the attempted introduction of a name to fail to designate anything.[6] Failure is significantly more of a threat in the case of substance terms, and Kripke briefly mentions several types of case where it may turn out that there just *is* no single, distinctive substance of which the bulk of the specimens are made. One problem case, for instance, arises when the original samples turn out to be of several different and unrelated compositions, so there is no such thing as *the* substance of which the bulk of the samples are made.[7]

Supposing there are no such slips at the beginning, and the term is successfully introduced, it is thereafter passed on from speaker to speaker. Kripke observes that the way in which new speakers pick up the term can differ between the case of common substances and the case of rare ones. With common substances such as water, new speakers may acquire the term in connection with exposure to samples, though of course these will not be the very *same* samples as at the initial introduction. This is comparable to a case where we learn a new personal name by being introduced to the person bearing the name while at the same time being told the name: 'I'd like you to meet Ms Wutzerneym.' With rarer substances such as gold, probably some speakers will pick up the term in the first-hand way through exposure to samples, while others will pick up the term only second- or third-hand. With very rare substances, technetium or neptunium, say, almost everyone will be getting the term *n*th-hand, as we all do when first picking up proper names for historical personages long dead.

Now there seem to be very few interesting identities where on both sides of the equals sign we have simple natural substance terms of the kind Kripke considers, though 'tungsten = wolfram' does provide one example. The interesting examples in Kripke are identities with a simple natural substance term like 'water' on one side, and a more complex term like 'H_2O' on the other. Unlike the simple terms 'water' or 'gold' or 'hydrogen' or 'oxygen,' the complex term 'H_2O' cannot plausibly be claimed to lack any descriptive sense or connotation. Rather, at least to a first approximation, it is something like an abbreviation for 'the substance whose molecules consist of two atoms of hydrogen and one of oxygen,' and this longish description is something like a definition of 'H_2O.'

It is the fact that 'H_2O' does bear such a meaning that makes the identity 'water = H_2O' an important scientific result. This result is, of course, anything but a priori: Not only did the ancients and medievals think water was an element, but from Dalton until Avogadro chemists thought water's chemical formula was HO, which is to say, they thought water was a substance whose molecules consisted of one atom each of hydrogen and oxygen. Nonetheless, Kripke claims the identity in question is necessary. He makes a similar claim for 'gold = the element with atomic number 79,' which he seems to understand as synonymous with something like 'gold = the element the nucleus of each of whose atoms contains 79 protons.' This is an even more recent discovery than the exact chemical composition of water, but Kripke denies it is contingent.

Kripke acknowledges overlap between some his conclusions and work of Hilary Putnam having its roots in the early nineteen sixties (but given canonical expression only in Putnam (1973), somewhat after the publication of N&N). Though Putnam's interests and emphases are different from Kripke's, his way of bringing out the intuitions may be considered with profit alongside Kripke's discussion. Putnam's main imaginative method is similar to Kripke's duplication method, except that instead of imagining a counterfactual situation or way the world could have been, he imagines a distant planet. Kripke, we have seen, generally insists that possible worlds are *not* like distant planets; but where it is qualitative features that are of concern, the differences become less important. Kripke's treatment of the example 'water = H_2O' is very reminiscent of things said by Putnam.

Putnam asks us to imagine, somewhere in the universe, a planet 'twin earth' not on superficial examination perceptibly different qualitatively from earth, but where the substance that fills the rivers and lakes and rains down from the sky and is drunk by the inhabitants turns out on closer scientific investigation to have the some complicated chemical composition he abbreviates to XYZ rather than the chemical composition H_2O. Putnam elicits the intu-

ition that this is *not* a planet where the water is XYZ rather than
H_2O, but rather is a planet where some substance other than water
fills the rivers and lakes and rains down from the sky and is drunk
by the inhabitants – and is called 'water' by them. The Kripkean
argument for the necessity of 'water = H_2O' would be very nearly
the same, but with a 'possible world' in place of a distant planet.[8]

Natural Kinds

Let us turn next to Kripke's examples of simple terms for natural
kinds: 'tiger' and 'cat' and 'whale.' Kripke argues that in the case
of such examples the same sort of rough analogy with proper
names that we saw with certain terms for substances is present.
Kripke's discussion of these matters moves rather briskly along, as
if he were supposing that those who have caught the spirit of his
earlier, slower-paced discussions will be prepared to fill in the gaps
themselves by this point. Again it is claimed, as it was in the case
of substance terms, that fitting a given description is neither a priori
required nor a priori sufficient for a natural-kind term to be applicable, and that what kind of thing such a term designates is determined by an historical chain of communication leading back to an
initial baptism, rather than by associated descriptions.

More importantly, it is claimed that identity statements linking
two such terms are necessary, though often a posteriori. Actually,
outright identities such as 'groundhogs = woodchucks' or 'gorse
= furze' are not the really interesting examples of a posteriori necessities in this area. Interesting examples are provided, rather, by
statements of inclusion such as 'Tigers are mammals' (Kripke's
own main example)[9] or 'Cats are animals' (an example he quotes
from Putnam), along with statements of exclusion, such as 'Whales
are not fish.' Against a background of evolutionary biology, the a
posteriori necessity of inclusion and exclusion statements between
natural kinds of biological taxa will be seen to be more or less
parallel to the a posteriori necessity of parentage and ancestry in
the case of individuals, since taxonomy is or aspires to be geneal-
ogy writ large.

Kripke's claim that it is a posteriori that tigers are mammals may
be reworded as the claim that *for all we can know a priori* tigers may
actually be something other than mammals. To establish this claim
all we need do is imagine a scenario, consistent with everything
we can know a priori, according to which tigers are reptiles or

automata or demons or anything but mammals. In imagination we
may set aside everything we think we know about how things
actually are (including, of course, tigers *not* being reptiles or automata or demons), so long as that knowledge was actually obtained
empirically and was unobtainable any other way. And if we do
thus set aside all knowledge of tigers dependent on field observation or laboratory work, can we not easily imagine future DNA
studies finding that tigers, totally contrary to everyone's expecta-
tions, show no genetic relationship to the felines among whom they
have traditionally been classed, but rather, incredible as it may
seem, a fairly close relationship with crocodiles? There have been
many surprises, though perhaps none quite as great as this, since
biologists began reconsidering traditional classification schemes
in the light of DNA evidence. (Kripke, writing before the era of
routine DNA studies, imagined rather a detailed investigation of
the internal anatomy of tigers finding typically reptilian rather than
mammalian features.)

Kripke's claim that it is necessary that tigers are mammals
amounts to the claim that, *given how the world actually is*, and in
particular given the fact that tigers are by descent members of the
panther genus of the cat family of the order of carnivores
within the class of mammals, there is no way the world could
potentially have been in which tigers would not have been
mammals. The defense of the claim consists in showing that when
we try to imagine a way the world could have been in which tigers
would not have been mammals, we end up imagining something
else, typically a world where there are some non-tigers that look
and act very much like tigers in our world, but where there are no
tigers.

We can, for instance, easily imagine that, long before any lineage
of the cat family developed into impressively large and fierce pred-
ators, all the ecological niches such creatures might have occupied
had been filled already by a lineage of the crocodile family that,
having long teeth already, had gradually evolved in addition longer
legs and a slimmer tail, a fur-covered hide, orange and black stripes,
and so on. But all this is just to imagine that some other creatures,
looking and behaving like tigers, came to live where tigers actually
live, long before there were any tigers to live there, leaving no room
for real tigers. Running the engine of evolutionary history in reverse
until back before the emergence of *Panthera tigris*, then running it
forward along a different track, we cannot recognize any newly
emergent species as *Panthera tigris* unless it derives from the same

Necessity 71

ancestral mammalian stock. The situation is entirely parallel to that
with Pericles' ugly, snub-nosed son and Socrates.

There are any number of subtleties here, however, as illustrated
by the following example (adapted from an example used to a
somewhat different purpose in Soames 2002, chapter 9). A placozoon is a member of a certain animal phylum (Placazoa), while a
trichoplax is a member of a certain animal genus (*Trichoplax*). The
genus mentioned is one that falls within the phylum mentioned,
and indeed so far as is known is the *only* one that falls within it.
Thus not only are all trichoplaxes placozoa, but also so far as is
known all placozoa are trichoplaxes. (A Google image search on
either the phylum or the genus name will lead the reader previously unacquainted with these tiny creatures to the same extensive
set of photomicrographs.) And yet, while the inclusion 'All trichoplaxes are placozoa' must seem to those who share Kripke's intuitions to be as necessary as 'All tigers are mammals,' by contrast
'All placozoa are trichoplaxes' seems contingent.

For it would not have been the case that all placozoa are trichoplaxes if some ancestral placozoon, already clearly differentiated
from all other phyla, had had in addition to its actual offspring (the
lineage leading to present-day trichoplaxes) some other offspring
whose descendants came to form a reproductively isolated population and through natural selection and/or genetic drift so evolved
as to leave them no longer cross-fertile with other lineages, and
different enough from them in other ways also to make for a distinct genus. Here we have an apparent counterexample to any
principle stating that inclusion statements involving natural kind
terms are in all cases necessary if true. If Kripke was aware at the
time of his lectures of such cases, he did not mention them. How
such apparent counterexamples are to be explained or explained
away on Kripkean principles remains controversial, one of several
significant loose ends left by Kripke's suggestive but far from con-
clusive discussion.[10]

Natural Phenomena and Natural Law

Let us turn finally to Kripke's examples of simple terms for natural
phenomena: 'heat' and 'light' and 'sound.' Respectable physicists
once held that heat is a material substance – a weightless, self-
repelling gas they called 'caloric fluid' – and we still speak today
in some ways as if it were, but according to the scientific account

accepted today, what heat really consists in is random molecular motion. Similarly, light consists of streams of photons, and sound consists of vibrations in air. (Actually, all three of these statements are shorthand for more complicated scientific accounts whose further details would be irrelevant and distracting.) In each case, the identification of the phenomenon with what science now says it is was an historically comparatively recent development, and the identity is as a posteriori as anything can be. Kripke nonetheless wants to claim that we have here a trio of examples of a posteriori *necessity*, though before 1970 such 'scientific identifications' had often been cited as supposed examples of 'contingent identities.' Kripke also wants to claim that the terms involved lack any descriptive sense or connotation.

Now certainly no would-be defender of descriptivism could claim that the description given by an advanced scientific account tells us what the term meant all along. For that description (known even today only to a fraction of the many speakers who use the term) was unknown to *all* the many speakers who used the term in ages past. There is, however, in the case of each term one maximally plausible candidate description that immediately suggests itself as a possible meaning or synonym or definition. For heat it would be *'whatever it is* that causes heat sensations' or perhaps *'whatever it is* that causes sensations like *these'* while having heat sensations and attending to them. For light and sound it would be the same but for 'visual sensations' and 'auditory sensations' in place of 'heat sensations.' It took advanced science to discover that random molecular motion causes heat sensations, but it requires no advanced science to know that *heat* causes heat sensations.

It is surely implicit awareness of some kind of close connection between heat and heat sensations, and between light or sound and visual or auditory sensations, that tempts many to say that the blind or the deaf, though they can talk about light or sound, must have a different concept of light or sound (as the case may be) from those who can see and hear, and that if there are any people congenitally entirely insensitive to heat, then they have a different concept of heat from the rest of us, too. Kripke acknowledges the initial plausibility of this line (so long as one does not interpret 'concept' too strictly), and yet he wants to oppose to it the view that the identity of heat with random molecular motion is necessary, while heat's causing heat sensations in us is contingent.

Kripke discusses light and sound more than heat, but the kind of thought experiment or imaginative exercise required reader can by now perhaps. Imagine a world in which people's wires are crossed, and the presence of lots of random molecular motion makes them feel the way we do when we feel cold, while the absence of much random molecular motion makes them feel the way we do when we feel hot. Now ask: Is this a world in which heat feels just the way heat does here, and cold feels just the way cold does here, but heat is the absence and cold the presence of random molecular motion, rather than the other way around? Or is this a world in which heat is what heat is here, but feels like cold does here, while cold is what cold is here, but feels like heat does here? I do not need at this point to tell the reader which would be Kripke's answer.

And yet Kripke does want to accommodate the feeling that there is something special about the connection between heat and heat sensations. He does so by suggesting that 'light is what causes visual sensations' or 'sound is what causes auditory sensations' or 'heat is what causes heat sensations' are used to *fix the reference*, rather than *give the meaning* of the terms. Now in most other cases, the role of a description in fixing reference is transitory, and once the reference is fixed, the description plays no further role, and may be forgotten. Kripke seems in this case to be suggesting that the reference-fixing role is something more long term, or even permanent, perhaps even something one must know if one is to have the full 'concept' (in some loose sense) of 'heat' or 'light' or 'sound.' But this is another loose end.

So much for the third of Kripke's three classes of cases. There remains a remark to be made about all three together. There was in the pre-Kripke literature some not very extensive or incisive discussion of what was variously called 'physical necessity' or 'natural necessity' or 'causal necessity' or 'nomological necessity.' This was variously conceived by different writers – who may not all have had exactly the same notion in mind – but perhaps what was meant was generally something like 'couldn't have failed to be without a violation of the laws of nature, or of general scientific principles.' All the scientific discoveries Kripke mentions (the composition of water, the atomic number of gold, the classification of tigers as mammals and not reptiles, and the identifications of heat and light and sound that we have just been discussing) are trivial examples of *this* kind of 'necessity,' insofar as they are all examples of established scientific principles, or natural laws in some broad sense. (What that status involves is, of course, the topic of a large philosophical literature of its own, about which I will say nothing.)

Kripke's claim is that all these examples enjoy what he calls the 'highest' kind of necessity. To use what has become the more common expression, they are supposed to be 'metaphysically' necessary. That is what his arguments are supposed to show, since in none of our imaginings did we strictly limit ourselves to imagining only what is compatible with the laws of nature so far as we think we know them. Kripke, in passing in the body of the lectures, darkly hints that it *may* be the case that *all* instances of 'physical' necessity are instances of 'metaphysical' necessity, of necessity *tout court et sans phrase*.

What such a claim might involve one can only conjecture. Couldn't the laws of physics have been different? For instance, it is generally accepted that the law of conservation of electrical charge holds exactly. Can't we imagine a universe quite like ours apart from some one, single exception? Must we say that in the imagined situation it isn't really electrical charge that is at issue, but merely something else very similar though not quite the same? That doesn't sound especially plausible, but Kripke does not elaborate on such issues; on the contrary he ends his addenda by explicitly leaving the question of how many physical necessities are metaphysical necessities as a matter for future research.

The Mystery of Modality

One reason Kripke in lecturing moves on fairly quickly, leaving many loose ends, is that the hour is growing late and the shadows are lengthening in the lecture hall, and he is eager to get on to applications of his views about the necessary or essential character of 'scientific identifications' to the mind–body problem. In this book, however, discussion of the mind–body problem will be deferred to the final chapter, where it can be considered together with other, related work of Kripke's. At this point, instead of following Kripke at once into philosophy of mind, I would like to go back to ask how Kripke would explain our ability to know anything about necessity and contingency, if as he says these do not simply reduce to the analytic and the synthetic. Let us ask, in a Kantian spirit: How is a posteriori knowledge of necessity possible? The first thing to note is that there are less interesting and more interesting cases.

The less interesting cases are those where in principle the knowledge could have been arrived at a priori, but it has in practice been arrived at a posteriori: What we know is a priori in the sense of being potentially know*able* by a route involving no appeal to empirical evidence, but our actual knowledge of it is a posteriori in the sense that our actual know*ing* came about by a route involving such appeal. Kripke in the addenda to N&N (item (c)) gives as an example knowledge of sums derived from a calculator, or by asking an expert, rather than from doing the computations ourselves. That the calculator or the expert tells us the sum is such-and-such is empirical evidence, and empirical evidence is required also to establish the reliability of the calculator or the expert. But the alternate route of doing the calculations for ourselves, which would avoid reliance on empirical evidence, remains in principle available, if in practice surely inconvenient and perhaps infeasible.[11]

The more interesting cases are those where reliance on empirical evidence is not just an option, but rather is mandatory: not a short-cut to the knowledge we seek, but the only route to it. That is supposed to be the status of the kinds of Kripkean examples we have been considering in this chapter: that Hesperus and Phosphorus are identical with each other but distinct from Mars; that Socrates' father was Sophroniscus and not Pericles; that water is H_2O and ammonia H_3N and not the other way around; that tigers are mammals and crocodiles are reptiles, and not the other way around; that heat is random molecular motion and not a weightless and self-repelling gas. How is knowledge of the Kripkean necessary a posteriori possible? This is the new form the mystery of modality takes in the wake of N&N.

Before considering Kripke's hints toward a solution, we must consider one more conceivable source of examples of the necessary a posteriori that Kripke briefly discussed in his introductory remarks, but that has not yet been taken account of here: mathematical conjectures. The reason examples of this kind haven't been considered sooner is that they aren't clear and clean examples.

A famous theorem of Gödel tells us that for any digital computer generating, without any external input, a list of mathematical truths, there is some mathematical truth it will never generate, no matter how long it runs. On the contentious assumption that 'the human mind works like a digital computer' it arguably follows that there are mathematical truths that are not knowable a priori. To get a vivid specific example, we have not only to accept this contentious assumption, but also to suppose or pretend to suppose that some particular well-known mathematical statement that was conjectured a long time ago but has not yet been proved is one of these mathematical truths that are not knowable a priori. Kripke chooses Goldbach's conjecture, though the particular choice, and what the chosen conjecture actually says, is not really relevant to the example.

So under our assumptions and suppositions, we now have a mathematical truth that is either knowable only a posteriori (perhaps by inductive reasoning from computer verification of particular consequences, or that combined with less direct heuristic considerations) or not knowable at all. And so, finally, we have a *necessary* truth that is either knowable only a posteriori or not knowable at all, since all mathematical truths are necessary.

The reason this example is brought in at this point is the following. There is some plausibility in the Kantian claim that experience by itself is never sufficient to give us knowledge of necessity, that some a priori element is always required. In the Goldbach's conjecture example, we see *exactly* where the a priori element comes in: in the principle that all mathematical truths are necessary, which tells us that if the conjecture is true, it is necessary, and that if the conjecture is false, it is impossible.

Now Kripke claims in his addenda (part (c)) that the situation is similar with *all* his examples:

> All the cases of the necessary *a posteriori* advocated in the text have the special character attributed to mathematical statements: Philosophical analysis tells us that they cannot be contingently true, so any empirical knowledge of their truth is automatically empirical knowledge that they are necessary. This characterization applies, in particular, to cases of identity statements and of essence. It *may* give a clue to a general characterization of *a posteriori* knowledge of necessary truths.

I should immediately point out that Kripke is *not* suggesting that in every case of a posteriori necessity, it is a priori that the statement in question is necessary if true. Kripke is only saying that his examples are of this type. From examples of this type one can easily cook up, by forming logical compounds, examples of necessary a posteriori statements that for all one could have known a priori might have been necessarily true, contingently true, contingently false, or necessarily false.[12]

In the case of each of Kripke's examples, he suggests, there is an a priori element, telling us that something is either necessary or impossible. Across the range of examples there are a range of a priori principles playing the role that in the Goldbach example is played by the principle that mathematical facts couldn't have been otherwise. Perhaps the principles at work are something like these: *Whatever parents a person actually had, any character having different parents wouldn't count as that person; whatever composition a natural substance actually has, any stuff having a different composition wouldn't count as that substance; whatever genus or family or order or class or phylum a species belongs to, a group belonging to a different one wouldn't count as that species;* and so on.

If Kripke's 'clue' is pointing in the right direction, then the mystery of modality comes down to the question: How do we know such a priori principles about necessity and possibility? Kripke says 'by philosophical analysis,' which is close to (if not quite the same as) saying that the principles are analytic, ultimately resting on rules of language. A lot of work would be needed to excogitate from Kripke's particular examples precisely what the general principles at work in them are. (For the versions given in italics above are only first approximations, at best.) A lot of further work would then be needed to make explicit what 'rules of language' make these principles 'true by virtue of meaning,' if that is what we want to claim about them. Only then would we have a candidate solution to the new mystery of modality.

It is perhaps only in the case of the mathematical type of example that we are close to being able to propose a plausible candidate for the 'rules of language' at work. The rule seems to be something like the following grammatical principle: Distinctions of grammatical tense and mood are not to be applied to purely mathematical statements. For mathematical statements, there is no distinction to be made among 'is' and 'was' and 'will be,' or among 'is' and 'would have been' and 'might have been.' Such distinctions have no use, and therefore no meaning, in our language. At any rate, that is the claim it seems likely that anyone seeking to demystify the 'eternal and necessary' character of mathematical facts will want to make.

We are now well beyond anything explicitly said by Kripke in his published writings (or even in any widely circulated *samizdat* material), and I do not plan to press on further. Let me just note that, once one has made it this far, *another* 'mystery of modality' looms, which perhaps we should have noticed or seen coming at an earlier point. The mystery is: Why does our language have a category of mood and modality at all?[13]

4

Belief

Let us now take up the topic, alluded to several times in preceding chapters, of belief attributions. (Kripke 1979), a follow-up paper to N&N that appeared between its anthology and book editions, will be the main text. In the last section, the recently published (Kripke 2011c) will also be taken up.

The plan will be to begin with the background to Kripke's puzzle about belief attributions, which lies in a difference of opinion between Kripke and some of the philosophers who have been most heavily influenced by him, the 'direct reference' theorists. As remarked two chapters back, at the end of N&N Kripke was left still owing us an account of the Hesperus *vs* Phosphorus and Pegasus puzzles. The disagreement just alluded to is in the first instance over what a Millian should say about Hesperus *vs* Phosphorus. Kripke's 'Puzzle about Belief' arises out of that question. Actually, there are two puzzles about belief, requiring separate consideration, the Pierre and the Paderewski cases. After considering these we will try to draw up a balance sheet on Hesperus and Phosphorus before looking at what Kripke has to say about Pegasus, to conclude the discussion of naming.

Direct Reference

So far I have attributed to Kripke a minimal Millianism, a denial that names have any descriptive meaning or sense or connotation.

A number of philosophers influenced by Kripke have gone on to adopt a kind of maximal Millianism known as 'direct reference' theory. It adds to Millianism a commitment to *propositions*. The very word 'proposition' was generally avoided in N&N, and toward the end of the preface to the book version, Kripke suggests that the apparatus of 'propositions' may simply break down in certain puzzle cases (those to be taken up in the next two sections of this chapter, in fact). Though Kripke has been called a 'direct reference' theorist, he is not one as I understand the term, since I understand the term as involving an unqualified acceptance of the apparatus of propositions. But just what does that apparatus involve? Three elements, mainly.

First, propositions are supposed to be what are expressed by sentences like 'Snow is white' and utterances thereof. If Jack says 'Snow is white,' then Jack expresses *the proposition* that snow is white. What proposition if any such a sentence expresses is determined by its meaning.[1] Sentences with the same meaning express the same proposition. Thus if Jacques says 'La neige est blanche,' then since his French sentence is synonymous with Jack's English sentence, Jacques expresses the same proposition as Jack; a proposition, unlike a sentence, thus belongs to no particular language. A sentence that has no meaning, because some component has no meaning, or because the components are somehow wrongly compounded, expresses no proposition. Thus if Jack says 'Bandersnatches are white,' then since 'bandersnatch' is a nonsense word, Jack expresses no proposition.

Second, propositions are supposed to be the primary bearers of the truth values, true and false. A sentence or utterance can be considered true or false only insofar as it expresses a proposition that is true or false. Sentences that express the same proposition have the same truth value; sentences that express no proposition have none.

Third, propositions are supposed to be the 'objects of belief': When one believes something, what one believes is a proposition, and belief is accordingly called a *propositional attitude*, an attitude toward a proposition. To believe that snow is white is to have an attitude of belief toward, or stand in the 'belief-relation' to, the proposition that snow is white. Propositions are likewise the 'objects of knowledge,' and knowledge is another propositional attitude. Being believed and being known are properties of propositions (rather than the sentences expressing them), and similarly for being knowable a priori.[2]

Now suppose we try to combine the Millian view that names have no descriptive meaning with the elements of proposition theory above. It seems to follow that all the presence of a name in a sentence can contribute to the proposition expressed by an utterance thereof would be the bearer of the name. This is the most fundamental principle of *direct reference* as I understand it. Two intermediate principles then seem to follow, though everyone allows some exceptions to these principles, at the very least for cases where a name is *mentioned* (as a word) rather than or in addition to being *used* (to designate something).[3]

> *Substitutivity*: If we have two names for the same thing, for instance 'Hesperus' and 'Phosphorus,' then switching one for the other in a sentence does not change the proposition expressed.

> *Vacuity*: If we have a name without a bearer, for instance 'Pegasus,' then sentences containing it fail to express propositions.

Given these principles, some counter-intuitive conclusions seem to follow. First, that because Pegasus does not exist, the sentence

(1)   Pegasus does not exist.

is not true. Of course, the intuitive view is that because Pegasus does not exist, the sentence (1) *is* true. This problem I will put aside for the moment.

Second, because Hesperus and Phosphorus are identical, the following pair must have the same truth value, and since the first is surely true, the second must also be true:

(2a)   Homer believed that Hesperus is Hesperus.
(2b)   Homer believed that Hesperus is Phosphorus.

Likewise with the pair:

(3a)   It is knowable a priori that Hesperus is Hesperus.
(3b)   It is knowable a priori that Hesperus is Phosphorus.

The intuitive view, by contrast, is that (2a) is true and (2b) false, and the view defended in N&N was that (3a) is true and (3b) false.

In the works of avowed direct reference theorists, notably Salmon (1986) or Soames (2002), the conclusion that (3b) is true is defended. On the direct reference view, the proposition expressed by 'Hesperus is Phosphorus' is a priori because it is the same as the proposition expressed by 'Hesperus is Hesperus.' But since it cannot be known a priori that 'Hesperus' and 'Phosphorus' have the same bearer, it cannot be known a priori that 'Hesperus is Phosphorus' and 'Hesperus is Hesperus' express the same proposition. This circumstance is supposed to explain away the intuition (or as the direct reference theorists would put it, the illusion) that (3b) is false.

Direct reference theorists reject Kripke's first example of something necessary but a priori, 'Hesperus = Phosphorus.' But writers like Salmon and Soames, though disagreeing with the letter of Kripke's doctrine on a detail they consider important for semantic theory, do greatly appreciate his achievements, and agree wholeheartedly with the spirit of Kripke's approach, thinking themselves to be truer to that spirit than Kripke himself is: more Kripkean than Kripke.[4]

Even while maintaining that 'Hesperus = Phosphorus' is not a posteriori, they do grant that 'Hesperus = Phosphorus' is synthetic. For while they regard being a priori as primarily a property of propositions, analyticity cannot be, at least not with the modern understanding of analyticity as 'truth by virtue of meaning.' For something to be true by virtue of meaning, it must *have* a meaning. Sentences have meanings, but propositions are closer to *being* meanings than to having them. To get 'Hesperus = Phosphorus' to come out analytic, you would need something like Marcus's doctrine about a dictionary or lexicon.

And even while maintaining that 'Hesperus = Phosphorus' is not a posteriori, they do grant that 'Venus ≠ Mars' or 'Augustus ≠ Antony' is a posteriori. While rejecting Kripke's *first* example of a posteriori necessity, direct reference theorists accept many of his other examples, beginning with the necessity of *non*-identity.

If the question of the status of examples like (3b) has been an issue between direct reference theorists and Kripke, the question of the status of examples like (2b) has been a major topic of disagreement between direct reference theorists and descriptivists. By way of background to Kripke's own puzzles, let me develop another example similar to (2b), such as a descriptivist might invoke in arguing against direct reference.

Consider the case of Marguérite, a speaker of French who has twice visited the former capital of the former South Vietnam. The first time she liked what she saw; the second time she didn't. The first time she heard the tour guides call the place 'Saigon,' and the second time 'Ho Chi Minh City' (or rather, they used the French equivalents of these names). We hear Marguérite speak, and report her speech using direct quotation as follows:

(4a)   Marguérite says, 'Saïgon est belle.'
(4b)   Marguérite says, 'Hô-Chi-Minh-Ville n'est pas belle.'

We translate her words into English and report her speech as follows:

(5a)   Marguérite says, 'Saigon is beautiful.'
(5b)   Marguérite says, 'Ho Chi Minh City is *not* beautiful.'

We 'disquote,' or in other words, change direct to indirect quotation, and report her speech as follows:

(6a)   Marguérite says that Saigon is beautiful.
(6b)   Marguérite says that Ho Chi Minh City is *not* beautiful.

Kripke's puzzle is going to concern the difficulty of getting from what people say to what they believe, but what are involved in his examples are not the *usual* reasons why this may be difficult. The usual reasons are that people don't always say what they believe: They sometimes hide their beliefs; they sometimes pretend to believe things they don't; they sometimes say things without thinking whether they really believe them or not. It is not these kinds of issues that concern Kripke, so let us once and for all assume away any of the usual difficulties over such points: Let us assume throughout that all speakers are forthcoming and not reticent, sincere and not dissembling, and reflective and not thoughtless.

Then it is an immediate step from (6ab) to the following:

(7a)   Marguérite believes that Saigon is beautiful.
(7b)   Marguérite believes that Ho Chi Minh City is *not* beautiful.

In the literature, the label 'disquotation principle' is indeed often applied to the principle allowing us (on the background assumptions of forthrightness and sincerity and thoughtfulness) to pass at once from (5ab) to (7ab), ignoring the intermediate step (6ab). Assuming further that Marguérite is not irrational, and does not believe any simple contradictions, from (7ab) we can to conclude also the following:

(8)   Marguérite does *not* believe that Ho Chi Minh City is beautiful.

And now, descriptivists will chide the direct reference theorists for holding the view that 'Saigon' and 'Ho Chi Minh City' should be freely interchangeable in reporting Marguérite's beliefs. For that assumption leads to the conclusion that in addition to (7ab) we have the following

(9a) Marguérite believes that Ho Chi Minh City is beautiful.

(9b) Marguérite believes that Saigon is *not* beautiful.

while the background assumption of no contradictory beliefs fails, and with it (8).

Kripke does not deny that the direct reference theorists' claims here are counter-intuitive, and he does not endorse those claims, but his puzzles do in an indirect sense support direct reference theory, since they tend to undermine the principles underlying the descriptivist's *criticism* of direct reference theory as just presented. For Kripke argues that *translation and disquotation*, which we used (along with background assumptions of forthrightness, sincerity, thoughtfulness, and rationality) to get from (4ab) to (7ab) and (8), *already lead to trouble all by themselves*, regardless of what theory of names one embraces.

Puzzling Pierre

The avowed primary aim of (Kripke 1979) is simply to introduce a certain puzzle about belief, illustrating the difficulty that can arise in certain cases when we want to report in our own language and idiolect a belief expressed by a subject with a different language or idiolect. Or rather, the primary aim of the paper is to present the puzzle and convince the philosophical public that it is genuinely puzzling, admitting no quick and easy solution. The sheer volume of the subsequent literature shows that Kripke has been brilliantly successful in achieving this aim.

A clear secondary aim of the paper, however, is to weaken the force of the objections to direct reference theories based on the examples like the Vietnamese case we have just been considering, by arguing that similar problems arise *independently* of any particular doctrine about proper names. (Another way to describe what Kripke will be trying to do is this, that he will try to present an example like the Vietnamese case, but where it is not plausible to claim that the two names involved differ in their descriptive meanings.) How far Kripke succeeds in the secondary aim is more debatable.

Without further preliminaries, here is the example. One Pierre grew up as a monolingual French speaker, and later in life learned

English by the 'direct' or 'immersion' method, being plopped down among monolingual English speakers and left to fend for himself, without help from bilinguals. Pierre as a child saw pretty pictures of a city the Francophones around him called 'Londres,' and as an adult had to spend some time in ugly surroundings in a city the Anglophones around him called 'London.' Speaking English, he says, 'I, Pierre, believe that London is not pretty,' or simply 'London is not pretty.' Speaking French, he says, 'Moi, Pierre, je crois que Londres est jolie,' or simply 'Londres est jolie.'[5] Kripke asks, 'Does Pierre believe that London is pretty?' By disquotation we would infer that he believes that London is *not* pretty. By translation-*cum*-disquotation we would infer that he believes that London is pretty. Yet surely, Kripke holds, we should not consider him an irrational person who holds overtly contradictory beliefs. So there is a puzzle.[6]

The problem, Kripke emphasizes, is not to describe the situation in a non-paradoxical way: He has done that himself in setting up the problem. The problem is to answer 'yes' or 'no' the specific question, 'Does Pierre believe that London is pretty?' or to answer 'oui' or 'non' to the specific question, 'Pierre, croit-il que Londres est jolie?' The difficulty in answering the question (attested by the diversity of answers defended in the ensuing literature) points to a fundamental problem about reporting in our own words beliefs expressed by a speaker of a language or idiolect not quite the same as our own.

Direct reference theorists will simply hold (what Kripke, in common with intuition, refuses to grant), that Pierre simply has contradictory beliefs. Salmon (2011b) defends this line in detail. Mark Richard (2011) has recently surveyed several other lines of response to the Pierre puzzle, including one of his own. I have in the past proposed a response of my own, based on the principle that before one infers a belief from someone's words, one must be assured not only that the speaker is forthright and sincere and reflective, but also – or rather, first of all, before anything else – that the speaker is linguistically competent. If we hear someone say, 'Assad is odorous!' then even if there is no questioning the speaker's forthrightness and sincerity and reflectiveness we may hesitate to attribute to the speaker a belief that Assad is smelly, if we have reason to suspect that what was meant was *odious*. This much is fairly uncontentious. What is controversial is the claim that Pierre lacks linguistic competence. How can that be, since the only languages involved are English and French, and Pierre is a native French-speaker and speaks English like a native, too?

Well, if Pierre sought a job as a translator, would he pass the qualifying examination? Any long text a translator is given to turn from English to French or vice versa is bound to contain many proper names. The great majority of the proper names that appear in the original will simply reappear in the translation unchanged (so far as spelling is concerned). A minority of proper names, especially of well-known places, may be changed. Thus the French 'Bourgogne' is conventionally anglicized as 'Burgundy,' and the English 'Cornwall' is conventionally gallicized as 'Cornouaille.' As for 'London,' when used as the name of the great metropolis in England it will be gallicized as 'Londres,' while when used as the name for the modest town in Ontario it will be left alone.

The fact on which the Pierre puzzle turns is that *prevailing customs and conventions of anglicization and gallicization cannot be predicted or projected just from knowledge of each of English and French separately.* That the great British metropolis and the modest Canadian town that share a name in English are treated differently in the course of gallicization is, for instance, something one could not conceivably guess just from Pierre's kind of linguistic knowledge. Such facts guarantee that Pierre is likely to fail his qualifying exam. What he submits as his French translation of an English text about, say, a trip from Burgundy by way of Dunkirk and Dover to Cornwall, will have all the names wrong. Despite his competence in the two languages separately, Pierre lacks full bilingual competence, such as would qualify him for work as a translator. For surely a professional translator ought to know that Dunkirk and Dover are 'Dunkerque' and 'Douvres' in French, for instance, just as a professional translator ought to know that 'Parme' in title of Stendhal's novel *La Chartreuse de Parme* is in English 'Parma.' If Pierre's linguistic incompetence disqualifies him for work as a translator, perhaps it should disqualify him also for the job of speaker in a philosophical example.

I don't wish to insist on this 'solution' – perhaps some would say 'evasion' – here. Indeed, I don't wish to pursue *solutions* at all. Kripke brings up his puzzle in part for its bearing on issues about naming, making it part of a rather indirect defense of direct reference theory by undermining the background assumptions of the Vietnamese and related objections. One might, however, prefer to consider the bearing of the puzzle on theories of naming in a different and more *direct* way, say by asking how well each of the main rival theories can do in explaining *why there seems to be a problem* in the Pierre case. Or rather, since the existence of people with Pierre's trouble is only one of many general facts about translation, and hardly the most important,[7] one might instead prefer to ask, as I will here, how well each of the rivals handles facts about translation generally. Even without attempting a comprehensive investigation of the issue, one can pretty quickly note the following points, which show that the facts about translation create some degree of embarrassment for *every* theory.

Against descriptivism in general: There is, to begin with, an argument of sorts against descriptivism implicit in the simple fact that names are never translated as descriptions, though according to descriptivists every name is synonymous with one.

Reply: To this a descriptivist might respond, however, that all we have here is an analogue or special case of the convention that abbreviations are to be translated as abbreviations rather than as their synonymous long versions: If the English texts says 'NATO,' the French text should say 'OTAN' and not 'Organisation du traité de l'Atlantique Nord.' If the French texts says 'SIDA,' the English text should say 'AIDS' and not 'acquired immune deficiency syndrome.'

Against Fregeanism in particular: Implicit in the fact that knowledge of French and English separately is insufficient to provide knowledge of conventional anglicizations and gallicizations is an argument of sorts against ideal Fregeanism, though a weaker one than the arguments from error and ignorance, since it depends on a couple of plausible but debatable assumptions. The first of these is just this, that 'London' and its gallicization 'Londres' are synonyms. Fregeanism is committed to 'London' being ideally synonymous with some name-free English description, and 'Londres' with some name-free French description. It then follows by the transitivity of synonymy (the principle that a synonym of a synonym is a synonym) that the English and French descriptions are synonymous. A second assumption is that for a pair of synonymous name-free descriptions, one English and one French, knowledge of each of the two languages separately should be enough to enable one to recognize their synonymy, as is surely the case with purely qualitative predicates. (If one knows what 'reddish' means in English, and what 'rougeâtre' means in French, surely one should be in a position to infer that the two terms have the same meaning.) Perfect knowledge of English by itself would include knowledge of the synonymy of 'London' with the English description, and perfect knowledge of French by itself would include knowledge of the synonymy of 'Londres' with the French description. But then, applying transitivity of synonymy, it should be feasible for Pierre to figure out that 'London' and 'Londres' are synonymous. Yet the foundation of the Pierre example is precisely the fact that one *cannot* figure out that 'Londres' is the gallicization of 'London' – or more precisely, of 'London, England' as opposed to 'London, Ontario' – just from knowledge of the two languages separately.

Reply: None of this would have troubled the historical Frege, who recognized that different speakers may associate different descriptions with the same name, and surely would have held, if the issue arose, that the same speaker may associate different descriptions with the same name at different times.

Against the metalinguistic view in particular: There is an apparent problem for the metalinguistic theory in that the meaning of 'London' is supposed to be something like 'that which is called "London,"' and the translation of such a description would be something like 'ce qui s'appelle "London"' rather than 'ce qui s'appelle "Londres,"' which is supposed to be the meaning of 'Londres.'

Reply: This argument – a new specimen of an old species of arguments from translation that were much used by Alonzo Church in the 1930s in providing counterexamples to various proposed analyses – turns on a view about the translation of quoted material that, though widely accepted among philosophers as theoretical principle, would evoke howls of protests from those same philosophers if applied in practice by publishers of translations of their own works. The normal procedure in translation, followed in the overwhelming majority of cases by translators and their publishers, though subject to special exceptions for special purposes in special circumstances, is illustrated by the fact that an English-speaking person who has never seen a letter of the Russian alphabet can read a complete English translation of *Anna Karenina* and still never have seen one. For though the novel is about Russian characters who speak to each other, often at great length, in the Russian language, sprinkled with occasional bits of French, a normal translation will be entirely in English, apart from the occasional bits of French. Dialogue material, found inside quotation marks in the original, and narrative material, found outside quotation marks, will be treated exactly alike, the Russian in both cases being put into English, with only the occasional bits of French left alone. (Indeed, the very quotation marks are 'translated,' the German or French style favored by Russian publishers being replaced by British or American style.) A translation by a disciple of Church, by contrast, would contain vast stretches of material in an alphabet unfamiliar to most English readers, and for this reason would not sell. Nor, presumably, would the many foreign translations of *Naming and Necessity* sell if they left all the many English-language quotations in English. The response to the translation argument against the metalinguistic theory is that 'London' means something like 'that which is called "London," ' which in a *normal* translation as opposed to a Church-style translation becomes 'ce qui s'appelle "Londres," ' which is something like the meaning of 'Londres.' Or so a metalinguistic theorist might maintain.[8]

Against direct reference: There is an argument against direct reference theory in the neighborhood, too. Such views seem unable to account for why, in a translation of some French screed by Trotsky, a translator would take care to render 'Djougachvili' as 'Djugashvili' rather than 'Stalin,' and 'Staline' as 'Stalin' rather than 'Djugashvili,' even though Stalin and Djugashvili are one and the same person, and Trotsky knew it, and anyone likely to be interested in reading Trotsky in translation probably knows it, too. On the direct reference theorist's principles, the 'meanings' or 'contents' of the names 'Stalin' and 'Djugashvili' are exactly the same, and switching one for the other in any sentence won't change the proposition expressed.

Reply: Evidently, the direct reference theorist will have to claim that mere identity of 'meaning' or 'content' or proposition expressed is insufficient for correctness of translation. Such a claim may raise a suspicion that the notion of 'meaning' or 'content' with which the theorist is working may be impoverished, excluding some factor that ought to be included; but a suspicion is not a disproof.

Poles Apart

We have seen that, looking directly at the facts about translation, they create some degree of embarrassment for every theory; but they do not conclusively refute any. And meanwhile, examination of translation reveals enough subtleties and pitfalls to suggest that no great reliance should be put on examples that depend crucially on it. Kripke, however, claims he can reformulate his puzzle so as to eliminate such dependence.

For opponents of direct reference, giving examples involving things said in foreign languages is no great loss. One can always find examples of mistaken beliefs about identity or non-identity that only involve English speakers and English names. Even these, however, will still depend on a disquotation principle, on moving straight from a person's words to a similarly worded attribution of a belief to that person. And so Kripke aims to give a Pierre-like puzzle turning only on the disquotation principle.

We imagine ourselves back circa 1920, when a character Peter has encountered, or anyhow heard of, Ignacy Jan Paderewski in two connections, as a famous and successful pianist, and as an equally famous though less successful politician. Peter has somewhere got the idea that the pianist and the politician are two distinct persons: the one an apolitical musician, the other an unmusical politician. Perhaps, misremembering something he was told about the two Poincarés, he thinks the two Paderewskis are cousins, which might explain any perceived resemblance between the pianist and the politician, if he happens to have seen 'one of them' in the concert hall and 'the other of them' at a party rally. If Peter thought the pianist was called 'Ignacy Paderewski' and the politician 'Jan Paderewski,' we would be back in a situation like the Saigon *vs* Ho Chi Minh City example. But Kripke supposes there are no first names involved, and simply asks, 'Does Peter believe that Paderewski has musical talent?'

The puzzle is, as in the case of Pierre, not to describe the situation in non-paradoxical terms, but to answer this specific question. As with Pierre, I would suggest that if we are interested in the bearing of the puzzle on issues about naming, we should not try to answer Kripke's question, but rather should ask, of each of the main theories, how it explains why Kripke's question appears difficult to answer. We may judge the different theories of naming by how plausible an explanation they are able to give.

If I say 'Please sit in the chair' to a student who correctly sees or erroneously seems to see *two* empty chairs in my office, the student may well ask, 'Which of the two chairs do you mean?' Likewise, if we asked Peter out of the blue, 'Do you think the well-known person called "Paderewski" has musical talent?' he would surely answer, 'Which of the two well-known persons called "Paderewski" do you mean?' Or anyhow, he would probably so answer unless our question happened to catch him right in the middle of a conversation about pianists, or one about politicians. Peter would give exactly the same kind of answer if one asked, 'Do you believe that Paderewski has musical talent?' So the Paderewski case is certainly no problem for the metalinguistic theory. That theory in a sense *predicts* there will be trouble with this particular question in a case of a subject like Peter, and there is.

In connection with the Fregean theory, it should first be noted that ambiguous abbreviations abound. In this era of interdisciplinary work between psychologists and philosophers, there is a real danger of misunderstanding involved in speaking of 'the A.P.A.,' since that abbreviation is shared by the American Philosophical Association and the American Psychological Association. And, of course, if there are cases where an abbreviation really is ambiguous, there can be cases where an abbreviation is mistakenly believed to be ambiguous. We can imagine a scenario in which Paderewski is awarded the honorific title 'Preeminent Polish Personage,' people beginning to call him 'PPP' (pronounced 'triple P' or 'P cubed') for short, and Peter somehow gets the idea that one of the Paderewski cousins has been awarded the title 'Preeminent Polish Pianist' and the other Paderewski cousin the title 'Preeminent Polish Politician,' with 'PPP' ambiguously abbreviating both. The way Peter would answer the question, 'Does Paderewski have musical talent?' exactly parallels the way he would answer the question 'Does PPP have musical talent?' So there is no embarrassment for the Fregean view that names abbreviate descriptions in the Paderewski case; there is trouble, but the Fregean theory predicts it.

By contrast with the intuitively satisfying explanations of what is going on in the Paderewski example that we get from either form of descriptivism, direct reference theory, being committed to the counter-intuitive claim that Peter has outright contradictory beliefs, cannot give an account of what is going on that is equally intuitive. It is therefore not easy to see, when we look at things from the point of view I have been suggesting here, any really powerful defense of direct reference in the Paderewski case.

I don't know how many readers have been keeping score, but at this point in the game it seems to me that the metalinguistic theory is ahead. On the one hand, it does not face the problems faced by minimal Millianism, which still owes us an account of the Hesperus *vs* Phosphorus or Saigon *vs* Ho Chi Minh City example, let alone by the heavily theoretically committed direct reference theory, with its distinctly counter-intuitive consequences. On the other hand, if formulated carefully enough, it seems able to dodge the error and ignorance objections directed by Kripke against Fregeanism. There remains Kripke's modal objection, but we have seen two strategies for evading that.

There remains to be considered, however, a reinforced version of the modal objection, deriving from (Soames 2002, chapter 2) rather than in any published work of Kripke himself. The problem involved is not just about what would have been the case in certain counterfactual circumstances, and not just about what someone believes, but about what someone would have believed in certain counterfactual circumstances. I have not considered this further objection sooner because it requires a little background first, but it is time to take it up now.

Counterfactual Attitudes

The formulation of the objection in question requires the distinction between *de re* and *de dicto* that was made in the case of necessity to be extended to the case of belief. Let us begin with this background. We may start with an old puzzle or problem that was posed by Quine around the same time he was pressing his objections to modal logic. To use the best-known example from Quine (1956), the sentence 'Ralph believes that somebody is a spy,' is ambiguous, and may mean either of two things, thus:

(1)   Ralph believes that there is some person such that he or she is a spy.
(2)   There is some person such that Ralph believes that he or she is a spy.

Note the difference in structure. In both there is the pronomial phrase 'he or she' whose antecedent is 'some person,' but in (2) 'believes that' comes between pronoun and antecedent, while in (1) it does not. The structure seen in (2) is in jargon called 'quantifying into a belief context,' another kind of 'quantifying in' from the modal kind we saw earlier.

To go with the difference in structure there is a difference in meaning. On the one hand, (1) has Ralph believing something that can be put in a declarative sentence expressing a complete thought: 'There is some person who is a spy.' The kind of belief involved here is *de dicto* ('of the saying'). On the other hand, (2) has there being some person such that Ralph stands in a certain relation to him or her, the relation of Ralph's believing *of that person* that he or she is a spy. The kind of belief involved here is *de re* ('of the thing,' only here the thing is a person, so it perhaps really ought in

92

Belief

this case to be *de homine*). Quine himself calls *de dicto* belief *notional* belief, and *de re* belief *relational* belief.

Quine sees a problem in making sense of the notion of *de re* belief, and therefore in making sense of quantification into a belief context, parallel to the problem he saw about making sense of *de re* modality and quantification into a modal context. The problem is that one and the same person may be characterized or specified in different ways, and with a first way Ralph may believe that the person so presented is a spy, while with a second way Ralph may not believe that the person so presented as a spy.

In Quine's example, Ralph sees a certain Bernard J. Ortcutt (whose name Ralph never learns) several times in brown hat, when the man seems to be behaving suspiciously, and once at the beach, where the man is pointed out as a pillar of the community. He does not realize the man he is shown at the beach is the same as the man he noticed in a brown hat. This appears to give us an example of 'substitutivity failure,' a contrast between two *de dicto* belief attributions, of which one is true and the other false, even though the two differ only by substituting one description for another description of the same man:

(3a)   Ralph believes the man in the brown hat is a spy.
(3b)   Ralph believes the man at the beach is a spy.

Quine sees a situation roughly parallel to that encountered in the modal case in his Morning Star and Evening Star examples. Quine wonders how one can attribute to Ralph a definite attitude of belief or doubt or disbelief in *the man's* being a spy, when what Ralph believes about him thus varies with the mode or characterization or presentation.

The parallelism, however, between the modal and belief cases is faulty. For while it would make no sense to suggest that Venus's identity with the Morning Star wavers over time between being necessary and being contingent, so that it has no firm, fixed modal status, it makes perfect sense to say that Ralph has no firm, fixed attitude toward Ortcutt, that his attitude wavers over time. Sometimes, to wit, when he thinks of Ortcutt's suspicious behavior, Ralph thinks the man a spy; sometimes, to wit, when he thinks of Ortcutt's reputation as a pillar of the community, he thinks the man a loyal citizen. Ralph's opinion might waver in this way even if he found out that the man in the brown hat and the man at the beach are the same, just as Marguérite's opinion of that city in Southeast Asia might still waver even if she found out that Saigon and Ho

Chi Minh City are the same municipality. (Do not many of us have love–hate relationships with big cities of our acquaintance?)

We will have no more use for Quine's example, but we do need his distinction between notional and relational, or *de dicto* and *de re* belief. One way of describing direct reference theory's counter-intuitive features is to say that for direct reference theorists, a *de dicto* belief in proposition expressed by a sentence involving a proper name cannot be distinguished from a *de re* belief about the bearer of the name (because all the presence of the name in the sentence contributes to the proposition expressed is its bearer). For Ralph to believe *de dicto* that Ortcutt is a spy is for Ralph to believe *de re* of Ortcutt that he is a spy. For Homer to believe *de dicto* that Hesperus is distinct from Phosphorus is for Homer to believe *de re* of Hesperus a.k.a. Venus and of Phosphorus a.k.a. Venus that the former is distinct from the latter. So the direct reference theorist must either deny that Homer believed Hesperus distinct from Phosphorus, or else (and this is the option usually chosen) affirm that Homer believed Venus distinct from Venus.

The Soamesian objection I wish to develop is that descriptivism cannot save us from consequences as puzzling or counter-intuitive as these, if it is defended against the Kripke's modal argument in either of the ways suggested two chapters back. This point will take some unpacking. Earlier I sketched two different strategies a descriptivist might use in dealing with modal objections, inserting the adverb 'actually' and making play with distinctions of 'scope,' and the problem arises in somewhat different forms for each of these. For present purposes I will discuss the problem only as it arises for the strategy of inserting 'actually,' since that seems to be the more popular of the two; but what I have to say will anyhow apply *mutatis mutandis* to the other strategy. Descriptivism, of course, comes in two versions, Fregean and metalinguistic. For present purposes I will discuss problems only for the metalinguistic version, since the Fregean version is already in enough trouble over the problems of error and ignorance, while the modal objection has to be the main objection against metalinguisticism.

So what is the modal problem for the metalinguistic theory? We want the following to come out unequivocally true.

(4)   In certain counterfactual circumstances, Plato would not have been named 'Plato.'

But what do we get if we substitute 'the person who bore the name "Plato" ' for 'Plato' in (4)? Just the following:

(5)   In certain counterfactual circumstances, the person who bore
       the name 'Plato' would not have borne the name 'Plato.'

And this is ambiguous as between a truth and a falsehood, thus:

(6a)   In certain counterfactual circumstances, the person who in
       actual circumstances did bear the name 'Plato' would not
       have borne the name 'Plato.'
(6b)   In certain counterfactual circumstances, the person who in
       those circumstances would have borne the name 'Plato'
       would not have borne the name 'Plato.'

And what is the strategy under consideration for defense against
this objection? Simply to insist that the description associated with
Plato should be, not 'the person who bore the name Plato' but 'the
person who *actually* bore the name Plato,' so as to knock out the
unwanted reading (6b), leaving only the true reading (6a).

And what is the trouble now? Well, if we describe a certain
person in terms of properties he has in the actual world, then while
Socrates in another possible world might well have had various *de
re* attitudes toward that person, it does not seem that Socrates could
have had *de dicto* attitudes toward that person *under the description
we have used* (or a classical Greek equivalent thereof), a description
in terms of properties he has in *our* world. For to do that, Socrates
would have to be thinking about our world specifically, out of all
the many alternatives to his world; and this does not seem feasible.
If this is not clear, here is one of those places where the analogy
between the modal and the temporal may help. Socrates in the
other world could hardly be thinking about our world specifically,
out of all the many alternatives to his world, for much the same
reason that Socrates in times gone by did not think about our time
specifically, out of all the many future times beyond his time: There
are simply too many alternatives to make it plausible to suggest
that he could have had or did have a specific one of them in mind.

For instance, we may describe Plato and Aristotle as the elder
and the younger of the two Greek philosophers who are most
famous today. Socrates (d. 399 BCE) never got to know Aristotle (b.
384 BCE), but Socrates knew and doubtless had many *de re* beliefs
about Plato. Yet Socrates presumably had no *de dicto* beliefs about
Plato under a description mentioning his reputation *today*. For
under what description could that be? Certainly it could not be
under a description of today as 'today' (or its Greek equivalent),
since for Socrates 'today' would have been *his* day, not ours. Nor

could it be under a description of today as a certain day in 'the second decade of the twenty-first century CE' or the like, since that would involve a chronological system unknown to Socrates. Was it perhaps then under some description in terms of the such-and-suchth year of the six-hundred-ninety-somethingth Olympiad? That's not absolutely inconceivable, but it's extremely unlikely. Though Socrates doubtless had general thoughts about 'future ages,' he undoubtedly did *not* have thoughts quite as chronologically specific as *that* about future ages.

The foregoing considerations suggest that the metalinguistic theory is required to to treat all reports of beliefs in past situations, and by parity of reasoning, all reports of beliefs in counterfactual situations, as *de re* beliefs. And why is that a problem? Well, it means that the metalinguistic theory seems to lose what was supposed to be one of its main advantages over Millian or direct reference theories. For consider

(7)   If the Greeks had never learned the results of Babylonian astronomy, Aristotle have believed that Hesperus and Phosphorus were distinct.

Taken *de re* this amounts to

(8)   Consider on the one hand Hesperus a.k.a. Venus, and consider on the other hand Phosphorus a.k.a. Venus. If the Greeks had never learned the results of Babylonian astronomy, Aristotle would not have believed that *the former* and *the latter* were distinct.

That is not what we want. It is essentially what direct reference theory gives us, Aristotle believing Venus is not Venus. What we want, and what descriptivism seemed originally to promise us, was intuitively speaking a *de dicto* reading of (7) that has Aristotle in the counterfactual possible world saying to himself, 'Is Hesperus identical with Phosphorus? I don't believe so,' (or the Greek equivalent) and meaning by it what Homer in the actual world meant by it.

Is there any response the metalinguistic theorist can make here? Well, it seems that what we want would be supplied by a reading of (7) that goes, at least to a first approximation, as follows:

(9)   Consider the names 'Hesperus' and 'Phosphorus.' If the Greeks had not learned the results of Babylonian astronomy, Aristotle would have believed that the object bearing *the former* and the object bearing *the latter* were distinct.

This still attributes to the Aristotle of the alternative possible world a *de re* and not merely a *de dicto* belief, but it is not a *de re* belief about Hesperus and Phosphorus, which is to say, about Venus and Venus; it is a *de re* belief about the *names* 'Hesperus' and 'Phosphorus.'

Now if we think of a name as merely a sequence of phonemes or letters, (9) will still not be quite right. For couldn't Aristotle have *correctly* believed that the bearer of 'Hesperus' and the bearer of 'Phosphorus' were distinct, simply because he was using 'Hesperus' as a name for the moon, and 'Phosphorus' as a name for the sun, making the bearers of the two names in *his* usage distinct, though they are identical in *our* usage? In response, we must insist that a name is not just a sequence of symbols or sounds, but something more, a sequence of symbols or sounds with a tradition of usage. Alternatively, we could replace (9) by something more like the following, explicitly mentioning a tradition of usage:

(10) Consider the names 'Hesperus' and 'Phosphorus' as used in the tradition to which our own usage belongs. If the Greeks had not learned the results of Babylonian astronomy, Aristotle would have believed that the object bearing *the former* and the object bearing *the latter* were distinct.

Here it should be noted that the reason we can have Aristotle believing something *de re* about the tradition to which *we* belong is not because we imagine Aristotle having a *de dicto* belief about that tradition under a description mentioning *us*. It is not that we imagine Aristotle in the counterfactual world thinking specifically about certain people, ourselves, in some specific alternative to his world, our own, and living at a specific future time, our days, and about their tradition of usage. Rather, we imagine that Aristotle in counterfactual circumstances would have thought *de re* about the tradition to which *he* counterfactually would have belonged, and because this presumably would have been the same tradition to which he actually did belong, and because *that* happens to be the same tradition to which Homer belonged before him and we belong after him, little as any ancient Greek did or would have anticipated *us*.

One last quibble: Of course, Aristotle did not use 'Hesperus' and 'Phosphorus' with quite the pronunciation, let alone anything like the spelling, that we do. I have said that a name may be more than a sequence of symbols or sounds, but it may also be in a sense less, since in the course of a tradition of usage, both pronunciation and spelling can change. When we use the anglicizations 'Hesperus' and 'Phosphorus,' we are not actually *expressing* the very thought that Aristotle had or would have had, which would have involved his pronunciation and perhaps spelling of the names; we are only *evoking* it, so to speak. This is common in cases where we have to rely on translation, with its many subtleties and pitfalls.

By contrast with all of this, if we want to describe a belief that would have been expressed using names for which there is no tradition of use among us, we must first introduce that usage, as in the following example:

(11)   The astronomers of Yuggoth called Venus 'Azathoth' when they saw it in the morning, and 'Yogsothoth' when they saw it in the evening, and they believed that Azathoth and Yogsothoth were distinct planets.

Here the second occurrence of 'Azathoth' amounts to a truncation of 'the bearer of "Azathoth"' (as used in the Yuggothian tradition), and similarly for 'Yogsothoth.'

What I have been presenting here in the form of (10) is a version of the metalinguistic theory, perhaps immune to the objection that has occupied us in this section, that is inspired by the version of the metalinguistic theory in the work of the linguist Matushansky (2008). In her theory there is, in the supposedly psychologically real though subconscious syntactic structure of a sentence involving a proper name, an unarticulated constituent, a slot for what she calls a 'naming convention,' this being more or less what I have called a 'tradition of usage.' The slot is filled in contextually, rather as if the description were 'the individual named "____" [according to the pertinent naming convention],' where context determines what naming convention is pertinent. The default setting is simply the naming convention used by the speaker and (rightly or wrongly) presumed by the speaker to be shared by the addressee. Non-default settings are possible where there is explicit mention of naming in the sentence. This last proviso is intended by Matushansky to cover cases like the Thumper example, among others, and would cover examples like (4) and (11) above.

Obviously, I have drifted quite some distance from Kripke in this last section.[9] So, indeed, has the discussion of naming in the literature. That topic is now being addressed by linguists with a formidable technical apparatus, and in Matushansky's case a formidable body of cross-linguistic data, drawing on dozens of languages to illustrate various subtle phenomena. But just as not all the points raised in the discussions of the linguists are readily appreciated by philosophers, so also not all the points raised in the discussions of philosophers are readily appreciated by the linguists. We can look forward to a period of active exchange between the disciplines in the future.

Empty Names

I noted earlier that Kripke in N&N leaves us without an account of empty names, but then set that issue aside. Within a few years of his Princeton lectures, Kripke delivered the Locke Lecture series at Oxford, giving as his title 'Reference and Existence,' and taking as his topic empty names. The text of these lectures has been in (officially unauthorized) circulation around philosophy departments for many years. Only very recently has another paper covering the same ground been published as Kripke (2011c), to which the present section will be devoted.[10]

In the paper in question, Kripke's views on empty names are developed against the background of a view on fiction: What he would have to say about 'Pegasus' is developed against the background of a view on 'Sherlock Holmes.' The view involves a pair of distinctions. A first distinction is the obvious one between discourse within the story and discourse about the story. Apropos of discourse within the story Kripke insists that storytellers do not make assertions, but only engage in a pretence of doing so. They do not assert anything false and do not assert anything true, since they do not assert anything at all. If on a true–false test it is appropriate to mark 'Sherlock Holmes used cocaine' as true, that is only because the whole test is framed by the tacit understanding that it is about what is true-in-the-story or false-in-the-story, not what is really true and really false.

A second distinction is between two uses of, say, 'Sherlock Holmes.' In the first use, it is used as a putative name for a human being. The storyteller *pretends* to be using the expression in this first way in the course of *pretending* to narrate certain historical events. A second use of the same expression is as the name for a literary character, a creation of Conan Doyle. The second kind of use is in evidence when one says, 'Sherlock Holmes is a greater creation than any of Conan Doyle's predecessors in the detective-fiction line ever produced.' The name is used *in earnest* in the first way if someone, overhearing the story and not realizing it is only a story, goes on to use the name in the erroneous belief that it designates a real person. The first kind of use is in evidence in the case of a naive reader who says, 'I need the services of a detective, and I want the best, so let's go to Baker Street and hire Sherlock Holmes,' and also in the case of a friend who by way of correction replies, 'But there is no Sherlock Holmes. The stories of Conan Doyle are pure fiction.'[11]

This kind of correction can also be offered even in some cases where there is no single, well-known fictional source in the background, as when some people say, 'Homer never existed: The *Iliad* and the *Odyssey* have different authorships, and both are accretions without a single principal author.' And *that* is the kind of case that really concerns Kripke. One thing he wants to say about it is that one should *not* think of 'Holmes does not exist' or 'Homer does not exist' as speaking of a fictional character, the Holmes of the stories or the Homer of tradition, and saying about him or it that he or it possesses the property of non-existence. The fictional characters do not possess the property of non-existence. On the contrary, they (in common with everything else) possess the property of existence, though they exist as some kind of abstract entity, not as flesh-and-blood people.

And, of course, if the negative existential judgments in question are true, as the one about Holmes surely is and the one about Homer perhaps may be, then using the expressions in the *first* way, as purported names of flesh-and-blood human beings, not names of abstract entities, Holmes and Homer do not possess the property of non-existence (nor any other), since they are not around to possess properties of any kind. Taking the non-existence assertions either way, they cannot be construed as picking out an individual and then ascribing a property of non-existence to him or her or it.

But how then *are* such singular negative existentials to be construed? Here Kripke confronts the problem that the Pegasus example raises for direct reference theory. Moreover, in Kripke (2011c), unlike N&N, Kripke does himself use the notion of 'proposition,' and he seems to concede the plausibility one key assumption of direct reference theory, the vacuity principle, which is the one that led to the paradoxical conclusion that since Pegasus does not exist, 'Pegasus does not exist' cannot be true.

If the problem were just about one isolated type of sentence, singular negative existentials, it might be feasible to treat sentences of this type as special idioms of some kind, and devise an *ad hoc* analysis. But as Kripke notes, the question is broader, since there

are other sentences that create similar problems. For instance, one
scholar has suggested that Homer was a woman. One might be
convinced, says Kripke, that *this* can't be right even while remaining doubtful or agnostic about whether Homer existed at all. Such
a view would naturally be expressed by saying,

(1)   If Homer existed at all, Homer wasn't a woman.

According to the vacuity principle, if Homer didn't exist, then (1),
because it involves 'his' name, can't be true. There are quite a large
number of conditional assertions on the order of (1) that one might
want to make in various connections, and in particular in discussing the evidence for and against the existence of Homer.

Abandoning Millianism for the metalinguistic approach or some
variation on it would seem to offer a cheap and easy answer to any
problems about such cases. A theorist who took this route might
simply say that (1) means something like

(2)   'Homer was a woman' does not express a true proposition.

This formulation *mentions* the name 'Homer,' but does not *use*
it. Kripke, however, rejects the metalinguistic theory, and rejects
the variation on it currently under consideration. Kripke is
unwilling to say that (1) is synonymous with (3), or in a simpler
case that

(3)   Homer does not exist.

is synonymous with

(4)   'Homer exists' does not express a true proposition.

Yet he *is* led in the end to take (3) to mean something like

(5)   There is no true proposition that Homer exists.

There is a worry here that if Homer does not exist, then since (5),
involving as it does *in*direct rather than direct quotation, *uses* the
name 'Homer' and does not just *mention* it, (5) itself may on his
principles fail to express a proposition, apparently leaving us no
further forward. In this connection he says, cryptically and without
much elaboration, that we can sometimes appear to reject a proposition meaning that there is no true proposition of that form,
without committing ourselves to mean that what we say expresses
a proposition at all. As far as the published record goes, that is
about where Kripke leaves the problem. I will have to leave the
problem in this unsatisfactory state, too.[12]

All the topics addressed in this chapter form one corner of a larger subject. Similar problems to those we have seen arising with 'believes that' also arise with 'knows that' and with 'fears that' and 'hopes that' and 'strives to bring it about that,' or even just the plain 'says that.' Contexts of belief attribution, knowledge attribution, and so on, are collectively known as *attitude* contexts, and attitude contexts together with modal contexts are collectively known as *intensional* contexts.

Just as belief is only one of a family of intensional notions, so also proper names form only one subclass of a larger class of expressions raising special problems for philosophers of language and theoretical linguists. Closely related to problems about naming in linguistic semantics and philosophy of language are problems about what linguists call *deixis*, or what philosophers call *indexicals* ('I' and 'now' and 'here' and others) and *demonstratives* ('this' and 'that'); closely related also are questions of *tense* (since the use of the present tense is closely related to the use of 'now').

A number of writers have adopted direct reference views of these further expressions. Such views lead to a coarse-grained notion of 'proposition,' under which my saying 'I am sleepy' and my saying 'JPB is sleepy' express the same proposition, and hence the same object of possible belief or knowledge or fear or regret. Such views imply that for me to believe or know or fear or regret that I am becoming sleepy is the same as for me to believe or know or fear or regret that JPB is becoming sleepy, even if I become so sleepy that I forget my own name.

This is counter-intuitive, and in contrast to it there are finer-grained notions of 'proposition.' But these are not immune to objections, either, for one reason because they result in there being many cases where colloquially we would say that two people were 'saying the same thing,' while according to the fine-grained theory they would be expressing distinct propositions. For instance, if I say to you, 'I am sleepy,' and you say back to me, 'You are sleepy,' on a fine-grained theory the propositions we have expressed, though in some sense equivalent, are not literally the same: I have said that the speaker of my utterance is sleepy, while you have said that the addressee of your utterance is sleepy.

There is a clash of two systematic views, each with its strengths and weakness, its intuitive and its counter-intuitive aspects. Now there is no *system* to be found in Kripke's published writings. To be sure, Kripke's published writings comprise only a fraction of his work: Audiotapes awaiting transcription, transcripts awaiting

editing, and edited material awaiting publication fill the archives
of the Kripke Center at the City University of New York. And
though he is now a septuagenarian, Kripke remains philosophically active and productive. But even if we had before us the *whole*
of Kripke's thought, published and unpublished and work-in-
progress, we would find no system in it. Kripke simply is not a
system-builder. In particular, Kripke has avoided taking a systematic stand in favor of coarse-grained or fine-grained propositions,
attaching more weight to intuitions about puzzle cases – above all,
the intuition that they are genuinely puzzling – than to any desire
for a systematic theory.

Nonetheless, in work only recently published – in some cases
only recently produced, in others produced much earlier but only
recently released – he has addressed a variety of issues and explored
a variety of phenomena of which any systematic theory would
have to take account. For the reader who wishes to pursue further
Kripke's treatment of such issues insofar as it is now available to
us in print, there are several items of interest (mainly transcripts of
talks with additions and amendments), all to be found in the first
volume of the *Collected Papers* (Kripke 2011a). Let me here, for the
sake of readers interested in going deeper into the issues, take brief
note of these writings, which together fill in some gaps in Kripke's
treatment of issues in philosophy of language.[13]

'Unrestricted Exportation…' (Kripke 2011e) is concerned with
when inference from a *de dicto* belief attribution such as 'Ralph
believes that the man in the brown hat is a spy' to an existential
generalization such as 'There is someone whom Ralph believes to
be a spy' is warranted. This was a problem that much exercised
Quine, and it has much exercised his successors. Ostensibly the
paper is merely an argument against one extreme view, that such
inference is *always* warranted, ingeniously showing how that view
leads to absurdities. But there are a great many incidental remarks
that indicate the complexity of the problem.[14]

'Frege's Theory of Sense and Reference' (Kripke 2008) is primarily historical, but it provides some very sensitive exposition and
development of a fine-grained approach to propositions or
'thoughts' [*Gedanke*] with which Kripke is fundamentally unsym-
pathetic. The bulk of the paper deals with a vexed issue in Frege
exegesis that has not concerned us,[15] but there are also discussion
of (i) the present tense and the indexicals 'now' and 'today' and (ii)
the first-person pronoun 'I,' indicating how these would optimally
be handled by a believer in fine-grained propositions.

'Russell's Notion of Scope' (Kripke 2005) is also historical, having been written for the occasion of the 100th anniversary of the famous paper of Russell introducing his theory of descriptions, though Kripke's paper also has clear connections with contemporary debates. Much of the paper is concerned with a technical question about how the theory is applied by Russell and collaborator Alfred North Whitehead in their monumental *Principia Mathematica*,[16] but there are also significant remarks on the importance of keeping scope distinctions straight in less formal intensional contexts.

'The First Person' (Kripke 2011d) is directly concerned with the indexical 'I' (and 'me' and 'my'), the first-person singular pronoun(s), and indirectly with larger questions. The discussion is wide-ranging, and part of it pertains to issues in philosophy of mind that I am deferring until my closing chapter. But there is also direct comparison of the views of David Kaplan and the views of Frege. Kaplan and Frege are the archetypes of coarse-grained and fine-grained proposition theorists, respectively. In particular, Kaplan's work on demonstratives had a profound influence on such direct reference theorists as Salmon and Soames. Kripke compares and contrasts the Kaplanian and the Fregean approaches to the indexical 'I' (and to some extent over the present tense and the indexicals 'now' and 'today'). Indeed, Kripke offers what is probably the most sophisticated version of a fine-grained theory, even though his personal sympathies tilt more toward the coarse-grained.

These works require rather more background than I have wished to assume, and that fact, together with their having only recently become publicly available, makes it seem to me inappropriate to try to go into them more deeply here.[17] As such works are increasingly assimilated and critically examined in the years ahead, a better picture of Kripke's views – and therewith, needless to say, a better picture of the phenomena his views are about – can be expected to emerge. Meanwhile there remains a major long-published and much-discussed work of Kripke's to be dealt with.

5

Rules

Kripke's work on the interpretation of Wittgenstein happens to be our main or only source for certain views of Kripke's own, and so even though the focus in this volume is exclusively on Kripke's work in philosophy, rather than his work in history of philosophy, Kripke's *Wittgenstein on Rules and Private Language* (Kripke 1982) cannot be overlooked.[1] Not all parts of the book, however, are equally relevant. Kripke's interpretation finds in Wittgenstein four elements: a 'skeptical paradox' (addressed in Chapter 2, after a longish preface and a short introductory Chapter 1), a 'skeptical solution' and an application to the problem of 'private language' (both addressed in Chapter 3), and an application to the problem of 'other minds' (addressed in a long postscript). Kripke clearly thinks the 'skeptical paradox' worthy of serious, sustained attention; he informs us of the fact of his rejecting the 'skeptical solution,' but not of his grounds for rejecting it, or of what alternative solution he would himself propose;[2] there is nothing to suggest that Kripke in his own person endorses any of the views he attributes to Wittgenstein in the two applications. Accordingly, my interest here being solely in Kripke's rather than Wittgenstein's views, Chapter 2 will be treated in more detail than Chapter 3, and the postscript will be neglected entirely.

The plan here will be first to offer a way into the problem entirely independent of Wittgenstein, then to dismiss of all questions of Wittgenstein exegesis, then to elaborate on the analogy with the thought of David Hume that is so striking a feature of Kripke's account, and only after all this to take up the problem that Kripke takes to be a serious one, and the solution that Kripke expounds but for unstated reasons rejects.

Conventionalism

So far I have mentioned Quine mainly as a critic of modal logic, whose criticism crucially depends on identifying necessity with analyticity, an identification Kripke emphatically rejects. Quine is most famous, however, for his rejection of the analytic–synthetic distinction itself. (In his critique of modal logic he sets his objections to the notion of analyticity aside, and plays along with the idea, simply because he wants to make the point that even if one accepts, as he himself does not, the notion of analyticity, still one should be dubious of modal logic.) Though Quine's best-known attacks on the analytic–synthetic distinction date from the nineteen fifties and sixties, there was an earlier critical discussion in Quine (1936). The closing paragraphs of that paper raise a serious issue about the conception of analytic statements as simply consequences of semantic rules or linguistic conventions.

In the background stands the gem Carroll (1895).[3] In this fable, Achilles wishes to defend an argument in Euclid, from premises

(A)   Things that are equal to the same are equal to each other.
(B)   The two sides of this triangle are things that are equal to the same.

to the conclusion

(Z)   The two sides of this triangle are equal to each other.

The tortoise refuses to accept the inference from (A) and (B) to (Z) without the further premise

(C)   If A and B are true, Z must be true.

But then, even after accepting (C), the tortoise refuses to accept the inference from (A) and (B) and (C) to (Z) without the yet further premise

(D)   If A and B and C are true, Z must be true.

And so on. Carroll does not state the moral of the fable.

Quine does state a moral. He observes that there are a potentially unlimited number of analytic truths and indeed of truths of pure formal logic. The following will do for examples:

(1.0)   Everything is self-identical.
(1.1)   Either everything is self-identical or at most one thing is not.
(1.2)   Either everything is self-identical or at most two things are not.
(1.3)   Either everything is self-identical or at most three things are not.

But we have time to establish only finitely many linguistic conventions. So it cannot be that each of the logical truths $(1.n)$ is established separately as an *immediate* convention. On the other hand, Quine writes

> [I]f logic is to proceed *immediately* from the conventions, logic is needed for inferring logic from the conventions.

To enlarge on what Quine says, suppose it is suggested that all the sentences $(1.n)$ follow from just *two* principles, which may be taken to be conventions, namely, (1.0) plus

(2)   Any sentence implies its disjunction with any other sentence.

Now how is the conclusion (1.1), for instance, supposed to follow? It seems we have to argue from (2) to

(3)   (1.0) implies (1.1)

and then from (1.0) and (3) to (1.1), and similarly in the case of any other $(1.n)$ for $n > 0$. But how are we getting from (2) to (3), or from (1.0) and (3) to (1.1)? Well, by logic. But if logic is supposed to be the product of convention, where are the conventions from which these bits of logic follow? It begins to seem that, in addition to the pair of conventions we have acknowledged, (1.0) and (2), we need some further conventions, thus:

(4)   A universal generalization implies any instance.
(5)   A premise and the further premise that it implies some conclusion together imply that conclusion.

But then how do we get from (4) and (2) to (3), or from (5) and (1.0) and (3) to (1.1)? Well, by logic. But if logic is supposed to be the product of convention, where are the conventions from which these bits of logic follow? It begins to seem that, in addition to the four conventions we have acknowledged, (1.0) and (2) and (4) and (5), we need some further conventions. Clearly we are headed down the same road as Achilles and the tortoise.

At this point it may be suggested that what we need to get the other (1.*n*) from (1.0) is not a convention in the form of a declarative *assertion* like (2), *stating* that inference from any sentence to its disjunction with any other sentence has the property of *permissibility*, but a convention in the form, so to speak, of a genuine *rule*, genuinely *premitting* the inference, or rather, *requiring* it – an imperative *command*, something on the order of the following:

(2')   From any sentence, infer any sentence under consideration that is a disjunction of the given sentence with some other.

But with the imperative as much as with the declarative, questions arise. In place of the question of what *justifies* the inference from (1.0) and (2) to (1.1) we now have the question of what makes the inference from (1.0) to (1.1) a *correct* application of (2').

If we are to be able to get to the conclusions we want *without* having to bring in any other conventions, we will have to understand that genuine acceptance of (2') as a genuine rule already *commits one in advance to all its potential applications*; and that means absolutely *all* of them, every last one, including the inference from (1.0) to (1.1), and to (1.2), and to (1.3), and so on. Such is, nearly enough for present purposes, the moral Quine draws from Carroll's example. But how *can* one undertake such a 'commitment in advance' to a potentially unlimited sequence of applications, most of which one surely has not explicitly and specifically contemplated in advance of accepting the rule? Quine hints that the notion of such 'commitment in advance' makes no real sense, that all there really is here is a certain behavioral disposition or habit, nothing more.

Quine's immediate target was Carnap, but the puzzle or mystery here is not just a problem for Carnap. It is a problem for any philosopher who makes use of the notion of analyticity (a class of philosophers that includes Saul Kripke). And it is not just a problem for philosophers, either. It is also a problem for all those linguists who posit 'psychologically real' phonological or syntactic or semantic rules; for they, too, are trading in the notion of something the commitment to which or internalization of which carries with it an advance commitment to a potentially unlimited number of unforeseen applications. Indeed, we have here a conceptual problem not just for contemporary linguistics but for the whole range of contemporary disciplines collectively known as 'cognitive science.' For Kripke the problem is all that, but it is first and foremost a problem suggested to him by his reading of Wittgenstein.

Kripkenstein

For better or worse, Kripke has given us his thoughts on such issues mainly in the form of a commentary on that celebrated Austrian philosopher. Unfortunately, Wittgenstein being not just an ordinary major philosopher but a cult figure, any sort of exegetical claim about him is bound to be enormously controversial. Consequently debates over whether Kripke is right or wrong in his interpretation of his source texts threaten to overshadow and distract attention from the merits or demerits of the argument that Kripke rightly or wrongly finds in them: The Kripkean message is in constant danger of being drowned out by Wittgensteinian noise.

Kripke tries so far as possible to defuse or deflect criticism on purely exegetical points. For while the body of the book is full of claims to the effect that Wittgenstein says this and Wittgenstein says that, there are framing passages, including much of the preface and the short introductory Chapter 1, indicating that one should not take such attributions one hundred percent literally. Kripke says he is expounding

> neither 'Wittgenstein's' argument nor 'Kripke's': rather Wittgenstein's argument as it struck Kripke, as it presented a problem for him. (Kripke 1982, 5)

But even in the very act of issuing in this semi-disclaimer, Kripke is taking a stand on the single most contentious issue in Wittgenstein exegesis.

The background is as follows. Early and late, which is to say, both in his 1922 *Tractatus Logico-Philosophicus* and in his 1953 *Philosophical Investigations*, Wittgenstein insists that philosophers should not propound theses, let alone arguments for theses. In the *Tractatus*, however, he fails to practice what he preaches, continually saying things that according to his own official doctrine cannot be 'said' but only 'shown.' This leaves him toward the end of the book in about the same dialectical position in which the ancient skeptic Sextus Empiricus found himself after propounding a battery of arguments to prove that no argument can prove anything. At that point Sextus, who was a physician as well as a philosopher, offered a pungent medical simile: Philosophy is like a laxative that purges the body of foul humors, and is itself purged along with them. He also offered a blander alternative simile: Philosophy is like a ladder one uses to climb to a higher place and then kicks away. The latter, ladder comparison made its way from Sextus's *Outlines of Pyrrhonism* into Arthur Schopenhauer's *World as Will and Representation* and thence to Wittgenstein's *Tractatus*. There it amounts to a confession on Wittgenstein's part of a failure to live up to his own stated principles about what philosophers should and should not do.

These claims about the relation of principles to practice in the *Tractatus* are about as close to uncontroversial as one ever comes in discussions of Wittgenstein. By contrast, about the most hotly debated issue in Wittgenstein studies is whether there is the same sort of gap between principles and practice in the *Investigations*, where there is no mention of kicking away ladders. Some are willing to speak of Wittgenstein's 'arguments' in his later book, while others hotly deny that there are any arguments in that posthumous work, claiming that in it Wittgenstein lives up to his professed principles as to how philosophy should be done, and never engages in argumentation, but only in 'therapy.' Now the wording of Kripke's semi-disclaimer quoted above seems to presuppose that Wittgenstein *does* have an argument, even if that argument isn't exactly what Kripke plans to present. Thus Kripke commits himself to one side, and perhaps the less fashionable side, in a heated controversy. (Moreover, though Kripke is not committed to attributing to Wittgenstein *precisely* the argument he describes, he does seem to remain committed to attributing to Wittgenstein *approximately* the argument he describes; and that claim will be controversial even among those who agree with Kripke that Wittgenstein does make some sort of argument or other.)

As the topic of this book is the philosophy of Saul Kripke, not Ludwig Wittgenstein, I would like to join those previous commentators who have tried to avoid questions about the interpretation of Wittgenstein, and to concentrate on the substantive philosophical merits of the argument presented by Kripke, regardless of that argument's provenance or pedigree. Some such commentators, finding 'Wittgenstein's argument as it created a problem for Kripke' too unwieldy a phrase, have taken to calling it 'Kripkenstein's argument.' Others have adopted the fiction that Kripke is writing, not about the famous *Philosophical Investigations* of the famous Ludwig Wittgenstein, but about another work of the same title by another philosopher of the same name, whom they distinguish from his more famous namesake by calling him 'Kripke's Wittgenstein' or 'KW.' The texts of the one *Philosophical Investigations* and

the other are word-for-word identical, at any rate in the passages
Kripke quotes, though the meanings may be very different, as in
the case of the *Don Quixote* of Miguel de Cervantes and the *Don
Quixote* of Pierre Menard in the well-known Borges story. Whatever
may be the correct interpretation of the text of the famous *Investigations*, it is supposed that Kripke is 100 percent correct in his interpretation of the other *Investigations*. In the pages that follow,
'Wittgenstein' will always refer to the fictional character Kripkenstein or KW. The historical figure will henceforth be mentioned
only in the notes, not the main text.

The Analogy with Hume

A provocative feature of Kripke's commentary is that he compares
his Wittgenstein to the celebrated Scottish skeptic David Hume.[4]
By way of outlining the argument Kripke attributes to his Wittgenstein, I would like to elaborate the analogy with Hume a bit beyond
anything Kripke says explicitly. More precisely, the analogy is with
a certain interpretation of Hume. It will not, for present purposes,
matter how accurate or inaccurate this interpretation of Hume may
be and, if the reader wishes, the Hume under discussion may be
taken to be a character related to a certain famous Scot in the same
way that the Wittgenstein under discussion is related to a famous
certain Austrian whom I have just said I will not mention by name
anymore except in footnotes. The goal is to get at what *Kripke* thinks
about linguistic convention or semantic rules, by way of what he
says about *his* Wittgenstein and *his* Hume.[5]

   With Hume, the text of primary importance is the discussion of
causation in §VII 'Of the Idea of Necessary Connection' in Hume's
Enquiry Concerning Human Understanding, a section that is divided
into two parts, a negative or critical phase, and a positive or reconstructive phase. Of secondary importance is a discussion of induction in §§IV and V of the same work, which also has a two-part
structure.[6]

   With Wittgenstein, the text of importance consists primarily of
22 pages of short, numbered paragraphs, §§143–242 of Part I of the
Philosophical Investigations (Wittgenstein 1953). Since, however,
the development in the *Investigations* is not linear, other sections
of the work may also be relevant. There is in Wittgenstein's argument the same kind of two-part structure that there is in Hume,

though there is no tidy sorting of sections into positive and negative. Kripke labels the two phases of the argument the 'skeptical paradox' and the 'skeptical solution.'[7]

In the background in Hume is a theory of meaning developed in §II of the *Enquiry*: Genuinely meaningful terms are associated with ideas. Complex ideas are compounds of simple ideas. Simple ideas derive from or are copies of 'impressions,' which is to say, of sensations or feelings.

In the background in Wittgenstein is a theory of meaning developed in the *Tractatus*: Not to put too fine a point on it, on this 'picture theory' declarative sentences are representations or 'pictures' of facts, or, more precisely, they are pictures of *putative* facts, and *if true* are pictures of facts. Knowing the meaning of a declarative sentence consists in understanding what putative fact it pictures. Note that this view gives declarative sentences a primary role; presumably the meanings of other sentences, imperatives and interrogatives, are to be understood in terms of their relations to declaratives. While many philosophers of language today would deprecate talk of assertions 'picturing' facts (which indeed Kripke himself avoids), and think it monumentally important to speak instead of assertions 'corresponding' to facts, or 'being made true by' facts, such terminological differences conceal fundamental similarities: Views that are, in all respects relevant to Wittgenstein's critique, nearly indistinguishable from the view that was Wittgenstein's most immediate target are still very much with us, despite changes of fashion.

The case of special interest to Hume is that of 'cause.' Hume analyzes the complex idea of cause into the simpler ideas of 'temporal succession' (the cause is earlier, the effect later) and 'necessary connection' (given the cause, the effect doesn't just *happen* to follow but rather *must* follow). Hume's problem is: From what impression is the idea of necessary connection copied? The negative phase of his argument is an exercise in impression-hunting that fails to locate the desired impression.

The case of special interest to Wittgenstein is that of meaning ascriptions, as when we say that the the preschooler Patricia, though still struggling with the concept of multiplication, has mastered the terminology and rules for addition, and means *plus* by 'plus,' or that the Frenchman Pierre, whose English lessons have not yet reached the chapter about numbers, has somehow picked up a wrong idea, and means *times* by 'plus.' Wittgenstein's problem is: What kind of facts do such meaning ascriptions picture? To what kind of facts do such meaning ascriptions correspond? What kind of facts make such meaning ascriptions true? The negative phase of his argument is an exercise in fact-hunting that fails to find the desired fact.

In the negative phase of his discussion of causation, Hume considers successively three cases: the action of one external body on another, as when a moving billiard ball strikes a stationary one and imparts motion to it; the mind's power over the body, as in the voluntary motion of a limb; and mind's power over its own ideas, as in recalling something to memory. In every case he fails to locate, among our impressions of the cause, anything that could be the source from which the idea of necessary connection is derived, the original from which it is copied. He states that we have not, in any of these three cases, any impression of the 'secret power' by which the effect is produced. He assumes that if it were not so, then on seeing the cause even for the first time, we would immediately be able to predict the effect, which we are not. We only learn what the laws of motion governing billiard balls are, or whether we can wiggle our ears, or how good our recall of past events is, by experience.

The negative phase of Wittgenstein's argument will be discussed in the next section of this chapter. The only thing that may be noted now is that, just as Hume looks in three principal places for the missing impression, so Wittgenstein examines three main candidates for the role of the missing fact, though since the structure of the *Investigations* is non-linear, there is no tidy division of the relevant paragraphs into three groups. (That there happen to be *three* main candidates both with Hume and with Wittgenstein is sheer coincidence. There is not even a superficial parallelism.)

Hume's solution to the problem he has uncovered in the notion of cause will be one that accepts and does not challenge the conclusion of the negative phase of his discussion, that among our impressions of any cause, or for that matter of the associated effect, there is nothing that could be the source from which the idea of necessary connection between the one and the other is copied. Nonetheless, Hume is or professes to be a mitigated (or 'Academic') and not an extreme (or 'Pyrrhonian') skeptic. He does not conclude that there is no genuine idea associated with the term 'cause,' or that talk of causes is mere sophistry and illusion. The negative phase of his argument may seem to point toward such a conclusion, but according to Hume, any argument for any radically skeptical conclusion

– and the conclusion that there is no such thing as causation, that talk of causes and effects is nonsense, would undoubtedly be a quite radically skeptical one – though it may cause momentary amazement, can produce no lasting conviction. If Hume sometimes appears to be advocating an *extreme* skepticism, that is largely because he sometimes gets carried away expressing the 'momentary amazement' that skeptical arguments can create.

Wittgenstein's solution to the problem he has uncovered will also be one accepting and not challenging the conclusion of the negative phase of his discussion, that there are no facts pictured by, or corresponding to, or serving as truth-makers for meaning ascriptions. Nonetheless, Wittgenstein does not conclude that no one ever means anything by anything they say, even if the negative phase of his discussion may seem to point toward such a conclusion. Wittgenstein does not conclude that meaning ascriptions themselves lack meaning, let alone that there is no such thing as meaning. If Kripke sometimes seems to be attributing to Wittgenstein the more radical conclusion that nothing means anything, it is because he sometimes gets carried away expressing the 'momentary amazement' that skeptical arguments can create.[8]

Misunderstandings may result from a certain ambiguity and awkwardness in Hume's use of the word 'reason,' though this is less a problem in his discussion of causation than in his discussion of induction. The negative phase of the induction discussion concludes that inference from past to future has no foundation in 'reason,' and this may easily be misread as an assertion that such inference is irrational or unreasonable and should be given up. That this is not Hume's intent emerges in the positive phase of his discussion, where he says that inference from past to future is founded on 'custom or habit'; for in so saying he describes this custom or habit as a principle 'of equal weight and authority,' and something we couldn't give up even if we wanted to. Part of the trouble is that sometimes Hume uses 'reason' in a narrower sense of 'reason' as contrasted with experience, 'reason' in the sense of *pure* reasoning of the kind for which 'rationalist' philosophers such as Descartes and Leibniz claimed great powers that Hume denies it to have; whereas at other times Hume uses 'reason' in a broad sense of 'reason' as contrasted with passion, 'reason' in a sense including *empirical* reasoning.[9]

Misunderstandings may result from a certain ambiguity and awkwardness in Wittgenstein's and Kripke's use of the word 'fact.' For one must distinguish the 'inflated' or metaphysical usage of 'fact' [*Tatsache*] in play in the *Tractatus* from the 'deflated' or pleo-nastic usage of 'fact' emphasized by F. P. Ramsey in the post-*Tractatus* period. On the deflated usage, to say 'yadda yadda yadda' and to say 'it's a fact that yadda yadda yadda' are virtually equiva-lent, so that advocating rejection of 'it's a fact that yadda yadda yadda' is tantamount to advocating rejection of 'yadda yadda yadda' itself. Kripke, who is certainly aware of the danger of mis-understanding on this point, and insistent that Wittgenstein never would advocate abandonment of the practice of saying 'Jones means *plus* by "plus"' or anything of the sort, picks up from the text of the *Investigations* the expression 'superlative fact' and some-times though not always inserts 'superlative' in front of 'fact' to make plain that he's not rejecting any and all claims to the effect that it's a fact that so-and-so means such-and-such, but only those in which 'fact' is taken in a nondeflated, nonpleonastic sense. For to repeat, to reject them when 'fact' is taken in a deflated, pleonastic sense would be tantamount to rejecting talk of meaning altogether, and this is something Kripke never wished to represent Wittgen-stein as wishing to do.

For one reason or another, there was quite a bit of misunder-standing of Hume. Kant writes in the Introduction to his *Prolegom-ena to Any Future Metaphysics* that it is positively painful to see how utterly Hume's opponents have missed the point of the problem. For the question was not, Kant insists, whether the concept of cause was right, useful, and even indispensable for our knowledge of nature, for this Hume never doubted. It was solely a question, according to Kant, concerning the *origin* of the concept.

For one reason or another, there has been quite a bit of misun-derstanding of Kripke. It is positively painful to see how utterly some of his opponents have missed the point of the problem. The question is not whether the concept of meaning is right, useful, and even indispensable, for this his Wittgenstein never doubts (as by contrast Quine, for one, notoriously did).

The positive phase of Hume's argument at last locates the missing impression that is the original from which the idea of nec-essary connection is copied, but locates it in a quite unexpected place. Having observed the 'constant conjunction' of A and B, having seen many cases of type A followed by cases of type B, and encountering a new case of type A, we anticipate or expect a new case of type B to follow. This sentiment or feeling of anticipation or expectation – of waiting for the other shoe to drop, so to speak

– is in the end identified as the long-sought impression from which the idea of necessary connection derives. The surprise is that the long-sought impression is to be found not in observation *of the cause*, or new instance of *A*, or for that matter of the effect, or new instance of *B*, but rather in observation *of our reactions to observing the cause*. If there is a mistake in our thinking about causation, for Hume this consists in projecting onto the world something that really comes from ourselves.

The positive phase of Wittgenstein's argument will be discussed in the last section of this chapter. The only thing that needs to be said in advance is that there is at this point in some respects a *dis-analogy* with Hume, since while Hume does at last find the impression he has been seeking, though not in the place where one might have expected to find it, Wittgenstein holds that we must educate ourselves away from looking for the non-existent meaning-facts, and adopt a different understanding of what meaning-ascription talk, and ultimately talk in general, is *for*, if not for depicting or reporting facts.

There is an important corollary to the positive phase of Hume's argument. On Hume's account, the notions of cause and effect can be applied to given *a* and *b* only insofar as they can be regarded as instances of general types *A* and *B*. There is no 'singular' causation. This corollary has significant implications for the evaluation of the traditional argument from design in natural theology.[10] Kant hints at this point by suggesting that tied up with the question of the origin of the concept of cause was the question whether that concept was independent of all experience, with perhaps a more extended use not restricted merely to objects of experience. (In plainer terms, the question is whether it even makes sense to speak of an unseen God as the *cause* of the visible world.)

There is an important corollary to the positive phase of Wittgenstein's argument as well, ruling out 'private' language, with implications for the so-called problem of other minds potentially as subversive as Hume's implications for the problem of the existence of God.[11] Concern with these matters is reflected in the phrase 'and Private Language' in the title of Kripke's book, and in the presence at the end of the book of a long postscript on other minds; but for reasons I have indicated, I am not going to pursue these matters. It thus now remains 'only' to give an account of the negative and positive, or critical and reconstructive, phases of Wittgenstein's discussion.

The Skeptical Paradox

Suppose the character Jones means *plus* by 'plus.' In other words, suppose that Jones means what *we* mean by 'plus.' Suppose he attaches the standard English meaning the word 'plus.' He does not mean *times* rather than *plus* by 'plus,' or *multiplication* rather than *addition* by 'addition,' or *product* rather than *sum* by 'sum.' Nor does he mean *quus* by 'plus' or *quaddition* by 'addition' or *quum* by 'sum,' where these are Kripke's labels for the strange operation that works like *plus* with its standard English meaning when applied to numbers both less than 57, but yields a constant value of 5 in other cases, so that whereas 68 plus 57 equals 125, 68 quus 57 equals 5. Supposing all this, the declarative sentence 'Jones means *plus* by "plus"' is true. And now comes the embarrassing Wittgensteinian question: Of what fact is this true declarative sentence, this true meaning ascription, a picture? To what fact does it 'correspond'? What fact 'makes it true'?

Perhaps the first answer that occurs to one is this, that the sentence pictures or corresponds to or is made true by the fact that Jones has internalized a *rule* for addition. When – as a preschooler, one may suppose – he was first taught addition, he wasn't just given some examples, but was told, say, that one can find the sum of *m* and *n* by counting out *m* marbles, making a pile of them, and then counting out *n* marbles, making another pile, and then combining the piles and counting how many marbles there are altogether. But even if Jones does not merely retain this rule as a subconscious memory but can actually *recite* it, we encounter another problem, a problem about the meanings of the words used in the enunciation of the rule. The fact that Jones associates addition with this rule only implies that Jones means *plus* by 'plus' on certain assumptions about what he means by the words 'combine' and 'count' among others.

We must assume that Jones means *combine* by 'combine,' and not the bizarre operation *quombine*, which involves putting two piles together if neither has 57 or more things in it, but saving five things and getting rid of the rest otherwise. We must assume that Jones means *count* by 'count,' and not the bizarre operation *quount*, which agrees with ordinary counting unless applied to a heap that has been put together out of two smaller heaps, at least one of which had 57 or more things in it, in which case the result of quounting is simply 'five.' We have not fully uncovered what fact it is that

'Jones means *plus* by "plus"' depicts or reports until we have
uncovered what facts they are that 'Jones means *combine* by
"combine"' and 'Jones means *count* by "count"' depict or report.
And if we try to cite further rules for 'combine' and 'count' as we
cited the rule for 'plus,' we will encounter further problems, problems about the meanings of the words used in the enunciations of
these rules. We need 'a rule for interpreting the rule,' and that will
either land us in a circle if the new rules for 'combine' and 'count'
themselves involve 'plus,' or else launch us on an infinite regress
of the Achilles–tortoise type.[12]

Kripke opens with this kind of example (considering his own
meaning *plus* by 'plus' rather than Jones's doing so), and alludes
to §§185ff in the *Investigations*, which contains related discussions
(involving a different kind of candidate rule for addition, but a
similar infinite regress). Those passages culminate in §201, from
which perhaps I should quote, and a little more fully than Kripke
does:

> This was our paradox: no course of action could be determined by
> a rule, because every course of action can be made out to accord with
> the rule. ... It can be seen that there is a misunderstanding here from
> the mere fact that in the course of our argument we give one inter-
> pretation after another; as if each one contented us at least for a
> moment, until we thought of yet another standing behind it. What
> this shews is that there is a way of grasping a rule which is *not* an
> *interpretation*, but which is exhibited in what we call 'obeying the
> rule' and 'going against it' in actual cases.

So the 'meaning fact' we have been looking for is not to be found
in *rules* and *interpretations*, but must be sought elsewhere, in what
'is exhibited' when a rule is obeyed or gone against. But exhibited
to whom? To the external observer watching the subject Jones as he
obeys or goes against the rule, what is 'exhibited' or observable is
behavior in particular cases, in which the observer may seem to
perceive a pattern, the manifestation of a general *disposition* to
behave in a certain way. To the subject Jones himself are 'exhibited'
introspectively certain *feelings*, for instance, of being *guided*, that
may accompany his actions in obeying or going against a rule. And
so the further candidates to be considered for the role of facts pictured by or corresponding to meaning ascriptions, once we have
reached the conclusion of first subphase of the negative phase of
the argument, include facts about, on the one hand, behavioral
dispositions, and on the other hand, introspectable feelings. Or

anyhow, these are the other two candidates that Kripke discusses in the second and third subphases.

About dispositions, Kripke first points out that if Jones means *plus* rather than *times* or *quus* by 'plus,' then '125' rather than '3876' or '5' the *right* answer to the question 'What is 68 + 57?' if the plus-sign means what Jones means by it. But merely to say that Jones is *disposed* to give the answer '125' rather than some other is not to say that Jones is *right* to do so. The dispositional account simply leaves out this crucial *normative* aspect of meaning.[13] After all, Jones might be *disposed* to give *wrong* answers in certain cases, this one included. (And one may add that it does not help to bring in second-order dispositions to accept corrections to his first-order dispositions, since he might go wrong about these, too. He might even have the first-order disposition to give the correct answer '125' while also having the second-order disposition to timidly retract his answer it if bullied and browbeaten.)

Though the point about normativity is his *main* argument, Kripke adds that it is not just a possibility but a virtual certainty, given human fallibility, that Jones will go wrong in some cases, and an absolute certainty that he and all the rest of us as well will be disposed to give no answer at all, but just boggle, in many others, where the numbers are so large that calculating with them is beyond human powers. The function that for input m and n gives the value that Jones is disposed to give if asked, 'What is $m + n$?' in the best case agrees imperfectly with the addition function up to some finite bound, and becomes undefined thereafter.

At this point Kripke's mentions, as one of the replies he has heard in discussion, the suggestion that one shouldn't understand 'disposition' in too crudely literal a sense. It is not so much what Jones with his actual limitations is disposed to do, but what he would be disposed to do 'other things being equal.' The quoted phrase is one that, in its Latin version *'ceteris paribus,'* is often found in the proposed analyses of various notions in philosophy of science and elsewhere. Here Kripke does not object to bringing in a counterfactual, but merely insists that if one is to do so, one must spell out what is meant. And here one faces a dilemma.

On the one hand, what is meant may be that if Jones's brain 'had been stuffed with sufficient extra matter' and his life prolonged (in a healthy state) for sufficient time, then given two even quite large numbers m and n, he would return their sum. About this Kripke quite rightly says that we do not know what the result of such brain-stuffing and life-prolongation might be. It might lead Jones to go insane, for instance: 'Surely such speculation should be left to science fiction writers and futurologists.'

On the other hand, what is meant may be that if nothing (in the way of insufficient memory capacity, too short a lifespan, or anything else, including insanity induced by brain-stuffing and life-prolongation) interfered with Jones's current intentions, then given two even quite large numbers *m* and *n*, he would return their sum. This is true, Kripke says, if Jones's current intentions are taken to include an intention to perform *addition* and not *quaddition* on the two numbers, an intention to return their *sum* and not their *quum*. But that, obviously, can only be so only if Jones's current intentions include meaning *plus* and not *quus* by 'plus.' And so the proposed analysis is circular, assuming what is in doubt, that our saying that Jones means *plus* by 'plus' is depicting or reporting some fact about Jones. The analysis does not *locate* or *identify* the supposed fact, which was the problem.

Another suggestion would be that it is not so much facts about behavioral dispositions themselves that meaning ascriptions picture or correspond to, but facts about something in the structure and functioning of the brain causally underlying them: For Jones to mean what the rest of us mean by 'plus' is for him to be in relevant respects in the inner state (details of which are at present unknown) the rest us are in. Wittgenstein barely alludes to this kind of suggestion, and Kripke's treatment of it is correspondingly compressed (and the most significant part of it confined to a long footnote beginning on page 35, occupying the whole of page 36, and not ending until page 37). What he has to say there pertains to the issue of 'functionalism' in cognitive science and philosophy of mind, which I am reserving to the next and final chapter of this book.

Suffice it to say that by the end of the second subphase of the negative phase of the argument, not only rules (and/or interpretations) have been eliminated, but also dispositions (and/or neurology). The third and last candidate identified for consideration as perhaps constituting the fact depicted or reported by meaning ascriptions is the occurrence of some introspectable feeling. To summarize very briefly a discussion of the 'phenomenology' involved that goes on at some length, both in the Wittgensteinian text and in the Kripkean commentary, it is on the one hand doubtful that the fact of experiencing a certain feeling could play the role required of the supposed fact supposedly depicted or reported by a meaning ascription. How could Jones's *feeling* that '125' is the right answer make it to be the case that '125' *is* the right answer?[14] Might not the feeling perhaps be induced even in cases where Jones does *not* mean *plus* by 'plus,' simply by administering some drug? And it is on the other hand doubtful upon introspection that there *is* any distinctive feeling of 'meaning.' Indeed, Kripke concludes by saying that if there really were a unique introspectable feeling of meaning *plus* by 'plus' it would have stared one in the face from the beginning, and the skeptical challenge would never have gotten off the ground.

Now there is no argument – say by successive dichotomies – offered in Wittgenstein or Kripke to prove that the three candidate facts thus far considered and rejected are the *only* candidates, and in this sense the argument is a challenge rather than a proof: *What else* could be the missing fact of which a meaning-ascription is a picture, the fact to which a meaning-ascription corresponds, the fact that makes a meaning-ascription true? Kripke briefly considers one last attempt to respond, sometimes encountered in the literature, all too often expressed in impenetrably obscure prose. The attempt simply posits an unexplained 'primitive' state, not to be assimilated to sensations or dispositions or whatever, but uniquely of its own kind, *sui generis*: a finite something of unknown or ineffable nature that in some unknown or ineffable way makes one answer right and all other answers wrong in infinitely many cases, and that is not liable to quus-like misinterpretation. In the end, Kripke rightly dismiss this suggestion as desperate.[15]

The Skeptical Solution

If the arguments roughly and briefly outlined in the preceding section are accepted, then the model on which declarative sentences picture or correspond to or are made true by facts, and on which to grasp the meaning of such a sentence is to grasp what putative fact is involved, has been undermined in the special case of declarative sentences ascribing meanings. Though most of the discussion to this point has proceeded as if there were a *contrast* here between meaning ascriptions and other kinds of assertions where the facts depicted or reported were presumed to be readily locatable, if one stops to think about it there is something dizzying in trying to hold onto the view of declarative sentences as in other cases still depicting or reporting facts when it is conceded that sentences about what a given speaker means by a given sentence

– sentences about which fact a given speaker takes a given sentence to depict or report – do not themselves depict or report facts. Whether the link is logical or merely psychological is not a matter about which Kripke says a great deal, but when his Wittgenstein gives up anything like the picture theory of language as applied to meaning ascriptions, he gives up anything like the picture theory of language altogether.

This leaves him and us needing a whole new theory of meaning, whose application to all areas of thought would need to be worked out. A large part of the *Investigations*, including its whole second part, is indeed devoted to its application to psychology, as is a large part of Kripke's commentary, including the long postscript. The preface to the *Investigations* mentions that a comparable examination of mathematics would also be possible, as do several of Kripke's footnotes. Here, however, there will be space to consider the application of the new theory of meaning to meaning ascriptions, the special case that first led us to the general problem.

The new general model of meaning that Wittgenstein proposes looks something like the following. For any sentence, we characterize its usage through a simile comparing seriously uttering the sentence to making a move in a game. The key questions are: What previous moves warrant making the move of uttering the sentence? And what subsequent moves are warranted by the move of uttering the sentence? The account of usage given by the answers to these questions, the account of *how* and expression is used, must be accompanied by an account of utility, of *why* the expression is used, or to restate the question using two of Wittgenstein's favorite bits of jargon, what role the 'language game' plays in our 'form of life.' An account of *use* in the full double sense of usage and utility is what is called for when an account of meaning is called for.

Note that this model assigns no special, privileged role to *declarative* sentences as opposed to imperatives or other kinds. If the sentence in question does happen to be declarative, as with 'Jones means *plus* by "plus"' and other meaning ascriptions, then since serious utterance of a declarative sentence amounts to assertion, the question of what previous moves warrant such utterance becomes the question of what conditions must hold for the sentence to be assertable. The question of what subsequent moves utterance of the sentence warrants and the question of what the whole game is for may be run together into the question of how the assertion is applied, what use is made of it. So an account of the meaning of a declarative sentence should include an account of its assertability conditions and of its application.[16] In particular, what is demanded in the case of meaning ascriptions is not an account of what 'facts' they picture or correspond to or are made true by, but rather answers to the following questions: Under what conditions may one assert that Jones has learned the meaning of the word 'plus,' or has come to mean *plus* by 'plus'? And if another member of our speech community makes this assertion and we accept it, how if at all can we apply it and make use of it?

Let me begin by giving an answer that is only a first approximation, later indicating *why* it is only a first approximation. To a first approximation the new account or meaning ascriptions runs somewhat as follows. As to assertability, when Jones (typically after some considerable training involving being exposed to various examples and generally also being told certain rules) has been observed in enough cases to answer addition problems more or less as others in our community would do, we may assert that he means *plus* by 'plus.' As to applicability, if we are told Jones means *plus* by 'plus,' then we may treat his answers to future addition problems more or less as we would treat those of other members of the community.

By contrast, if instead Jones is observed answering addition problems more or less as others in our community would answer multiplication problems involving the same numbers, we may assert that he means *times* by 'plus.' And if we can discern no pattern in his answers, we must confess to not knowing what, if anything, he means by 'plus.' If we are told Jones means *times* by 'plus,' then we may treat his answers to future addition problems more or less as we would treat the answers of other members of the community to multiplication problems involving the same numbers. But if instead we are told Jones attaches no discernible meaning to 'plus,' then we are warned against relying on his answers to addition questions.

Wittgenstein concedes, or rather emphasizes, that assertability conditions and applications such as those just roughly sketched above in the case of 'Jones means *plus* by "plus"' resist anything like precise formulation. And Kripke would emphasize that however they were formulated, skeptical doubts would still be possible to raise about their correct interpretation as they apply to any given move. But what matters for the role of the language-game in our form of life is only that members of the community generally *do not in practice* disagree on how the rules apply. It does not matter that a skeptic *might in principle* do so or pretend to do so.

Here one may quote two of the last things Wittgenstein says in the part of the *Investigations* on which Kripke focuses:

> 240. Disputes do not break out (among mathematicians, say) over the question whether a rule has been obeyed or not. People don't come to blows over it, for example. That is part of the framework on which the working of our language is based (for example, in giving descriptions).

> 241. 'So you are saying that human agreement decides what is true and what is false?' – It is what human beings *say* that is true and false; and they agree in the *language* they use. That is not agreement in opinions but in form of life.

These passages, coming at the end of the suite of paragraphs that Kripke deems central, represent the bottom line, the ultimate conclusion, in the positive phase of the main argument.

Now the language-game of meaning ascription can contribute positively to the form of life of our community only because human beings generally are such that, if they are (typically after some greater or lesser amount of training) observed to use a word as other members of the community do in a large and varied enough selection of cases, then they can be relied upon to continue using the word for the most part as other members of the community do. Yet while the features of human behavior just indicated underlie the language game of making meaning ascriptions, and while doubtless features of the human brain underlie these features of behavior, nevertheless it is still supposed to remain the case that – as the negative, skeptical phase of the argument concluded – 'Jones means *plus* by "plus"' does not *picture* and does not *correspond* to and is not *made true* by facts about a speaker's behavior or brain.

This is why the account of the language-game of meaning ascriptions that has been given so far is too crude and only amounts to a first approximation. It hardly distinguishes the role of 'Jones means *plus* by "plus"' from the role of 'Jones uses "plus" as we do' or 'Jones is, as regards what causally underlies his use of "plus," in the same kind of state as we are.' But there certainly is supposed to be a difference. For the move of asserting 'Jones means *plus* by "plus"' is supposed to warrant the further move of saying, 'Given what Jones means by "plus," the *right* answer for him to give when asked "What is 68 + 57?" is "125" and nothing else,' whereas the move of making an assertion merely about behavioral dispositions or presumed underlying inner causes is not supposed to warrant, all by itself, any move in the language game of 'right' and 'wrong' – with, one may add, the associated distribution of praise and blame, reinforcement and deterrence, which an anthropologist would perhaps not feel free to bestow on the members of an alien culture whose ways were being observed, but which we do feel free to bestow on fellow members of our own community.[17]

For Wittgenstein, according to Kripke, one has only given a full account of 'Jones means *plus* by "plus"' when one has given an account also of the language-game move of saying, 'The answer Jones *ought* to give is …' If we want to move beyond a first-approximation account, perhaps it is best to speak metaphorically: Saying 'Jones means *plus* by "plus"' is like awarding Jones a kind of certificate of competence, entitling him to certain forms of employment (for instance, as a bookkeeper). To say 'Jones uses "plus" as the rest of us do' is to say that Jones has performed in a certain way, a way that as it happens amounts to fulfilling the criteria for certification; but we only actually hand him the certificate when we say, 'Jones means *plus* by "plus."' That is why what is effected by saying 'Jones means *plus* by "plus"' is not reducible simply to the depicting or reporting of a fact. But Kripke, though he certainly warns more than once or twice against taking meaning ascriptions simply to depict or report facts about Jones's behavioral dispositions or their presumed underlying causes, overlooking the normative element, does not provide overmuch in the way of detail and elaboration.

In any case, Kripke, as I stated earlier, gives an indication that he does not accept Wittgenstein's new model of meaning, though he withholds any indication of *why* he does not accept it. About his reasons I will not even speculate, but only very briefly indicate why one might have doubts about the new model of meaning, without in any way claiming to be speaking for Kripke here. Perhaps the most basic difficulty with the Wittgensteinian account is that trying to think of meaning in terms of assertability and application seems to underestimate the importance of *interactions* among different kinds of sentences. Such interactions give rise to many *indirect* ways of justifying assertion, beyond whatever may be thought of as the primary assertability condition, and many *indirect* applications, beyond whatever may be thought of as the primary application.

For one example, an obvious problem with the Wittgensteinian account as sketched so far is that the assertion conditions and applications it suggests both alike presuppose direct contact between our community and the speaker in question, so that his speech can be tested and, once the test is passed, made use of. But cases where we can sensibly ask about what some speaker means by some word seem to extend far beyond cases where there is interaction with the speaker in question.

To give an illustration different from the one most often discussed in the literature – the case of Robinson Crusoe[18] – it is generally agreed by classical scholars that the emperor Claudius knew the Etruscan language. But this assertion is *not* made on the basis of having examined surviving Claudian inscriptions in Etruscan and checked that they use the language correctly. Nor is it applied by reacting to newly excavated Claudian inscriptions in Etruscan by treating what they say in the same manner as we treat testimonies from other Etruscan sources. For the actual opinion of the classical scholars is that Claudius was one of the *very last* people who knew the Etruscan language, and the scholars freely confess that they themselves do not. They would not be in a position to evaluate whether a Claudian inscription uses Etruscan correctly, were such an inscription unearthed. Nor would they be in a position to make use of what such a hypothetic Claudian inscription said, in the way they make use of the numerous known Claudian inscriptions in Latin. For being ignorant of Etruscan they simply would not *know* what such an inscription would be saying.

The attribution of knowledge of Etruscan to Claudius is based on indirect grounds, partly on testimonies in ancient sources from persons better placed than we are to know whether he had such knowledge, and partly on testimonies that Claudius went about seeking knowledge of a rapidly disappearing language in much the way a modern anthropological linguist might, by questioning aged peasants in remote rural districts. And the potential *application* of the ascription of knowledge of Etruscan to Claudius, to the extent that there is any, is really very indirect indeed, and seems to be something like this, that if a newly excavated Claudian inscription in *Latin* were discovered, that happened to mention the meaning of some Etruscan word, scholars would add that bit of information to the scanty list of Etruscan words whose meanings they think they know (as they have added the information incidentally mentioned in passing by Suetonius, that 'aesar' is Etruscan for 'god'). They would add it as one more contribution to a long-term project they hope will eventually leave us with a list long enough to allow us to translate some informative Etruscan inscriptions.

Another obvious problem with the Wittgensteinian account as sketched so far is that it only covers meaning ascriptions that are categorically asserted, and tells us nothing about appearances of meaning ascriptions as subordinate clauses in longer sentences. For instance, it tells us nothing about the appearance of a meaning ascription as the antecedent of a conditional imperative, as in 'If he's the sort of person who means *reluctant* by "reticent" and *center* by "epicenter," then don't offer him the editor's job.' Indicating when declarative meaning ascriptions may be categorically asserted, and how categorically asserted meaning ascriptions may be applied, still leaves us without an account of conditionals or hypotheticals, and of imperatives as opposed to declaratives. And the cases of conditional commands whose antecedents concern meaning and of attribution of knowledge of the meanings of dead languages to historical figures are only two of many cases that the basic Wittgensteinian account sketched above seems to make no provision for.

Now if the cases of the scholarly emperor and of the unsuitable editor obviously do not quite fit the account of the assertion conditions for and application of meaning ascriptions that was roughly sketched earlier, these cases equally obviously are not entirely unrelated to cases that fit better with that account. Perhaps an account of what is going on in the two problem cases can be somehow derived from the account roughly sketched earlier of what goes on in paradigm cases. Wittgenstein seems to have been always ready and even eager to recognize multiple uses of expressions, linked only by 'family resemblance' and not shared essence. So perhaps he would not have seen it as a problem to worry over if meaning ascriptions had to be recognized as having, besides their basic use as sketched above, a whole indefinitely large family of other variously related uses somehow indirectly derivative, each in a different way, from the basic or central one.

Others may worry that on the Wittgensteinian approach there would be so many different kinds of case as to make it difficult to credit the hypothesis that we learn to use the word 'means' by receiving training on what are the relevant assertion conditions and applications one-by-one and separately in each of these different cases. That is one reason, among others, for suspecting that something more systematic must be going on, even if it is not visible right out there on the surface. Perhaps Kripke, though he is no builder of comprehensive philosophical systems, nonetheless would like to see in semantics something a little more systematic than Wittgensteinianism can allow. But it would be sheer specula-tion on my part for me to make any positive assertion about why Kripke does not accept the Wittgensteinian view: I freely confess that I am in no way able to supply what we really want here, Kripke's own statement of his objections to the Wittgensteinian 'skeptical solution,' and above all, Kripke's own account of *his* solution to the Wittgensteinian 'skeptical paradox.'

For *that* we will have to await the release of more unpublished Kripkeana.[19] Meanwhile, we should be grateful to Kripke for for bringing vividly to our attention a puzzle at which writers since Lewis Carroll at least have been hinting, the puzzle of how it comes about that the *right* application of a previously stated rule to a present case is the one that goes *this* way rather than *that* way, the problem of the source of the 'must' in the assertion, 'if we are to follow the rule, we must do *this* rather than *that*.' This is another, and perhaps for Kripke a deeper, mystery of modality, beyond the surprises of a posteriori necessities and a priori contingencies.

6

Mind

At last we come to Kripke's deep – but so far as the published record is concerned, all too brief – contributions to the philosophy of mind. The two most relevant passages in Kripke's published writings have already been identified: the last part of the third lecture on N&N and the corresponding late parts of (Kripke 1971), and the brief discussion of what causally underlies behavioral dispositions in the Wittgenstein book (especially the lengthy footnote 24). There are besides some occasional remarks in the recently published lecture (Kripke 2011d).

The plan here will be a simple one, to review some background, first on materialism or 'physicalism,' then on 'functionalism,' a fashionable variety of or variation on physicalism, before proceeding to accounts of Kripke's criticisms, first of functionalism, then of physicalism. The discussion will end with some brief parting reflections on where Kripke leaves us.[1]

Physicalism

The mathematician and philosopher Descartes was one of the chief advocates of the program in 'the new science' of the seventeenth century that put the emphasis, in theorizing about the natural world, not on the qualitative factors that we all find so striking – the colors, the sounds, the smells – but on factors that can be measured and quantified. As the old 'natural philosophy' became the new 'natural science,' and 'physics' ceased to be the name for a branch of philosophical speculation, and became the name of a branch of scientific research, mathematically formulated descriptions of kinematic and dynamical features of physical phenomena came to predominate.

The leaders of the scientific revolution originally did not anticipate that it would be possible to describe *all* the physical behavior of physical objects in terms of mathematically formulated laws of completely general applicability. It was expected, rather, that departures from the laws applicable to dead matter would be found when one came to study living beings; or that, if there were after all no break at the boundary between the mineral and vegetable, there would be one at the boundary between the vegetable and animal kingdoms. Even Descartes, who expected that the behavior of non-human animals would be explicable in wholly mechanical terms, thought that the activities of conscious, rational human agents would resist such reductive explanation. The succeeding centuries of the development of science have not, however, turned up any clear violations of the laws believed to govern matter when it is *not* part of the body of a sentient, thinking being by matter that *is* part of such a body. The history of 'psychical research' and 'parapsychology' has been one of dismal failure to come up with any reliably reproducible results.

On the other hand, neurology, the medical study of injury and disease of the nerves and brain, has again and again found that such injuries and diseases are generally accompanied by sensory and cognitive deficits, and that where such deficits appear, corresponding injuries or diseases are generally to be found (if only upon autopsy). There have been some signal successes in linking various sensory and cognitive deficits to injury and disease of specific *parts* of the brain. And so it appears not only that matter obeys the same laws when it is part of a brain that it obeys when it is not, but also that everything in consciousness is dependent on something corresponding in the brain. To be sure, this principle is today, when so very much still remains to be discovered in neuropsychology, more in the nature of a methodological precept, to the effect that one should *look* for physical phenomena underlying mental phenomena, than the statement of an established result. Many philosophers, however, anticipating future successes, regard it as virtually a settled scientific law, whatever exactly that status involves. And if the principle that the mental depends on the physical, and specifically on the neural, does have that status, then the continuation of mental life when the body and brain have suffered death and decay would be a miracle in the most literal sense: a violation of the laws of nature.

As the late David Lewis more than once remarked to the present author, back in the Victorian era one who held such a view, and combined it with something like Hume's skepticism about miracles, would generally have been called a 'materialist.' It is not clear that Darwin's bulldog T. H. Huxley, or even Marx's sidekick Friedrich Engels, were 'materialists' in any stronger sense than this. But present-day materialists generally claim more. Most often, they have claimed that everything mental does not just *correspond* to and *depend* on something neural, but rather that everything mental literally just *is* something neural. This is the so-called *identity thesis* in philosophy of mind.

In the nineteenth century, energy joined matter as central to physics. In view of this change in the conception of the physical, and in view of the potential for further such changes in the future, many materialists today prefer to be called 'physicalists.' But if our conception of *the physical* has changed since Descartes' day, by embracing energy as well as matter, our conception of *physics* has perhaps changed less. It is still a science that ultimately expresses its theories in mathematical form, and this is a fact that has important consequences.

Consider, for instance, what goes on when a motorist approaches a crossroad, sees the light turn yellow, quickly (in a thought-process that is only partly conscious and hardly at all put into words) estimates that there is not enough time to get through the intersection before the light turns red, and presses on the brake pedal. A physical description of what is going on here would mention electromagnetic radiation or streams of photons with certain characteristics passing from the traffic light to the motorist's retina, to be followed by certain electrochemical events in the optic nerve and visual centers of the brain, themselves followed by activities in other parts of the brain, and finally in motor neurons and leg muscles, resulting in contractions whose effect is to depress the brake pedal, after which various mechanical or hydraulic events take place in the car, ultimately resulting in its coming to a halt. (Needless to say, a lot of the middle part of this description is something no one is quite in a position to write today, what with the gaps in our knowledge of brain activities.) All of this would or could be formulated mathematically, and as a result would be fully intelligible to a physicist who is totally color-blind, and has never shared the motorist's experience of seeing yellow. Gray is all theory.

This means that there is not, in the physical description of the episode, any overt, explicit mention of what is most striking to the motorist herself: seeing the color of the light. Nor is there any overt, explicit mention of the experiences of having the quick thought 'Better stop' or of feeling herself make the effort to press down on the pedal.

The philosophical identity theorist maintains, however, that the physical description has in fact left nothing out: that the experience of seeing the color of the light consists of *nothing more than* the occurrence of certain events in the visual areas of the brain, and has been mentioned in the physical account under the latter description, and similarly with the other subjective experiences. These mental events just *are*, according to such philosophers, the 'corresponding' neural events. What a cautious psychologist may call the 'neuronal correlate of consciousness' – the phrase is used often enough the psychological literature that the abbreviation 'NCC' has become current – the bold or reckless philosopher will simply identify with consciousness itself.

Actually, the identity theory comes in two versions. According to the *type–type* version, each *kind* of mental event is identified with a corresponding *kind* of neural event. In discussions in the literature it is generally assumed, for instance, that what pain corresponds to is the firing of C-fibers.[2] The type–type identity theorist will therefore say that being in pain just *is* having one's C-fibers stimulated. According to the *token–token* version – also called *anomalous monism* – while each individual mental event is identical with some neural event, this is *not* in virtue of belonging to some *kind* of mental event systematically correlated with some corresponding kind of neural event. There is no law or rule or pattern to the identifications. One pain may consist in some C-fiber firings, and another in something quite different, an excess of some neurotransmitter in some lobe of the brain, perhaps. To many this version of physicalism seems very much less plausible. It will be neglected in what follows, since Kripke's remarks are mainly addressed to the type–type version (though meant to apply *mutatis mutandis* to the token–token version).

Functionalism

I have so far described physicalism as identifying a subject's being in a certain mental state with the subject's being in a certain *neural* state, which is to say, with the subject's brain's being in a certain *electrochemical* state. There is, however, another view currently popular among philosophers of mind, one that some its adherents have considered a version of physicalism and others of its adherents have considered an alternative to physicalism – the issue is purely terminological – and one that conceives the relationship between the mental and the neural state somewhat differently. The view I have in mind goes by the name of *functionalism*.

Functionalism rests on an analogy – the 'computational theory of mind' – between the brain and a computer, and conceives of the relationship between mind and brain as comparable to that between computer software and the hardware on which it is executed. Toward seeing how the analogy is supposed to work, consider a calculator performing an addition following a certain program. Asked what the machine is doing at a given step, there are two kinds of answer that might be given. Speaking in software terms, one might say, 'The machine is carrying one from the tens to the hundreds place.' Speaking in hardware terms, one might say, 'The machine is sending a pulse from this node to that node.' Here program state or event contrasts with electrical state or event. There is a distinction to be made between the software state of the machine ('carrying one') and the hardware state of the machine ('sending an impulse'). The relationship between the two is often described by saying that the hardware state *realizes* the software state.

Insistence on distinguishing between a software state and the corresponding hardware state is not just pedantry. For the same program can be executed on different kinds of machines. With an old-fashioned mechanical adding machine, executing the software instruction 'carry one' might be realized at the hardware level by movement of some gear from one position to another, rather than by transmission of some electrical impulse. Thus the same kind of software state may be realized by quite different kinds of hardware states, electrical in some cases, mechanical in others. This key feature of the software/hardware relationship is called *multiple realizability*.

According to functionalism, the brain is, metaphorically speaking, running some program. Mental states are to be identified with software states while neural states constitute the hardware states that realize them. Thus the relationship between a mental state, say that of being in pain, and the correlated neural state, commonly supposed to be that of C-fibers firing, is the relation not of identity but of realization. What being in pain is *identical* with is the brain's carrying out a certain kind of instruction in its program.

The identification of mental states or events with software rather than hardware states or events has a significant consequence. Owing to multiple realizability, beings of some other kind from us might be in that same software state even though it was being realized by hardware quite different from a human brain. For instance, crash-test dummies of a new kind might be designed so that when they have been damaged they take themselves over to the repair shop or, if they are too damaged to do that, sound a siren as a signal to their human handlers, or perhaps other crash-test dummies, to take them there. If crash-test dummies were made sophisticated in this way and in enough other sorts of ways also, then we might come to a stage where a functionalist would find it plausible to suppose that the chips implanted in the dummies are in effect executing the same program that our brains execute, or if not our brains, then at least the brains of some simpler creatures, perhaps rats.

In that case, according to machine-state functionalism, the dummies would be in pain, since all being in pain *amounts to*, according to functionalism, is just executing a certain instruction in a certain program. And so presumably the crash-test dummies ought to become objects of moral concern, with animal-rights groups spinning off robot-rights groups, and ethics boards that superintend the use of laboratory animals such as rats spinning off subcommittees to deal with automata such as crash-test dummies. This is perhaps the most surprising implication of the functionalist view.

Actually, what I have so far been describing as functionalism is only one version thereof, the version called *machine-state* functionalism. There is a rival version called *causal-role* functionalism, having only a loose family resemblance with the machine-state variety. According to causal-role functionalism, there is a whole network of interrelated concepts including 'belief' and 'desire' as well as 'pain' and others, and certain precepts or platitudes of 'commonsense psychology' or 'folk psychology' posit all sorts of causal laws relating them to each other and to behavior. An example might be, 'In general, a belief that some activity will cause pain tends to lead to avoidance of that activity.' The various precepts or platitudes taken together specify certain *roles* for belief, desire, pain, and so on to play in a causal network leading to various types of human behavior in various types of external circumstances, and the functionalist's distinctive claim is that to be in pain just *is* to be in whatever physical state it turns out to be that plays this causal role.

One similarity between causal-role and machine-state functionalism is that the former, quite as much as the latter, is committed to multiple realizability. For the relevant causal role may be differently 'realized' in different creatures. As David Lewis, an early and forceful advocate of causal-role functionalism, once argued, while for human beings the pain-role may be realized by stimulation of the C-fibers, for Martians the pain-role might be realized by the inflation of certain microscopic cavities in the feet.

One difference between causal-role and machine-state functionalism is that the former, unlike the latter, is often put forward not just as a metaphysical view about what, say, pain *is*, but also as a semantical view about what 'pain' *means*. To say someone is in pain is, on this view, just to say that he or she is in the state that occupies a certain place in a causal network, an intermediary, for instance, between hitting one's thumb with a hammer and howling out impolite expressions. Put forward this way, the causal-role version of functionalism may seem extremely implausible.[3] It will be neglected in what follows, since Kripke's remarks are mainly addressed to the machine-state version (though meant to apply *mutatis mutandis* causal-role version).

So much by way of background.[4] Kripke's contributions to philosophy of mind consist on the one hand of a critique of functionalism, and on the other hand of a critique of physicalism as such. Different kinds of concerns are involved in the two critiques, the one being directly related to issues about rules of the kind addressed in the immediately preceding chapter, the other to issues about identity addressed in earlier chapters.

Against Functionalism

The problem with (the machine-state version of) functionalism can be brought out by considering a simple adding machine, such as the *pascaline* devised by Descartes' near-contemporary Blaise Pascal. Just looking at the physical device – say the specimen known as the Marguerite Périer in the Musée Henri Lecoq in Clermont-Ferrand – a question arises as to what program it should be thought of as executing.

There is a problem right at the beginning in recognizing inputs and outputs, but since the machine has eight dials each with ten settings, let us just take it as understood that it is natural numbers less than one hundred million that can be entered as inputs or read off as outputs. The real problems arise when we ask what function, with inputs and outputs of this kind, the *pascaline* should be thought of as computing.

One candidate is the function f that returns for inputs m and n less than one hundred million the output $m + n$. Another is the function g that returns for such inputs the output $m + n$ modulo one hundred million. If we regard the machine as computing g, it does a fairly good job, or rather, would probably have done so when it was new. If we regard the machine as computing f, it does not do so well, since when the sum is greater than one billion, it fails to register the leading digit one. Yet another candidate would be some function h resembling f or g, but with the addition of a random factor depending on the time the operation is performed, so that one does not always get the same output from the same numerical inputs.[5] The machine in a sense does best of all as a realization of a computation of such a function h, since it is, like any real physical machine, subject to random events of dials sticking or gears slipping or whatever.

The point of all this is that the physical object in the museum case can be construed as an approximate physical realization of an ideal machine or abstract program in more than one way. Which way is the *right* way to regard it? We cannot say to what program state a given physical configuration, a given setting of the dials and gears, corresponds unless this question has been answered, and we know which program is the relevant one.

The answer to the question is provided, in the case of the pascaline, by the intentions of the designer, which can be recovered from Pascal's own diagrams and notes, instructions for operating the machine, and so forth, which have (at least in part) survived and been published in volume 5 of the *Œuvres de Pascal*. On this basis we can say with confidence that when the *sautoir* is 'jumping' from the second to the third wheel, what is going on is the physical realization of the instruction 'carry one from the tens column to the hundreds column.'

The human brain, unlike one of Pascal's creations, is a piece of meat. It certainly does not come with a manual of instructions for operation. It does not have a designer whose blueprints and explanations have been made available to us in a volume of his collected works. Presumably materialist or physicalist philosophers would hold that it does not have a designer at all. (It is of no use to speak metaphorically of natural selection as a designer, since natural selection is not an agent with intentions.)

The long and short of it is, what program state a given physical state realizes or embodies depends on what program the physical device is construed or interpreted as realizing or embodying. In the case of artifacts built as calculating machines, there is privileged construal or interpretation, determined by the intentions (which may be known to us, or may be unknown but recoverable by us, or may be both unknown and irrecoverable, but at any rate at least *exist* or at the very least once *existed*) of the designer or designers of the machine. In the case of natural growths such as the brain, there is no such privileged construal or interpretation.[6] But surely whether I am in pain or not does not depend on how you choose to construe my brain, and whether you are suffering or not cannot be dependent on how I elect to interpret your nervous system!

Such, in a nutshell, is Kripke's objection to functionalism. I leave it to the reader to make the connection here with Kripke's remarks on the role of intention in his discussion of *ceteris paribus* version of dispositionalism in the negative phase or 'skeptical paradox' in the argument he attributes to his Wittgenstein. The objection, surprisingly, has provoked comparatively little comment in the literature, perhaps because Kripke has persisted in withholding his fuller expositions of it from publication. (Early advertising for Kripke (2011a) indicated one important text on the topic would be included in that collection, but in the event it was omitted.) So far there has been no major response from any cognitive scientist working in the 'computational theory of mind' paradigm.[7] I will therefore at this point set functionalism aside, and move on to consider Kripke's objections to the identity thesis.

Against Physicalism

Aristotle, we are told, thought the brain was an organ for cooling the blood. Today we know better, but still are ignorant of a great deal. Such knowledge as we do have of the correlations that obtain between aspects of consciousness and features of the brain is emphatically the product of empirical investigation, not armchair methods. The discovery that there is any bodily correlate of pain at all is just as much an a posteriori discovery as the discovery that the bodily correlate involves the brain rather than spleen, which in turn is just as much an a posteriori discovery as the discovery that it is the C-fibers in particular that are involved.

Prior to 1970, physicalists would often cite equations of the type 'pain = firing of C-fibers' as examples of 'contingent identities' along with other scientific identifications such as 'water = H_2O' or 'heat = random molecular motion.' Kripke, having taught us in the first two lectures of N&N to distinguish the distinction between a priori and a posteriori from the distinction between necessary and contingent, turned in his third lecture to the examination of this doctrine. All three of the equations just mentioned, he taught, are indeed not a priori. Of the equations 'water = H_2O' and 'heat = random molecular motion,' we know a priori that if true at all, they are necessarily true. And they *are* true, and hence necessary. As for 'pain = firing of C-fibers,' according to Kripke (i) we also know a priori that it is necessary *if true*, but (ii) it is *not* necessary – and therefore it is *not* true, contrary to the physicalists.

There has been comparatively little opposition to Kripke on point (i): After N&N one quickly began to hear very much less talk of supposed 'contingent identities' than one used to. Opposition has centered mainly on point (ii). But even here, too, the issue is often no longer framed in terms of identity. For Kripke, in rejecting the identification of pain with C-fiber stimulation, maintains something more, that even the *correlation* between the two is contingent. (Whatever may be the case with physical laws, if there are psychophysical laws correlating bodily with mental states, these do not enjoy the 'highest' kind of necessity.) What the materialist or physicalist side most crucially maintains is, on the contrary, that mental states, even if not *identical*, at least 'supervene' on bodily states: It is 'metaphysically' necessary that if C-fiber stimulation occurs, pain occurs.

Now we can *imagine* C-fiber stimulation occurring painlessly, though we cannot imagine *pain* occurring painlessly. It seems coherently conceivable that an episode of C-fiber stimulation is not to be identified with the corresponding episode of pain sensation. What Kripke wants to claim is that it is not just coherently conceivable that the C-fiber stimulation should occur painlessly, but genuinely possible, making the correlation between the bodily and the mental state contingent.

We seem to be able to imagine a great deal more than painless C-fiber stimulation. For we seem to be able to imagine the whole mathematically formulated, color-blind physical description of the universe, the description that leaves out overt, explicit mention of everything that is most striking to the universe's sentient inhabitants, being true, without any of the creatures moving around in the universe being sentient at all, or ever having any subjective experience. We can imagine a world whose inhabitants consist solely of 'philosophical zombies,' creatures physically indistinguishable from us, but where 'nobody's home' inside their skulls. Some of the zombies even emit *sounds* aurally indistinguishable from the speech of philosophers lecturing for or against materialism; but none of the zombies has materialist or antimaterialist or any other conscious *thoughts*.

The question is, when we imagine painless C-fiber stimulation, or the zombie world, are we imagining something genuinely possible, or do we have here an a posteriori necessity, and misdescription of what it is we are imagining? Kripke must argue that the case here is *unlike* his other examples of a posteriori necessities, where we seem to be able to imagine a violation, but none is in fact 'metaphysically' possible. The ensuing dialectic has been largely concerned with whether or not in his argument in N&N carries this point.

Kripke's claim is that if we look closely at, say, the case where we seem to be able to imagine random molecular motion without heat, we see that what we are really imagining is random molecular motion occurring without its being *felt* as heat: The heat is still there, but we don't feel it. But it seems absurd to say, 'Where we seem to be able to imagine C-fiber stimulation occurring without pain, what we are really imagining is C-fiber stimulation occurring without its being *felt* as pain: The pain is still there, but we don't feel it.' For how could pain be present and not felt?[8] Pain is a *feeling*; that much is analytic. And other cases of a seeming ability to imagine 'metaphysical' impossibilities that Kripke has suggested how to explain away seem even less helpful precedents for the physicalist to consider.

Kripke seems to be in effect assuming there is a *defeasible presumption* that what is coherently conceivable is genuinely possible, and that to defeat the presumption one must offer some positive explanation of the illusion of possibility. Kripke has shown that an illusion of possibility can be explained away in some cases, and pointed out that the ways in which this is done in the cases of the illusions that he discussed in N&N is not available in the case of concern to the materialist or physicalist. The burden of proof is therefore on them to find some other way, or so Kripke seems to be assuming. (Some commentators seem to attribute to Kripke a dogmatic assumption, sometimes called 'textbook Kripkeanism,' to the effect that the *only* way in which something coherently conceivable could fail to be genuinely possible would be in the way represented by the heat case. I see no textual basis for such an attribution. Without such an assumption, we get no knock-down argument for the antiphysicalist conclusion, but only a shift of the burden of proof to the physicalist side; I see no textual basis for attributing to Kripke a claim to have a knock-down argument.)

Some of Kripke's opponents seem just to reject the background assumption about defeasible presumption, in effect simply adopting a stance of skepticism about the prospects for achieving knowledge of possibility through conceivability. Some write as if the fact that imagination fails in some cases *for reasons we can explain* means that it is not to be relied on in any case *even if we have no reasonable explanation of why it should fail*. To the extent that some of the discussion has taken this turn, it presents us with another instance of the common tendency of philosophical debates to get bogged down in issues of burden of proof.

There is another respect in which the case of C-fibers and pain differs from Kripke's examples of a posteriori necessities. As we have seen, Kripke hints in the addenda to N&N that there is in his other examples somewhere in the background principle to the effect that whichever way the facts are about a certain question, they are that way of necessity, a principle that is a priori and perhaps even analytic and founded in rules of language. With 'water = H_2O,' for instance, the principle might be that whenever we have a genuine natural kind of substance, it has a definite composition, so that no substance with a different composition can count as *that* substance, however similar it may be in observable properties. The empirical discovery is then twofold. First, it is found a posteriori that water is a genuine natural kind of substance, that samples of water are not, for instance, samples of two different natural kinds of substance, as in the case of jade. Second, it is found a posteriori that the composition that water has is that of a compound rather than an element, and a compound with the formula H_2O and not Dalton's HO or Putnam's XYZ.

Again, nothing parallel seems to be available to the physicalist. It seems difficult to maintain that we know a priori that if pain is correlated with some bodily state, then the correlation holds of necessity. Kripke has not pressed this line of thought, presumably because he does not want to put too much weight on what after all is for him only a 'clue.' But perhaps only a definite solution to the mystery of modality, revealing the ultimate source of modal distinctions, can fully resolve questions about when conceivability can be relied on to establish possibility and when not.

The Mystery of Mentality

Kripke regards materialism as a scientistic prejudice of the present day, though this opinion is something one finds conveyed in quotations in press interviews available online, rather than something openly stated in so many words in his professional publications, where etiquette perhaps does not permit so blunt an expression of opinion. But if it is clear enough, from one source or another, what Kripke is *against* in philosophy of mind, it is less clear what he is *for*.

In Kripke (2011d, footnote 21) he has some fun at the expense of materialist philosophers of mind, whom he describes as writing in a way that would lead one to believe they must be robots.[9] But even in this talk, despite much sympathetic discussion of Descartes, he does not openly embrace 'Cartesian dualism' of mind and body. In N&N, he points out that Descartes' position is incompatible with his own principle of the necessity of parental origins.

Now it is clear where this principle of parental origins is coming from. If we run the engine of history in reverse back to a time before Socrates was born or thought of, and then run it forward again along a different track, we will have trouble recognizing a person we encounter as Socrates unless we have previously recognized Sophroniscus and Phaenarete, and this person is their child. Nonetheless, though I may not be able to recognize you, and you may not be able to recognize me, except through parental origins, may we not each recognize him- or herself?

I seem to myself to be able to imagine having been born to different parents – how many children in moments of frustration have expressed a wish they had been! – and even in a different century. According to Kripke, I must be misdescribing what I am imagining when I project myself sympathetically into the position of, say, some eleventh-century Byzantine courtier; but Kripke does not supply much of an explanation of the nature of the error, the way he does in the heat case, for instance.

If one accepts the 'hint' in the addenda to N&N, it seems there must be an a priori principle in the background guaranteeing that whatever parents I had, those are the only ones I could have had. To assert there is such a background principle would be, in a way, to make a rather remarkable claim. After all, a large portion of the human population of the earth, so far from subscribing to a materialistic ideology or scientistic prejudice, embraces religious conceptions according to which I not only could have had different parents from the ones I grew up with, but actually have had such parents – and many pairs of them, and not all of those human.

Is Kripke committed to the claim that the concepts of reincarnation and so forth are not just false but incoherent? Well, perhaps the a priori principle in the background, if there is one, is that my origins *whatever they may be* are necessary. That my only origins are my biological origins would then be an additional assumption that might be considered a scientific discovery by some, a scientistic prejudice by others.

What Kripke actually says in N&N (footnote 77) is the following:

> If we had a clear idea of the soul or the mind as an independent, subsistent, spiritual entity, why should have to have any necessary connection with particular material objects such as a particular sperm or a particular egg? A convinced dualist may think that my views on sperms and eggs beg the question against Descartes. I would tend to argue the other way; the fact that it is hard to imagine me coming from a sperm or egg different from my actual origins seems to me to indicate that we have no such clear conception of a soul or self.

He adds, 'In any event, Descartes' notion seems to have been rendered dubious ever since Hume's critique of the notion of a Cartesian self.' It is clear from (2011d), however, that Kripke has since re-evaluated the famous Descartes–Hume disagreement, and now apparently tilts toward Descartes.

Nonetheless, there is no indication that he has in the intervening forty years or so changed his mind about the *last* thing he says in the longish footnote from which I have been quoting: 'I regard the mind–body problem as wide open and extremely confusing.' And so Kripke leaves us without a definitive solution, or even a full statement of a settled position, on this central philosophical problem. One might have hoped for more, but is not Kripke's freely confessed sense of puzzlement or mystery better by far than a glib false certainty based on ideological prejudices of the day?

Appendix A: Models

What follows is a brief, not-very-technical account of the work that first made Kripke famous. Kripke has given one semi-popular exposition of his work on modal logic in the first two-thirds of (Kripke 1963), the written version of a talk at a famous 1962 Helsinki conference on modal logic, whose proceedings were published the next year in a special issue of *Acta Philosophical Fennica*. Details of the work appeared in technical publications 1959–65, though some material never did see print, and none of the technical papers will be seriously discussed here.

Here I will do no more than attempt a popularization of the gist of Kripke's approach, considering in turn: the state of modal logic before Kripke; two parts of Kripke's achievement, his work on modal versions of the two branches of logic called sentential logic and predicate logic; and lastly certain misrepresentations and misunderstandings about Kripke's work in this area that have grown up in the subsequent literature.

The Logic of Modality

Let me begin with a broad-brush history of the logic of necessity and possibility before Kripke's intervention.

Formal logic is concerned with logical form. A premise logically implies a conclusion just in case the logical forms of premise and conclusion are such that in *any* example of a premise and a conclusion of the same logical forms, if the premise is true, then the conclusion will be true also. Thus 'Jones is a man and Jones is unmarried' logically implies 'Jones is unmarried' because in *any* example, if a premise in the form of a conjunction is true, the conclusion taking the form of its second conjunct will be true also. Modern logic represents logical forms by symbolic formulas. Thus the general principle just indicated will be stated compactly with symbols, thus: p & q logically implies q.

Note that though there is a symbol for 'and' in this formulation, there is none for 'logically implies.' In its simplest branch, *sentential* logic, formal logic is concerned with how complex statements are formed from simpler ones by *connectives*, by negation and conjunction and disjunction and the conditional, expressed using the words 'not' and 'and' and 'or' and 'if,' and symbolized ~ and & and ∨ and →. There is no symbol for logical implication, that being a notion used in talking *about* relationships between logical forms, not in representing logical forms themselves. In jargon, the notion of logical implication is said to belong to the '*meta*language' rather than the 'object language.'

The idea of C. I. Lewis, founder of modern modal logic, was to a first approximation that there *should* be a symbol ⇒ added to the usual list to stand for logical implication, so we can write p & q ⇒ q. More precisely, the new symbol was supposed to stand for what he called *strict* implication, where if one reads him closely it emerges that he understood strict implication not as implication by pure formal logic alone, but as implication by that plus definition or meaning or synonymy. Thus for Lewis not only 'Jones is a man and Jones is unmarried' but equally 'Jones is a bachelor' strictly implies 'Jones is unmarried.'

Later Lewis proposed adding a diamond symbol ◇, pronounced 'possibly,' and treating p ⇒ q as an abbreviation for ~◇(p & ~q). Still later it was proposed to add a box symbol □, pronounced 'necessarily,' and to treat ◇p as an abbreviation for ~□~p and p ⇒ q as an abbreviation for □(p → q). Thus the premise that p strictly implies the conclusion that q just in case it is *necessary* that if p then q. Given what 'strict implication' is supposed to mean, this equivalence only works on the understanding that 'necessary' here means 'analytic.' But that was the prevailing understanding of necessity at the time, and Lewis's understanding in particular.

Lewis preferred to think, however, not in terms of necessity or analyticity, but directly in terms of strict implication, and consulted 'intuition' in deciding what laws to admit and what laws to reject for that notion. Unfortunately, when it comes to complicated formulas with iterated, nested, embedded double arrows, 'intuition' proves an uncertain and fallible guide. Lewis began by endorsing the following candidate law:

$$(p \Rightarrow q) \Rightarrow ((q \Rightarrow r) \Rightarrow (p \Rightarrow r))$$

but later retracted his endorsement, endorsing only a weaker alternative:

$$((p \Rightarrow q) \& (q \Rightarrow r)) \Rightarrow (p \Rightarrow r)$$

Try saying these in words (*p*'s strictly implying *q* strictly implies that *q*'s strictly implying *r* strictly implies *p*'s strictly implying *r* *versus* *p*'s strictly implying *q* and *q*'s strictly implying *r* together strictly imply *p*'s strictly implying *r*) and you will see why some of Lewis's disciples had trouble following their master on such subtle points. Soon there were five candidate systems of modal logic, numbered in order of increasing strength **S1–S5** (though **S1** and **S3** pretty quickly dropped out of the running).

Not long after there were dozens, as contributors to the technical development of modal logic simply devoted themselves to exploring various systems, setting aside all questions of intuitive interpretation, and making no attempt to settle any of the *dubia* of the subject, or pin down which modal logic was the right one. In the long run, that proved to be a productive attitude. For in the case of a number of the types of exotic logics devised by twentieth-century philosophers, useful interpretations having nothing to do with any philosophical notion of necessity were later found by computer scientists and others, much as for a number of types of exotic geometries devised by nineteenth-century mathematicians, useful interpretations having nothing to do with the space in which we live and move were later found by physicists and others.

Philosophers also devised new interpretations in which the $\Diamond$ might be read as 'it is permissible to bring it about that' or 'sometime in the future it is going to be the case that' or something else, thus giving rise to subjects labeled deontic logic, temporal logic, and more. In contrast to these special flavors of 'modality,' the original plain vanilla kind came to be called 'alethic.' The use of the label 'alethic necessity' by an author did not indicate that the author had in mind something other than Lewis's interpretation of necessity as 'analytic necessity,' but more often tended to indicate rather that the author simply was not giving questions about the nature of necessity much thought. Meanwhile, the contemplation of deontic, temporal, and other alternative interpretations led to the further proliferation of modal systems.

Kripke's first great achievement as a logician was to bring order to the chaos of competing systems by introducing a notion of *model*. To understand the problem Kripke was addressing, we need to review briefly the situation in classical, non-modal sentential logic.

This was originally presented by Frege, Russell, and others as what is called an *axiomatic system*. Certain formulas were endorsed as axioms not requiring proof, for instance $(p \lor p) \rightarrow p$, and certain rules were endorsed as usable in proofs, for instance, inference from $A \Rightarrow B$ and A to B. A *proof* was then defined to be a sequence of formulas, called the *steps* of the proof, each of which was either an axiom or followed from earlier steps by a rule. A formula was defined to be *provable* or a *theorem*, if there was a proof of it, which is to say, a proof having it as the last step.

Now the formulas we should *want* to have as theorems are the ones that represent laws of logic. Here formula represents a law of logic if and only if it represents a logical form that is true in every instance, a formula that is true regardless of what specific sentences are put in for the letters p and q and so forth. Thus $p \,\&\, q \rightarrow q$ represents a law of logic, since every instance, such as 'If Jones is a man and Jones is unmarried, then Jones is unmarried,' is true.

Now all that really matters for the truth value, true or false, of an instance of some complicated formula A is the pattern of truth values of the sentences put in for p and q and so forth. This is because the truth values of compounds formed using $\sim$ and $\&$ and $\lor$ and $\rightarrow$ can be determined given the truth values of their components: For $\sim A$ is true if and only if A is not true, and $A \,\&\, B$ is true if and only if A is true and B is true, and so on. A *model* in classical sentential logic is just a valuation, or assignment of truth values to the sentence letters p and q and so on. A model represents just as much about an instance, or substitution of specific sentences for the letters, as is relevant to determining the truth of compounds. Given the model, or valuation of the sentence letters, we can evaluate any desired compound. For instance, if the model makes p false and q true and r true, then it will make $(p \,\&\, \sim q) \lor (\sim p \,\&\, r)$ true. A formula is said to be *valid* for or *validated* by this notion of model if it comes out true in every model. Intuitively, a valid formula represents a logical form that is true in every specific instance or, in other words, if it represents a law of logic.

This means we should want the theorems of an axiomatic system to turn out to be precisely the valid formulas. That they are precisely what we want is what we are told by a pair of results, converses of each other. The *soundness* theorem says that every provable formula is valid, while the *completeness* theorem says that every valid formula is provable. Soundness tells us that if there is a *countermodel* for a formula, which is to say, a model where it is false, then that formula is *independent*, which is to say, is not a theorem. Completeness tells us that for any independent formula, there will be a countermodel.

In the case of classical logic, though the models historically came later, they are now widely thought of as conceptually prior: The model theory is widely thought of as telling us what such symbols as ~ and & *mean*, and this is perhaps one reason for the popularity of the alternate label 'semantics' for model theory. The test of a good axiomatic system is that it should be possible to establish soundness and completeness for it.

In the case of modal logic, the situation was rather the reverse. Lewis presented his modal logics as axiomatic systems very much in the style of Russell. The various axiomatic systems, S2, S4, S5, and more, were historically given, and the problem was to find for each a notion of model for which soundness and completeness hold. After we have found the model, and after we have begun to distinguish different kinds of modalities, we can perhaps look at the models and see whether or not they heuristically suggest anything about whether the axiom system for which soundness and completeness hold is or is not appropriate for this or that kind of modality. But that is a separate project: The first problem is to find the models.

Since the various axiomatic systems have different sets of theorems, different models will be needed for each. The problem is thus, more precisely, to develop a general *type* of model, which can be made to fit different axiomatic systems by adjusting some parameter. This is the problem to which Kripke gave the definitive solution.

Kripke Models

It remains to outline that solution. First note that nothing so simple as an assignment of truth values to sentence letters (a classical model) will do as a model in modal logic. For the truth value of p does not determine the truth value of $\Box p$ or of $\Diamond p$ the way it determines the truth value of $\sim p$. Some truths are necessary, others contingent, while some falsehoods are possible, others impossible; hence simply from the assumption that p is true one cannot tell whether $\Box p$ is true or false, and simply from the assumption that p is false one cannot tell whether $\Diamond p$ is false or true. Kripke's first idea, in devising a model theory for modal logic, was that to determine the truth value of such a compound as, say

$$p \mathbin{\&} q \mathbin{\&} \Diamond(\sim p \mathbin{\&} q) \mathbin{\&} \sim\!\Diamond(p \mathbin{\&} \sim q)$$

it would be enough to know (i) which combination of truth values the letters *do actually* have, and (ii) which other combinations of truth values the letters *could possibly* have had.

In the system **S5**, every modal formula, even ones with very complicated iteration or nesting or embedding of boxes and diamonds, is provably equivalent to one of the fairly simple kind exhibited above, without any such iteration or nesting or embedding. And so for **S5** Kripke defines a model to consist simply of (i) one classical model or valuation, representing how things actually are, and (ii) a set of other classical models or valuations, representing all the other ways things possibly could have been. He calls the valuations in (i) and (ii) 'possible worlds,' among which he distinguishes the valuation in (i) as the 'actual world,' and the valuations in (ii) as the *merely* possible worlds. A necessity-formula $\Box A$ counts as true (at any world) if and only if A is true at *all* worlds, while a possibility-formula $\Diamond A$ counts as true (at any world) if and only if A is true at *some* world. A formula counts as true in the model as a whole if and only if it is true at the actual world of the model. Kripke then establishes soundness and completeness: The formulas that are theorems of **S5** (the ones for which there are proofs using the axioms and rules of that system) and the formulas validated by Kripke's model theory (the ones true in all Kripke models) coincide.

Soundness is by far the easier of the two directions. Its proof consists simply in checking that each axiom has the property of being true in all models, and that each rule preserves this property, so that if the premises have it, so does the conclusion. From this it follows that in any proof each step, including the theorem at the end, has this property, the property of being valid. The whole business is mainly a matter of tedious but routine verifications.

Completeness is trickier, since one most go from the *non-existence* of something (a proof of a given independent formula) to the *existence* of something (a countermodel for the formula). The trick is to work with a method of constructing countermodels and find a way of converting obstructions to the construction into proofs; then with an independent formula, one that has no proof, there will be no obstructions, and the method will produce a countermodel. Kripke found in the work of E. W. Beth a method of model-construction for classical logic, called the *tableau* method, which he was able to adapt to modal logic and use in this way.

For systems other than **S5**, the task of devising a model theory is more difficult. In **S5**, $\Box \Diamond p$ and $\Diamond \Diamond p$ collapse to plain $\Diamond p$. But there are systems where this collapse does not occur, and for such a system one is going to have to distinguish *actual possibilities* from *possible possibilities* (and indeed, *actually possible possibilities* from *possibly possible possibilities*, and so on). Worse, consideration of such a formula as

$$p \,\&\, q \,\&\, \Diamond(p \,\&\, {\sim}q \,\&\, \Diamond q) \,\&\, \Diamond({\sim}p \,\&\, {\sim}q \,\&\, {\sim}\Diamond q)$$

shows that in general one is going to have to keep track of which possible possibilities are possible relative to which actual possibilities. (There must be a possible possibility that q that is possible relative to the actual possibility that $p \,\&\, {\sim}q$, but not possible relative to the actual possibility that ${\sim}p \,\&\, {\sim}q$.) Worse still, consideration of such a minor variant as

$$p \,\&\, q \,\&\, \Diamond(p \,\&\, {\sim}q \,\&\, \Diamond q) \,\&\, \Diamond(p \,\&\, {\sim}q \,\&\, {\sim}\Diamond q)$$

shows there may be distinct possibilities where p and q and perhaps all letters have the same truth values. So a 'possible world' cannot just be a valuation or classical model, but must be something that has a classical model somehow attached to it.

In the end, Kripke's notion of model involves (i) a set X of 'possible worlds' (in the broadest sense, including the merely possibly possible, the merely possibly possibly possible, and so on) with one element thereof, x_0 distinguished as the 'actual world,' together with (ii) a relation R of 'relative possibility' (sometimes called 'accessibility') between worlds, plus (iii) an assignment V to each world of a classical model or valuation, telling us what the truth values of the different sentence letters are at that world. $\Diamond A$ is true at a given world w if A is true at some world v possible relative to w, while $\Box A$ is true at a given world w if A is true at all worlds possible relative to w. (Worlds not possible relative to w don't count.) This is the model theory for modal logic one finds presented in textbooks today.

The model theory comes in different versions distinguished by conditions placed on the relation R: The conditions placed on the relation R constitute the parameter that can be adjusted to fit different modal systems. If we require R to be *reflexive*, for instance, meaning that we always have Rww for every world w, then the formula $\Box p \to p$ is validated: truth at all worlds possible relative to the actual world implies truth at the actual world, since reflexivity guarantees that the actual world will be among the worlds possible relative to the actual world. Similarly, if we require R to be *transitive*, meaning that we have Rwu whenever we have Rwv and Rvu, for any worlds w and v and u, then the formula $\Box p \to \Box\Box p$ is validated. Likewise, if we require R to be *symmetric*, meaning that we have Rwv whenever we have Rvw, for any worlds w and v, then the formula $p \to \Box\Diamond p$ is validated. (The reader without previous familiarity with these matters may find it an instructive exercise to try to think these through.) Kripke manages to prove soundness and completeness results characterizing the theorems of various modal systems from the literature in terms of classes of his models characterized by various combinations of simple conditions the relation R of the model.

He even identified a minimal system – subsequently dubbed **K** for Kripke – for which his methods as sketched so far work. He then extended his methods to handle some other systems, notably **S2**, adapted them to what is known as 'intuitionistic logic' as well as to the 'deontic logic' and 'temporal logic' alluded to earlier.

The Curse of the Barcan Formulas

So far I have said nothing of *predicate* as opposed to sentential logic. I have said nothing about *quantifiers*, universal and existential – in words, 'all' and 'some'; in symbols, $\forall$ and $\exists$ – as opposed connectives. Even for classical logic the situation here is much more complicated. A classical model has two components: first, a *domain* over which variables x and y and z and so on range; second, an assignment to each of the one-place predicate letters F and G and H and so on an *extension*, or set of elements in the domain that is true of, or as is said, that *satisfy* it, and to each of the two-place predicate letters R and S and T and so on an extension, or set of *pairs* of elements in the domain that satisfy it, and so on.

The definition of truth in a model is more complicated than in the sentential case and has to take a detour through an auxiliary notion of satisfaction, sometimes a stumbling block to beginning students. While the condition for $p \vee q$ to be true is simply that either p should be true or q should be true, the condition for $\exists x P x$ to be true is not stated in terms of the *truth* of a simpler formula. It is rather that there should be an *object* in the domain that *satisfies* the formula Px.

Kripke's work extends beyond modal sentential logic to modal predicate logic, also called quantified modal logic (QML). Essentially, one has the set X of possible worlds, which Kripke belatedly recognized might better have been called possible *states*; and one has one element of X distinguished as actual; and one has a relation R of relative possibility. This much, sometimes called a *frame*, is just as with sentential modal logic. But what gets attached to each element of X is now not a model for classical sentential logic, but something like a model for classical predicate logic. Intuitively, specifying the domain of the classical model attached to a given state w in X is like saying what things there would be if the world were in state w; specifying the extensions of the one-place predicate letters is like saying what properties which of them would have; specifying the extensions of the two-place predicates is like saying which relations which of them would stand in to which others of them, and so on.

There are some subtleties about the definition of model and the associated definition of truth in a model that cannot be gone into here.[1] Kripke deals with the subtleties in a way that solves an old puzzle that had frustrated attempts to develop an intuitively satisfying system of QML. The first attempts in this direction, beginning with Marcus (1946), were purely formal experiments in combining the classical axioms and rules for quantifiers and connectives with one or another system of axioms and rules for modalities and connectives. But these attempts involved certain intuitively very dubious-looking formulas, called the (direct and converse) *Barcan formulas*, turning up among the axioms or theorems.

The formulas in question read as follows:

$$\forall x \Box F x \to \forall x F x \qquad \Box \forall x F x \to x \Box F x$$

And what is wrong with these? Well, the formula on the right says that if necessarily everything that exists has some property F, then everything that exists necessarily has the property F. And this seems implausible if the property in question is existence. Necessarily everything that exists exists, but is it the case that everything that exists necessarily exists? Traditionally, necessary existence was thought to be a special attribute of God, perhaps shared with numbers, but certainly not with people. As for the formula on the left, if a and b and c and... are all the things that exist, then since anything is necessarily identical to itself, everything that exists is necessarily either identical to a or identical to b or identical to c or... But then the formula under discussion tells us that necessarily anything is identical to one of a or b or c or..., which is to say, to one of the things that actually exists: Nothing could possibly exist that doesn't actually exist.

In Kripke's model theory, the first formula is not validated unless we assume that whenever world v is possible relative to world u, then only things in the domain of the model attached to u are in the domain of the model attached to v; the second formula is not validated unless, conversely, only things in the domain at v are in the domain at u. Together, they impose the assumption that the same domain of things is involved at every world. But such assumptions, Kripke insists, ought not to be built in to the very framework of QML. They should rather be left as optional extras that one can assume or not as one chooses, like the sentential axioms (characteristic of the systems **S5** and **S4**) that would equate $\square\diamond p$ or $\diamond\diamond p$ with plain $\diamond p$.

Kripke's model theory does allow this, but the problem is that among the pre-existing axiomatic systems there was none for which his model theory is sound and complete: In the existing systems, what ought to be optional additional assumptions are made mandatory. The evil spirit of the Barcan formulas haunted all early work on QML. Nor is this feature of the early formal systems by any means a product of simple carelessness on the part of the pioneering workers in the field: It really is quite difficult to avoid the Barcan formulas in devising an axiomatic system, and Kripke himself by his own account puzzled for some time over derivations in Prior (1956) that seem to show these formulas are inevitable.

Kripke did, however, eventually find a way to avoid them, based on a careful diagnosis of the source of the problem. It turns out that the operation of 'combining classical predicate logic and modal sentential logic' is not well-defined. There are (A) several different systems of axioms and rules all leading to the same set of theorems of classical predicate logic, and (B) for any target system of modal sentential logic, several different sets of axioms and rules all leading its set of theorems. Yet, owing to interaction of rules, the different combinations of 'one from column A, one from column B' yield different set of theorems for QML. One has to make the *right* choice, which is by no means the usual or obvious choice, if one wants to escape the Barcan formulas. What Kripke chooses from column (A) is not one of the axiomatic systems one will find in mainstream textbooks, but a variant due to W. V. Quine.[2]

Kripke published his work on sentential S5 and the simplest system of QML based thereupon, *with* the Barcan formulas, in Kripke (1959a). The same year he published the abstract (Kripke 1959b) announcing the rest of his work, but this work did not appear until the mid-nineteen sixties, and some of it, pertaining to QML based on systems weaker than S5, *without* the Barcan formulas, was not published at all, beyond the sketch in Kripke (1963). Had he written up the rest in detail for publication, he would surely have found (and repaired) a gap that Kit Fine (1983) found (and repaired): The list of axioms in Kripke (1963) omits one needed to get the equivalence of $\forall x \forall y$ to $\forall y \forall x$.[3] One moral to be drawn from this little episode is that there is generally something to be gained by not keeping one's work to oneself, but writing it up to share with the professional community. Another is that one has to be *extra* cautious when striving to exorcise any spirit as malign as that of the Barcan formulas.

Controversy and Confusion

Here I will digress briefly to discuss some less-than-edifying aspects of the literature on Kripke's work on modal logic, with the ultimate aim of underscoring how little Kripke's work on models foreshadowed what was to come in N&N.

No major innovation occurs entirely without precursors. Footnotes in Kripke's publications on modal models cite quite a few (including all those I will mention by name below), and if one looks up the works cited, some of their footnotes cite yet others, and subsequent scholarship has turned up even more. This being the situation, one may wonder just what is distinctive about Kripke's contribution.[4] A complete answer to such priority questions could be supplied only by going through all the early papers in chronological order, carefully noting for each just what is and what isn't to be found in it, and being alert, as any good historian must be, against anachronistically reading later ideas back into earlier work. This has in fact been done in a magisterial survey by Robert Goldblatt (2005), which makes clear, for readers with the requisite background, why and how Kripke's contribution was the decisive one. Copeland (2002) is also of interest, as containing a number of quotations from communications of Kripke answering inquiries of the author about historical matters. I cannot go into the whole long history here, but three points stand out.

First, Kripke alone published completeness proofs. Authors as early as Kanger (1957) had *some kind of* set X and *some kind of* relation R and saw *some kind of* connection between conditions like reflexivity and transitivity and symmetry on R and modal axioms like $\Box p \to p$ and $\Box p \to \Box\Box p$ and $p \to \Box\Diamond p$. But of other early workers, only one, Jaakko Hintikka, even announced any completeness theorems; and Hintikka never published his proofs.

Second, Kripke develops a clearly, cleanly set-theoretic notion of model, the notion still in use today. His X is an arbitrary set of indices, and need not be a set of classical models (as with Kanger) or a set of sets of formulas (as with Hintikka), or anything of the sort; his relation R is arbitrary as well, except insofar as one chooses to impose conditions such as reflexivity or transitivity or symmetry; and his assignment V of classical models to indices is arbitrary, too, and permits the assignment of the same classical model to two different indices. Such features are crucial in technical work, as Goldblatt emphasizes. It is Kripke's models, not Hintikka's or Kanger's models, that one works with today in modal logic, temporal logic, intuitionistic logic, and more. *Experto crede.*

Third, Kripke could easily have been 'scooped' by ten years or so, at least as regards the sentential modal logic **S4**, perhaps the key test case. For there were two results in the literature by the early nineteen fifties, one due to McKinsey building on work of Alfred Tarski itself building on work of Adolf Lindenbaum, and the other to Bjarni Jónsson and Tarski, that if laid side by side could have been immediately combined to yield a completeness proof for Kripke models for **S4**.[5] Yet no one, least of all Tarski (who seems to have kept his work with his student McKinsey and his work with his student Jónsson in separate compartments in his mind), ever did lay them side by side until many years later, so what one has here is simply an intriguing case of a missed opportunity, though one that makes most other priority issues pale by comparison.

All these matters would be of interest only to historians of logic were it not for the fact that in the literature controversies over priority issues have become inextricably intertwined with issues about the relationship between (Kripke 1963) and N&N.[6] For it has repeatedly been suggested by Hintikka and others that the nature of Kripke's model theory in his earlier work *already* commits him to the kind of 'metaphysical' understanding of necessity that we find in his later work. This suggestion seems to have resulted from

Hintikka's trying to read Kanger's early work, which has rightly been described as difficult to decipher, in hopes of finding anticipations of Kripke, and then becoming infected with the curious standpoint assumed by Kanger, which involves a deviation from the normal understanding of the role of sentence letters p and q and so on.

The issue can be illustrated in the case of the very simple models for the sentential modal logic **S5**. On the normal understanding, p and q may stand for any statements whatsoever. They *may* be logically independent, as when p is 'Snow is white' and q is 'Grass is green'; but they may instead be equivalent, p being 'Snow is white' and q being 'Yes, it is'; or they may be contradictory, p being 'Snow is white' and q being 'No, it isn't.' With the normal understanding, regardless of any opinions about the nature of necessity, one must consider, as Kripke does, multiple models. Because p and q might be standing for the *equivalent* statements, one must allow models in which the only assignments represented are ones that give p and q the same truth value. Because p and q might be standing for *contradictory* statements, one must allow models in which the only assignments represented are ones that give p and q opposite truth values. And so on.

On the deviant understanding, distinct letters p and q must stand for logically independent statements. With this understanding, if the notion of 'necessity' at issue is 'logical necessity' in the sense of 'truth by virtue of logical form alone,' then there will be only *one* model to consider, the one in which *every* assignment of truth values to sentence letters is represented. For if the letters are assumed to stand for logically independent statements, no assignment of truth values is excluded by virtue of logical form alone. With this understanding, to consider models in which *not* all assignments of truth values to sentence letters need be represented is to consider some *stronger* notion of possibility, and correspondingly some *weaker* notion of necessity. And so it appears as if Kripke were committing himself to some non-logical notion of necessity.

If so, it might be concluded that he already had something like 'metaphysical' modality in mind at a much earlier period than the one to which he himself dates the main ideas of N&N. This would be an historical error, but more serious is a logico-philosophical error that also threatens. For it might be concluded that Kripke models, which time has shown to be the most important technical tools for modal logic, are somehow inappropriate for or inapplicable to *logical* modalities. Indeed, this unfortunately *has* been concluded by some, and remains an influential view in certain circles. But the appearance of a commitment on Kripke's part to a nonlogical notion of necessity is simply an illusion, a misperception resulting from adopting an abnormal way of looking at the role of sentence letters.

The great virtue of Kripke's model theory is in fact its *neutrality* about how the box and diamond are supposed to be interpreted. It is because of this neutrality that the method initially proved adjustable to fit a wide variety of modal, temporal, deontic, and other systems, and ultimately proved useful in pure and applied logic in entirely unanticipated ways. The 'vice' corresponding to this virtue is that the model theory leaves almost untouched all large philosophical issues about the nature of necessity: Being applicable to many conceptions of modality, Kripke's model theory does not help steer us toward any particular one.[7] As Kripke himself once said, there is no mathematical substitute for philosophy.[8]

Appendix B: Truth

What follows is a brief, not-very-technical account of Kripke's work on one of the oldest of all philosophical puzzles, the so-called liar paradox. The 'Outline of a Theory of Truth' (Kripke 1975) occupies an isolated position among those of Kripke's productions that are addressed to a philosophical audience; the other items in Kripke's *oeuvre* most closely related to it are not philosophical works but published and unpublished mathematical results from the 1960s (not to be covered here) in which Kripke contributed to founding the subject known as 'recursion on transfinite ordinals.'

The plan here will be to begin with a review of the basics about the liar and other so-called semantic paradoxes. The most influential treatment of these paradoxes historically has been that of the mathematical logician Tarski, in his monumental 'Concept of Truth in Formalized Languages' and other papers in Tarski (1956), so next some features of Tarski's approach must be reviewed, along with some of Kripke's objections to it. There will then follow a rough sketch of the basic form of Kripke's construction ('the minimal fixed point') and an even rougher sketch of alternative forms of Kripke's construction ('non-minimal fixed points') and the classification of paradoxical and pathological sentences these constructions make available. Finally there will be some remarks on the relation of Kripke's theory to our intuitive notion of truth.

Paradox and Pathology

Philosophers have traditionally debated the nature of truth: Is what makes a belief true correspondence with reality, or coherence with other ideas, or usefulness in practice?[1] But to logicians, our intuitive notion of truth has often appeared to be a quite simple one, governed by a single principle:

(1)   T-Scheme: '____' is true if and only if ____.

However, the T-scheme, though it may appear simple and obvious, quickly gets us into trouble, when combined with our language's power of referring to its own expressions through quotation and other means.

Suppose I say, 'What I am now saying is not true.' Or suppose I set down, as the second displayed statement item in this appendix

The second displayed statement in this appendix is not true.

Or more economically, suppose I set down

(2)   (2) is not true.

Then we have a *liar* sentence, saying of itself that it is untrue.[2] And once we have such an example, a contradiction quickly follows:

(3)   (2) is '(2) is not true'
(4)   (2) is true if and only if '(2) is not true' is true.
(5)   '(2) is not true' is true if and only if (2) is not true.
(6)   (2) is true if and only if (2) is not true.

Here (3) has been made true by definition, so to speak; (4) follows immediately from (3); (5) is an instance of the T-schema (1); while (6) follows immediately from (4) and (5). But (6) is a logical contradiction! Such is the *paradox of the liar*.

The liar goes back to antiquity, and a variation goes back to the middle ages. Suppose Plato says, 'What Aristotle is saying is true,' while Aristotle says, 'What Plato is saying is false.' Or suppose (in a modernized version) that what is written on one side of a postcard is, 'What is written on the other side is true,' while what is written on the other side is, 'What is written on the other side is false.' Or suppose I set down

(7)   (8) is true.
(8)   (7) is false.

Again a contradiction quickly follows (though we leave it to the interested reader to work out how). Examples with a cycle of three or more rather than two are also possible. So are examples with an infinite regress, like so:

(9.1) All statements 9.n with $n > 1$ are false.
(9.2) All statements 9.n with $n > 2$ are false.
(9.3) All statements 9.n with $n > 3$ are false.

though such examples seem to be of comparatively recent date.[3]

Though not 'paradoxical' in the sense of leading to contradictions, *truth teller* examples on the order of 'What I am now saying is true' or simply

(10) (10) is true.

are 'pathological' in the sense that, while assuming (10) true it follows that it is true, and assuming (10) false it follows that (10) is false, there seems to be no basis for assuming either.

Despite such paradoxes and pathologies and their notoriety among philosophers and logicians, probably most speakers go through life without ever encountering any problems with the internal logic of the truth concept. But if susceptibility to paradox and pathology thus leads to no immediate practical problems, it does make the concept of truth one to be avoided in a logically rigorous subject such as pure mathematics. Tarski, seeing this objection but at the same time seeing the potential for mathematical applications of the truth concept, worked out a restricted, paradox-free version of the concept for use in mathematics. (Kripke 1975), undoubtedly the most influential work on the paradoxes since Tarski's, constantly refers to Tarski, comparing and contrasting the approach to truth being advocated with Tarski's approach. A review of Tarski's approach is thus needed as a background to Kripke's.

Kripke *vs* Tarski

The means by which Tarski avoids paradox is simply to restrict his ambitions, and concern himself only with defining truth for a limited fragment of language (though one extensive enough to express important mathematical notions). The restricted fragment of language *for* which he is defining truth is called the 'object language,' while the larger fragment of language *in* which he is defining truth is called the 'metalanguage.' The object language may or may not have the resources to mention its own expressions and their 'syntactic' properties. What it will *not* have will be the resources to mention the 'semantic' property of truth for its own sentences. Truth for the object language will be something we can mention only in the metalanguage.

Tarski has two goals for his definition of truth. First, it should be 'formally correct' or fully rigorous mathematically, in order to overcome opposition among mathematicians, who firmly oppose introducing 'metaphysical' or 'psychological' notions into mathematics. Second, it should be 'materially adequate' or recognizably a restricted version of our intuitive notion of *truth*. The test or criterion for fulfillment of this second condition Tarski takes to be just this, that it should be possible to prove for each sentence A of the object language the instance of the T-schema for it.[4] Tarski succeeded in achieving his double goal, and his approach can be found expounded in his original or some variant version in all standard logic textbooks today.

Without getting involved in all the technicalities, let me outline how Tarski proceeds in the case of the *language of arithmetic*.[5] This language has in it in the first place a unity symbol **1** and an addition symbol **+** and a multiplication symbol **·** plus parentheses for punctuation. From these we can build up terms such as

$(1 + 1) \cdot ((1 + 1) + 1)$

Intuitively, each such term t has a certain numerical value $|t|$. In particular, the terms **1** and **1 + 1** and **(1 + 1) + 1**, which we may abbreviate **1** and **2** and **3**, have the numerical values one and two and three, and continuing this series there is for every positive integer n a term **n** that can serve as a numeral for it.

The language also contains an identity predicate **=** and an order predicate **<**. The logically simplest, or *atomic* sentences of the language are of the forms $s < t$ and $s = t$ where s and t are terms. With this much apparatus we can express simple numerical equations and inequalities that intuitively can be tested by computation, for instance the following:

$(1 + 1) + ((1 + 1) + 1) < (1 + 1) \cdot ((1 + 1) + 1)$

Further sentences are built up using the connectives ~ and & and ∨. (We need not list → because we can think of $A \to B$ as an unofficial abbreviation for ~$(A$ & ~$B)$.) Also we can use the quantifiers ∀ and ∃, but to go with these we need variables, to be thought of as ranging over positive integers. We can get indefinitely many variables from just two symbols if we take our variables to be z and z' and z'' and so on, though it will be convenient to abbreviate these informally as z and y and x and so on.

With this logical apparatus, we can now express serious notions of number theory. For example, that z is even (a multiple of two) as opposed to odd, can be expressed as follows:

$$\exists y(z = 2 \cdot y)$$

That z is prime (greater than one and not expressible as a product of two numbers greater than one) as opposed to composite can be expressed as follows:

$$1 < z \ \& \ {\sim}\exists y \exists x(1 < y \ \& \ 1 < x \ \& \ z = y \cdot x)$$

Goldbach's conjecture, which says that any even number greater than four is a sum of two odd primes, can be expressed as follows:

$$\forall z(4 < z \ \& \ z \text{ is even} \rightarrow \exists y \exists x(y \text{ is prime} \ \& \ x \text{ is prime} \ \& \ {\sim}x \text{ is even}$$
$$\& \ {\sim}y \text{ is even} \ \& \ z = y + x))$$

What Tarski wants is to define truth for this language.

It will be convenient to consider falsehood along with truth (though this is a *dispensable* convenience, since falsehood could simply be defined as truth of the negation). What Tarski in effect does is to begin with specifications for atomic sentences and then add specifications for logical compounds:[6]

(1) (a) If $|s|$ is the same as $|t|$, $s = t$ is true.
     (b) If $|s|$ is different from $|t|$, $s = t$ is false.
     (c) If $|s|$ is less than $|t|$, $s < t$ is true.
     (d) If $|s|$ is greater than or equal to $|t|$, $s < t$ is false.
(2) (a) If A is true, ${\sim}A$ is false.
     (b) If A is false, ${\sim}A$ is true.
(3) (a) If A is true and B is true, $A \ \& \ B$ is true.
     (b) If A is false or B is false, $A \ \& \ B$ is false.
     (c) If A is true or B is true, $A \vee B$ is true.
     (d) If A is false and B is false, $A \vee B$ is false.
(4) (a) If $A(\mathbf{n})$ is true for all n, then $\forall z A(z)$ is true.
     (b) If $A(\mathbf{n})$ is false for some n, then $\forall z A(z)$ is false.
     (c) If $A(\mathbf{n})$ is true for some n, then $\exists z A(z)$ is true.
     (d) If $A(\mathbf{n})$ is false for all n, then $\exists z A(z)$ is false.

Intuitively, the clause (1) suffices to assign a unique truth value, true or false, to every atomic sentence of the language. Clauses (2)–(4) then extend the assignment to *all* sentences of the language.

We may think of the assignment of truth values as occurring in stages. At stage zero, just the atomic sentences are given truth values, as per (1). Going from a given stage to the next stage, we apply (2)–(4) to sentences that have been given truth values already, to get truth values for further sentences. Thus at stage one we get truth values for negations and junctions and quantifications of atomic sentences, then at stage two we get truth values for negations and junctions and quantifications of those, then at stage three we get truth values for negations and junctions and quantifications of *those,* and so on. Intuitively, if a sentence involves, say, seventeen occurrences of logical symbols, it will get a truth value at the very latest by the seventeenth stage. Tarski turns these intuitions into a completely rigorous definition of a truth-predicate for our language of arithmetic.

Let us call the language of arithmetic, the object language we have been considering, L_0. This L_0 has, ignoring unofficial abbreviations, just fourteen symbols: $1, +, \cdot, (,), =, <, \sim, \&, \vee, \forall, \exists, z, {}'$. These can be assigned code numbers 10, 11, 12, 13, 14, 15, 16, 17, 18, 19, 20, 21, 22, 23. Then any sequence of them can be assigned as code the number whose Arabic numeral one gets if one writes down in order the Arabic numerals for code numbers of the symbols in the sequence. For example, the simple truth $1 = 1$ has code number 101510, so the number one hundred one thousand five hundred ten has the property of being the code number of a true sentence. (This particular code numbering can, using 24 through 99, accommodate as many as 76 additional symbols, if we want to enrich our language later on.)

The notion of being the code number of a true or of a false sentence of L_0 cannot be expressed in L_0. We can add symbols T_0 and F_0 for these notions to the language if we wish, thus obtaining a slightly larger language L_1. Tarski's method can then be applied to define truth for L_1. We just need additional clauses to handle atomic sentences of the form $T_0 t$ and $F_0 t$. The needed clauses would read as follows:

(5)   If $|t|$ is the code number of a sentence A of L_0, then:
    (a)   If A is true, then $T_0 t$ is true.
    (b)   If A is false, then $T_0 t$ is false.
    (c)   If A is true, then $F_0 t$ is false.
    (d)   If A is false, then $F_0 t$ is true.[7]

In the language L_1 we are able to express the notions of being a code number of true or of a false sentence of L_0, but we will not be able to express the notions of being a code number of a true or of a false sentence of L_1. We can add symbols T_1 and F_1 for these notions to the language if we wish, thus obtaining a slightly larger language L_2. In the language L_2 we will able to express the notions of being a code number of true or of a false sentence of L_1, but we will not be able to express the notions of being a code number of a true or of a false sentence of L_2. We can add symbols T_2 and F_2 for these notions if we wish, thus obtaining a slightly larger language L_3, and so on. Such is the 'Tarski hierarchy' of languages. But as we climb the hierarchy, we will never catch up with ourselves. That is to say, we will never in this way get a language containing *its own* truth predicate.

That is precisely how Tarski's method avoids the paradox of the liar. There is a sentence A_1 of L_1 in effect saying of itself that it is not a true sentence of L_0,[8] and a sentence A_2 of L_2 in effect saying of itself that it is not a true sentence of L_1, and so on; but none of these is paradoxical. The A_n are in fact all true: A_1, for instance, says it isn't a true sentence of L_0, and it isn't, because it isn't a sentence of L_0 at all, just a sentence of L_1. There is no sentence of L_0 saying of itself that it is not a true sentence of L_0, nor any sentence of L_1 saying of itself that it is not a true sentence of L_1, and so on.

Could these ideas be applied to ordinary language? Well, we can think of English as having a sublanguage English$_0$ in which one can say everything one can say in English that isn't about truth or falsehood or related notions. And we can think of using a restricted truth predicate 'is true$_0$' that would mean something like 'is a true sentence of English$_0$.' We can then think of English as having a larger sublanguage English$_1$ in which one can talk about truth$_0$, and think of a restricted truth predicate 'is true$_1$' that would mean 'is a true sentence of English$_1$.' And so on.

It would be extremely inconvenient to have to try to add a subscript every time the word 'true' or 'false' comes out of our mouths, but perhaps we wouldn't need to *say* or *think* the subscripts, but just let it be tacitly understood that when we use the truth predicate, it is supposed to have the lowest subscript that would make sense. So if you say, 'Snow is white,' and I say, 'That's true,' and you then say, 'And *that's* true, too,' my 'true' would be tacitly understood to be 'true$_0$' and yours to be 'true$_1$.'

Kripke's first important observation about these matters is that this hierarchical or subscripting approach leaves us unable to say a great many kinds of things we ordinarily *do* say, and most of the time without getting ourselves into trouble, either. (Kripke 1975) is a product of the Watergate era, and the most memorable of Kripke's examples pertains to the great Watergate scandal. He imagines Richard Nixon and John Dean speaking as follows:

(1)   Nixon: Most things Dean says about Watergate are true.
(2)   Dean: Most things Nixon says about Watergate are false.

There is no way to attach subscripts to these utterances. The subscript in (1) would have to be higher than that in any of Dean's statements, (2) included, while the subscript in (2) would have to be higher than the subscript in any of Nixon's statements, (1) included; and this is impossible. And yet, intuitively speaking, both (1) and (2) could well be true. If three quarters of Nixon's statements were not about truth at all, and clearly false, while three quarters of Dean's statements were not about truth at all, and clearly true, then both (1) and (2) would intuitively speaking be true.

Yet with unsubscriptible statements like (1) and (2) there is a *risk* of paradox. In very unfavorable circumstances one could get a situation analogous to the postcard paradox. This would happen, for instance, if apart from (1) and (2) each of Nixon and Dean made an even number of statements, with exactly half true and half false.

The broad general form of (1) and (2), each mentioning a totality of sentences to which the other belongs, is what makes them impossible to subscript, and what gives rise to a *risk* of paradox. But it need not give rise to an actual paradox, unless the stars are against us. The moral Kripke draws is that any approach that, like Tarski's, bans sentences on the basis of their broad general form is going to have to ban sentences where there is any *risk* of trouble, and that will mean banning many sentences where there is no *actual* trouble.

On a Tarskian approach, we try *first* to divide sentences into levels: first, those not mentioning truth; second, those mentioning truth only for sentences of this first kind; third, those mentioning truth only for sentences of the first two kinds; fourth, those mentioning truth only for sentences of the first three kinds; and so on. We then go through the levels assigning truth values first to those on the lowest level, then to those on the next level, then to those on the next level after that, and so on. This approach can't handle sentences that can't be assigned levels, though intuitively many such sentences are obviously true or obviously false.

Consider for instance the following:

(3)   Snow is white or most things Nixon says about Watergate are false.

(4)   Snow is black and most things Dean says about Watergate are true.

Regardless of the status of (1) and (2), the truth of 'Snow is white' and the falsehood of 'Snow is black' are arguably sufficient to make (3) true and (4) false. By contrast, the status of (1) and (2) would be crucial to evaluating

(3')   Snow is white and most things Nixon says about Watergate are false.
(4')   Snow is black or most things Dean says about Watergate are true.

Kripke's first vague hint of the alternative to Tarski that he is going to be proposing comes in the form of the slogan that sentences should be allowed to 'find their own level.' We don't try to assign levels or subscripts in advance, based on syntactic criteria or broad form. Rather, after the bottom level at which come sentences not mentioning truth, what should come next are not just sentence *that mention truth only for these bottom-level sentences*, as on the Tarskian approach, but any sentences *whose truth values are determined once the truth values of bottom-level sentences are given*. For Kripke, with 'Snow is white' and 'Snow is black' having been evaluated at the bottom level, (3) and (4) would be evaluated at the next-to-bottom level, while (5) and (6) would not, whereas for Tarski none of these come at any level at all.

Fixed Points

But how is one to make this idea of allowing sentences to 'find their own level' precise? (For Kripke does wish to be precise. Though this aspect of his work inevitably fails to show through in a semi-popular account, he does wish to match Tarski in precision and rigor.) Kripke's approach is perhaps best illustrated by reverting to the example of the language of arithmetic.

Let us consider a language L containing all the apparatus of the language L_0 of two sections back, plus predicates T and F intended to be read 'is the code number of a true sentence of L' and 'is the code number of a false sentence of L.' How can we assign truth values to sentences of this L? We can start with the clauses used for L_0, pertaining to (1) atomic sentences, (2) negations, (3) con- and disjunctions, (4) universal and existential quantifications, as in the preceding section. We will now want one more set of clauses, pertaining to the truth and falsehood predicates. There is only one obvious candidate. In place of (5) of the preceding section we should have the following:

(5)   If t is the code number of a sentence A of L, then:
       (a)   If A is true, then Tt is true.
       (b)   If A is false, then Tt is false.
       (c)   If A is true, then Ft is false.
       (d)   If A is false, then Ft is true.

Now we may think of sentences being evaluated in levels. At level zero, we first apply (1) to get truth values for all atomic sentences not involving T and F; and we then apply (2)–(4) to get truth values for all logical compounds of these, which is to say, for *all* sentences not involving T and F. At level one, we first apply (5) to these to get truth values for some atomic sentences involving T and F, namely, for Tt and Ft where the value of t is the code number of a level zero sentence; and we then apply (2)–(4) to get truth values for some logical compounds of these. We get to level two from level one as we got to level one from level zero, and repeat the process to get to higher and higher levels.

For instance, $1 = 1$ will be declared true at level zero. Consider now its code number a_0 and the numeral for it $\mathbf{a_0}$. (We earlier say that a_0 is one hundred one thousand five hundred ten, but the exact value does not matter for present purposes.) The sentence T$\mathbf{a_0}$ will be declared true at level one. (So will any disjunction T$\mathbf{a_0} \vee B$, regardless of the status of B, among other logical compounds.) Consider now *its* code number a_1 and the numeral for it $\mathbf{a_1}$. The sentence T$\mathbf{a_1}$ will be declared true at level two. (So will any disjunction T$\mathbf{a_1} \vee B$, regardless of the status of B, among other logical compounds.) And so on.

Kripke offers a heuristic analogy. Applying his ideas to ordinary language, we might imagine 'Snow is white' being declared true at level zero, and if 'Snow is white' appears in the *New York Daily News* for such-and-such a date, we might imagine 'The statement "Snow is white" appears in the *New York Daily News* for such-and-such a date' being declared true at level zero, too. For like the meteorological assertion 'Snow is white,' the bibliographical assertion about the *New York Daily News* does not involve truth, and belongs to 'English$_0$.' But then at level one ' "Snow is white" is true' will be declared true, and by logic ' "Snow is white" is true and the statement "Snow is white" appears in the *New York Daily News* of such-and-such a date' will be declared true, as will 'Some true statement appears in the *New York Daily News* of such-and-such a date.'

Some sentences will not get truth values at any of the levels zero, one, two, three, and so on. Such sentences are of two kinds. Intuitively, let us say that one sentence is *dependent* on another if we would have to determine the truth value of the latter before we could determine the truth value of the former. And let us say that a sentence A is *ungrounded* if there is an infinite sequence of sentences $A = A_0, A_1, A_2, \ldots$ where each sentence depends on the next. Ungroundedness includes the case where A depends on itself, as in liar and truth teller examples. (In this case all the A_n are just A.) Ungroundedness also includes the case where A depends on some B which in turn depends on A, as with the Plato–Aristotle or postcard paradox. (In this case, all the even A_n are A while the odd A_n are B.) An ungrounded $A = A_0$ cannot get a truth value at any level, because before that could happen, A_1 would have to have gotten a truth value already, and before *that* could happen, A_2 would have to have gotten a truth value already, and so on in an infinite regress.

But there is another type of sentence beyond the ungrounded that never gets a truth value in the process as described so far. Let us go back to the example of the sequence of sentences starting with $1 = 1$ and with each subsequent one asserting the truth of the one before. We were calling the code numbers of these sentences a_0 and a_1 and a_2 and so on, and we noted that Ta_0 and Ta_1 and Ta_2 were declared true at levels one and two and three. Now there is a sentence A^* that in effect asserts that *all* the sentences in this sequence are true. Then intuitively, this A^* is true. But it can't be declared true at stage one, because at that stage none of the Ta_n have as yet been declared true. And it can't be declared true at stage two, because at that stage none of the Ta_n for n greater than zero have as yet been declared true. And it can't be declared true at stage two, because at that stage none of the Ta_n for n greater than one have as yet been declared true. And so on. It is always 'too early' for this sentence A^* to be declared true.

It seems that what we want is a level *higher* than all the finite levels, at which A^* could at last be declared true (because all the sentences Ta_n will have been declared true at some lower level, which is to say, at some finite level). But we can't stop there, because if A^* as code number a^* with numeral $\mathbf{a}^*$, intuitively Ta^* is true, but even at the first infinite level it is still too soon to declare it so. Well, Georg Cantor, the founder of set theory, introduced some numbers beyond the finite ones precisely for counting the stages in a process or levels in a hierarchy that go beyond all finite ones, and at this point it is on his ideas that Kripke draws. Cantor's *transfinite ordinals*, as they are called, begin after $0 < 1 < 2 < 3 < \ldots$ with a limit called ω, which is followed by $\omega + 1 < \omega + 2 < \omega + 3 < \ldots$, which have a limit called $\omega + \omega$ or $\omega \cdot 2$ and so on.[9] In our example A^* would be declared true at level ω and $\mathrm{T}a^*$ at level $\omega + 1$. There is an A^{**} that would have to wait till level $\omega \cdot 2$, and $\mathrm{T}a^{**}$ would have to wait till level $\omega \cdot 2 + 1$. But drawing on the mathematical theory of transfinite inductive definitions, Kripke is able to show that we eventually come to an ordinal where we stop getting anything new.[10]

At this level, call it α, (5) ceases to tell us anything we don't already know. That means that for any sentence B with code number b and numeral **b**, the atomic sentence **T**b will have already been declared true by level α if the sentence B has been declared true by level α, and it won't be declared true *for the first time* at level α. Note that we can actually say that **T**b will be true at level α if *and only if* B is true at level α, since the only way an atomic sentence **T**b ever gets declared true is by application of (5), which requires that B has already been declared true.

This first level α where we cease to get anything new, or rather, the set of sentences declared true by that level, is called *the minimal fixed point*. Once we reach the minimal fixed point, the only sentences lacking truth values are ungrounded ones. Now the rule that permits the inference from '____' to 'it is true that "____"' is called T-*introduction*, and the rule that permits inference from 'it is true that "____"' to '____' is called T-*elimination*. In this jargon, what Kripke shows is that the set of sentences declared true by the minimal fixed point is closed under T-introduction and T-elimination.[11]

Such is Kripke's minimal fixed point construction, so far as it can be described without using his technical jargon of 'jumps' and 'monotonicity' and so forth, and without going into details about transfinite ordinals.[12] We start with *no* sentences declared true or false, then start declaring some one or the other (but not *both*) according to fixed rules, and reiterate the process until we stop getting anything new. The construction can also be described in terms not of which sentences have been declared true or false, but rather of which code numbers of sentences have been declared to satisfy the predicate T or F. Thus Kripke speaks of adding numbers level-by-level to the 'extension' and the 'anti-extension' of the truth predicate (where the anti-extension of the truth predicate amounts to the extension of the falsehood predicate). We start with the extension and anti-extension both empty, add numbers level-by-level to each according to fixed rules, and reiterate the process until we stop getting anything new.

It is natural to inquire what would happen if we didn't start with the extension and anti-extension both empty, but put some numbers in the one and other numbers in the other (but no numbers in both) at the outset, and only *then* began the process. One thing that could happen is that we might find ourselves reduced to *incoherence*, in the sense of finding ourselves forced by our rules to assign some number both to the extension and to the anti-extension of T. Suppose, for instance, that A is a liar sentence, in effect saying ~T**a**, where **a** is the numeral for the code number a of A. If we start by putting a into the extension of the truth predicate, we will soon find ourselves forced by our rules to put it into the anti-extension as well, and vice versa – though I will relegate the details about just how the incoherence comes about to a footnote.[13]

Suppose, by contrast, that B is a truth-teller sentence, in effect saying T**b**, where **b** is the numeral for the code number b of B. If we start by putting b into the extension of the truth predicate, we can carry out the whole Kripke construction without ever encountering incoherence, and we get a fixed point that differs from the minimal fixed point by counting the sentence B as true. Likewise, if we start by putting b into the *anti*-extension of the truth predicate, we get a fixed point that differs from the minimal fixed point by counting the sentence B as *false*. So we now have a way of describing the contrast between the kind of paradoxicality exhibited by liar sentences and the kind of pathology exhibited by truth-teller sentences: A liar is neither true nor false in *any* fixed point, while a truth-teller is true in some fixed points and false in others.

These are not the only possibilities. The liar A and the truth-teller B we have been considering are analogues of the informal examples

(6) (6) is not true.
(7) (7) is true.

But there are also analogues of the following:

(8) (7) is either true or not true.
(9) (7) is both true and not true.

A formal counterpart C of (8) will be true in any fixed point where B gets a truth value, and will have no truth value in any fixed point, such as the minimal one, where B has no truth value. It is ungrounded, but incapable of falsehood. A formal counterpart D of (9) will be false in any fixed point where B gets a truth value, and will have no truth value in any fixed point, again including the minimal one, where B has no truth value. It is ungrounded, but incapable of truth.

Subtly different from (8) and (9) are the following:

(10)   (10) is either true or not true.
(11)   (11) is both true and not true.

Formal counterparts E and F of (10) and (11) would be like (8) and (9) in being ungrounded but capable of taking only one truth value (truth in the case of (10), falsehood in the case of (11)). But E differs subtly from C in the following way: To make C true – that is to say, to obtain a fixed point for which C is true – we must give B a truth value, and whichever truth value we give it, it could have been given the opposite one. By contrast, E can be made true without making true anything that could have been made false and without making false anything that could have been made true.

As Kripke puts it, E is *intrinsically* true. Similarly, F differs from D by being *intrinsically* false. Kripke shows that there is a maximal intrinsic fixed point, where all and only the intrinsically true sentences are true, and all and only the intrinsically false sentences are false. In sum, the apparatus of fixed points, and the theory Kripke develops for them, gives a satisfying way of describing the intuitive differences among examples like (6)–(11). It provides a kind of taxonomy of pathologies.

The Intuitive Notion of Truth

But what, if anything, does all this theory have to do with 'true' as used in ordinary language, and 'truth' as understood in common-sense thought? What does it all have to do with our intuitive notion of truth? Here Kripke's attitude differs interestingly from that of most other writers on the topic, who tend to adopt one or the other of two opposed stances in addressing questions about the aims and claims a theory of truth.

One attitude, that of the *inconsistency theorists*, holds that every step of the reasoning in the paradoxes is fully in accord with our intuitive notion of truth, which notion must therefore be inconsistent. Another attitude, that of the *consistency theorists*, holds that our intuitive notion of truth is consistent, so that there must be some step in the reasoning in the paradoxes that is not fully in accord with it. Both groups are engaged in explicitly articulating consistent theories of truth. The inconsistency theorists put these forward as *emendations* of our intuitive notion, repairing its inconsistencies, while the consistency theorists put these forward as *exegeses* of our intuitive notion, revealing it to be consistent. Tarski was an inconsistency theorist. There is no single figure of equal stature on the other side; many different consistency theorists have offered many different accounts of just where the fallacy in the reasoning of the paradoxes is supposed to lie.

Kripke does not put forward his account as an exegesis vindicating our intuitive notion of truth as paradox-free, but neither does he put it forward as a replacement for an intuitive notion taken to be discredited by the paradoxes. It is supposed to be – or rather, to be an idealized model of – our intuitive notion of truth not as it is, but as it was naively, before philosophers began to reflect on it. Thus he writes:

> If we think of the minimal fixed point…as giving a model of natural language, then the sense in which we can say, in natural language, that a Liar sentence is not true must be thought of as associated with some later stage in the development of natural language, one in which speakers reflect on the generation process leading to the minimal fixed point. It is not itself a part of that process.…The ghost of the Tarski hierarchy is still with us. (Kripke 1975, 714)

Kripke's own account of truth is written from the later, reflective standpoint. He himself, for instance, says that a liar sentence is not true (and not false), whereas in the minimal fixed point, the formal counterpart of the sentence stating that of a given liar sentence A that it is not true, which is to say, the sentence $\sim$T**a**, where **a** is the numeral for the code number a of A, is itself not true (and not false).

In particular, the technical part of Kripke's work, which has inevitably been downplayed in the present semi-popular account, but is of considerable importance for Kripke himself, is a contribution to orthodox, classical mathematics, and as such freely employs all the modes of reasoning recognized by orthodox, classical logic, even though many of these methods seem to presuppose that every sentence to which they are being applied is either true or false, that there are no 'truth-value gaps.' Of course, the mathematical models that Kripke's mathematical results are *about*, the minimal and other fixed points, represent many sentences, including all liar sentences and other paradoxical examples, as exhibiting just such gaps. The logic appropriate for a situation where there may be such gaps is not, however, a logic that anyone would care to work with in proving mathematical results. As the prominent logician Solomon Feferman (who himself has made important contributions to the study of Kripke's theory on its technical side) has put it, 'Nothing like sustained ordinary reasoning can be carried out' with such a logic. So it is no surprise that Kripke does not, in writing about his idealized model, conform to the logic that would be appropriate if his own notion of truth were the 'naive' or 'pre-reflective' one the model is supposed to be a model *of*.

This fact in no way discredits the claim that the model is a good model of a notion of truth that Kripke (presumably along with most of the rest of us) has outgrown, any more than the fact that a developmental linguist writing about the grammar of three-year-olds will use grammatical constructions that are beyond even the most precocious three-year-old discredits the account of three-year-olds' grammar that the developmental linguist is offering. But did we really ever go through – either individually, as children, or else historically, as a culture – a 'naive' and 'pre-reflective' phase of which the minimal fixed point would be a good model? That would seem to be an empirical question, for developmental linguists (if it is an individual childhood phase that is in question) or historical philologists (if it is a collective cultural phase that is in question). At any rate, it is not a question that Kripke himself much discusses. Note that even the quoted passage above begins with the word 'If.'

It is the privilege of philosophers to speculate in advance of results from empirical disciplines. And some philosophical speculation there has been. Scott Soames, in his discussion of Kripke in his *Understanding Truth* (Soames 1999) is rather enthusiastic about the idea that a predicate can be introduced by partial specifications that leave the application of the predicate to certain examples undecided, an idea of which Kripke's approach to truth represents for Soames one conspicuous well-worked-out special case. Soames sees in this idea a clue as to the nature of not only of the notion of truth, but also of *vague* notions like 'bald,' whose application to borderline cases may seem as indeterminate as the application of 'true' to a liar sentence. There may be here a clue to the solution not only of the liar paradox and others pertaining to truth, but also of the notorious paradoxes pertaining to vagueness, such as the ancient *paradox of the heap*. (One grain of sand is not enough to make a heap. If some number n of grains of sand are not enough to make a heap, adding just one more grain won't be enough to make a heap, either. Therefore, a trillion grains of sand are not enough to make a heap.) Or so Soames speculates. Of course, as Soames is fully aware, in making such a suggestion he is extrapolating considerably beyond anything to which Kripke explicitly commits himself.

The present writer has reacted less enthusiastically to Kripke's suggestion, looking with a critical eye at a passage early in Kripke (1975) that Soames quotes approvingly. In this passage Kripke begins as follows:

> We wish to capture an intuition of somewhat the following kind. Suppose we are explaining the word 'true' to someone who does not yet understand it. We may say that *we are entitled to assert (or deny) of any sentence that it is true precisely under the circumstances when we can assert (or deny) the sentence itself.* Our interlocutor can then understand what it means, say, to attribute truth to ['Snow is white'] but he will still be puzzled about attributions of truth to sentences containing the word 'true' itself... [italics added] (Kripke 1975, 701)

Kripke then goes on to show how the subject can, by employing the italicized principle, end up asserting 'Some sentence printed in the *New York Daily News* for such-and-such a date is true,' an example I have already discussed. Kripke concludes:

> In this manner, the subject will eventually be able to attribute truth to more and more statements involving the notion of truth itself. There is no reason to suppose that *all* statements involving 'true' will become decided in this way, but most will. Indeed, our suggestion is that the 'grounded' sentences can be characterized as those which eventually get a truth value in this process.

Now all this comes in heuristic motivating remarks at the beginning of (Kripke 1975), and not too much weight should be put on it. But Kripke's discussion does raise the following question:

(1)   What would one have to tell a subject who has never heard the word 'true' before about how it is used in order to give him a notion of truth for which the minimal fixed point would be a good (though doubtless highly idealized) model?

And one thing that is certain about the answer to question (1) is that the italicized principle in the Kripke quotation above is not

enough. For that principle still eaves the subject unable to conclude, among many other things, the following:

(2)   Either every even number greater than four is a sum of two
      primes, or 'Every even number greater than four is a sum of
      two primes' is not true.[14]

In addition to the italicized principle, one could tell the subject the
rules for the logical operators (negation, junctions, quantification)
as displayed earlier in this chapter. That's already quite a few
clauses, and even so it's not enough. For it seems one would have
to give him clauses for atomic sentences, too. And once one goes
beyond arithmetic, with just two kinds of atomic sentences, to
ordinary language, with an indefinitely large or potentially unlimited number about meteorological and bibliographical and all sorts
of other phenomena, the number of rules that would have to be
imparted becomes enormous. This surely can't be the right
approach, but it remains far from clear what the answer to (1)
might be.

   In the absence of further light on the question from Kripke,[15] I
will speculate no further, but leave matters in this unsatisfactory
state. On the whole, the question with which we began this section
– 'What does it all have to do with our intuitive notion of truth?'
– has received less attention than the more technical side of Kripke's
theory, which has evoked a truly enthusiastic response, and given
rise to all sorts of spin-offs. Since this is not the place for a survey
of the technical developments inspired by Kripke's work, I must at
this point bring the discussion to a close.

Notes

Introduction

1   What abstract noun should go with 'a priori' the way 'necessity' goes with 'necessary' and 'analyticity' with 'analytic'? There is nothing really wrong with 'aprioriness,' but Kripke says 'aprioricity,' as if the phrase were 'a prioric,' while many commentators write 'apriority,' as if the phrase were 'a prior.' Other Latin prepositional phrases used in philosophy, such as 'ex nihilo' or 'ad hominem' or 'in re' and 'ante rem,' seem to be able to get along without corresponding abstract nouns and, so far as I am concerned, 'a priori' can do the same.

2   I owe such understanding as I have of the matters treated in this paragraph mainly to my colleague Desmond Hogan, though he is innocent of any responsibility for any misunderstandings on my part.

3   Kripke's criticism of the example 'Gold is a yellow metal' will be recalled in Chapter 3.

4   One subtlety I am eliding but that Kripke discusses is the slide from 'known' to 'knowable' here, from treating the a priori as a division within actual knowledge to treating it as a division within potential knowledge. Where potential know*ability* outruns actual knowledge, it is always the abilities of human-like cognitive agents that are in question.

5   It is really only a synonym if we stretch 'unmarried' to mean 'never married,' but let us follow tradition and ignore this complication.

6   Its prevalence prior to 1970 is evident in several of the quotations that Kripke produces in N&N, where the philosopher quoted writes 'necessary' or 'contingent' when clearly 'analytic' or 'synthetic' is what is meant. Kripke has been so influential that there is for

students of philosophy today a serious danger of anachronistic misreadings of earlier twentieth-century material, unless it is clearly recognized that the writers being read were for the most part simply oblivious to distinctions that philosophers since 1970 have thought crucial. The conflation, before Kripke, of the necessary, the a priori, and the analytic is a major theme of Scott Soames's survey of the history of twentieth-century analytic philosophy (Soames 2003).

7   Notes in this section will merely provide references to other works of the present author where some of the issues discussed in this book are treated in a different way. To begin with, in case any reader has seen my previous account of N&N in Burgess (2006), I should say that though there is inevitably some overlap, I here consider N&N at fuller length and in the wider context of Kripke's total *œuvre*, and with substantial attention to later developments, whereas the aim of the volume in which my earlier treatment appears is to provide concise, self-contained guides to specific works considered in themselves.

8   I have proposed a solution to the puzzle in a short note Burgess (2005), but will not insist upon the point of view of that note here.

9   The reader who would like to learn more, and is ready to tackle somewhat more technical material, may consult my fuller expositions in Burgess (2011a) or Burgess (2011c). From Burgess (2009), or any other textbook in the field today, one can see how absolutely central Kripke models have become.

10   My fuller outline of the 'Outline' can be found in Burgess (2011b), and the place of Kripke's work in current thinking on the nature of truth is also discussed in chapters 7 and 8 of Burgess and Burgess (2011).

1 Naming

1   By *descriptions* are to be understood what are more fully called *singular definite* descriptions, expressions like 'the most famous student of Socrates' or 'the most famous teacher of Aristotle,' in contrast to *plural* descriptions like 'the students of Socrates' or *indefinite* descriptions like 'a teacher of Aristotle.' By *names* are to be understood names in the ordinary sense, expressions like 'Plato' that traditional grammar calls 'proper nouns' and that established usage dictates should be capitalized.

2   Like the account of Kant, Frege, and Carnap in the introduction, the account of Mill, Frege, and Russell in this section has dealt in first approximations. The main references, in modern English editions, for the three historical figures I have mentioned are Mill (1950), 'On Sense and Reference' in Frege (1970) plus Frege (1956), and part VI of Russell (1985).

3 Versions were developed over the decades since 1970 by a number
   of philosophers and linguists such as Kent Bach, Jerrold Katz, Bart
   Geurts, and most recently Ora Matushansky (2008), whose treatment
   contains references to all important predecessors. Matushansky's
   version is substantially more sophisticated than any of those predecessors, and hers is the only version I will discuss.

4 Note that I write 'would say' and not 'says.' Socrates is the stock
   example I often use, not one of Kripke's own examples, though there
   is no doubt what he *would* say about it. With the exception of the
   Einstein case below, I generally do not reproduce Kripke's examples,
   so as not to spoil the fun of reading Kripke's own account of them,
   in his inimitable conversational style.

5 Even after Kripke's theory had been developed and, though not yet
   published, had been taken note of in the published literature (Kaplan
   1968, especially note 24), the cluster theory remained in fashion. For
   instance, there is a paper of Geach (1969), which (if the issue of the
   journal in which it is to be found actually came out by the December
   date on its cover) appeared on the very eve of Kripke's lectures.
   Geach's paper contains a passage strikingly parallel to the one from
   Searle quoted earlier:

> I introduced [in the opening of the paper] the proper name "Pauline" by
> way of the definite description "the one and only girl Geach dreamt of on
> N-Night"; this might give rise to the idea that the name is an abbreviation
> for the description. This would be wrong. A proper name can never be
> logically tied to just one definite description; so long as we agree in a good
> many of the judgments we make using a certain proper name, we can use
> that name for communication. And there is no one judgment, mentioning
> a peculiarity of Pauline, such that agreement on *it* is indispensable; in
> particular, not the one that would be expressed by "Pauline is the one and
> only girl of whom Geach dreamed on N-Night". If I told you a lot of things
> about Pauline under that name, and then suddenly remembered that my
> dream of her had occurred not on N-Night but the night before, I'd have
> to withdraw this definite description of Pauline, but I need not stop using
> the name. (Geach 1969, 289–290)

6 The cluster idea can also be found combined with the idea of distinguishing reference-determination from meaning-giving. Kripke cites
   Ziff (1960) in this connection.

7 Time has not been kind to Kripke's own example to illustrate this
   phenomenon, which involved the leading physicists Richard
   Feynman and Murray Gell-Mann. This example was spoiled in the
   nineteen eighties when Feynman became a celebrity, widely known
   as 'the scientist who explained the *Challenger* disaster.' As is remarked
   in Linsky (2011), this makes him a duplicate of the Einstein example.

8 Kripke notes that error is still possible with 'person thought to be...'
   if taken to mean 'person *generally* thought to be...' rather being taken

by each speaker to mean 'person I *think* is...' Kripke's own main
complaint about this particular amendment to Fregeanism is that
(especially if so formulated as to dodge the error objection) it makes
the connection between name and bearer problematic. In any case it
is, like all the other variations on Fregeanism that have been mentioned, and the metalinguistic theories to be discussed below, subject
to Kripke's modal argument, to be developed in the next chapter.

9   Geach (1969) puts even more emphasis than does Strawson on the
    history of a name, but still endorses the cluster theory, as we have
    seen.

10 More generally, linguists freely posit psychologically real but sub-
    conscious mechanisms at the phonological, syntactical, and semanti-
    cal levels. For a simple example, how many native English speakers,
    all perfectly able to form the plurals of English nouns, would be able
    state the rule for when one adds an -*s* and when a -*z* and when an
    -*iz* sound? Linguists, who would formulate the rule using technical
    terms like 'voiced' and 'sibilant' that are unknown to all but a small
    minority of English speakers, nonetheless may claim that the rele-
    vant *concepts* are possessed by ordinary speakers at some subcon-
    scious level, and that their very ability to form plurals correctly is
    proof that something like those concepts must be.

11 The distinction between what I have been calling the 'pure' intention
    to refer to the D *whatever it may be*, and the contrasting intention to
    refer to *what one thinks is* the D, is central in the account of Kripke's
    views in Berger (2002).

12 By way of further indication of the limited role of descriptions,
    Kripke mentions without elaborating that there may be other ways
    to fix the reference beyond ostension and description. It is not hard
    to think of cases. For instance, if I am introducing a code name just
    for my personal use in a secret diary, words may be entirely super-
    fluous, as naturally are gestures of the kind I might use to bring
    something to *your* attention. For though I do need to have *some* way
    of thinking about the object if I am to form the intention to use a
    certain expression as a name for *it*, still if the object is before me now,
    I may have sense-perception of it, or if it has been before me in the
    past, a memory-image. My private sense-perceptions and memory-
    images would not, of course, be useable in introducing a name for
    public use, at least barring telepathy.

13 Note the awkward disjunctive constructions 'whoever or whatever'
    and 'she or it' that are needed for grammatical correctness in the
    absence of basic classificatory information about the bearer of the
    name. It is not a weighty argument against the view that basic clas-
    sificatory information is part of the meaning of the name that the
    wife manages to use the name without that information. For one
    often succeeds in using a word whose meaning one does not fully
    know. The husband may, for instance, successfully relay a message

by telling a decorator 'My wife wants teal for the new curtains,' while not knowing whether teal is a color or a kind of fabric.

14 That is anyhow, as we will see when we come to Kripke's views on philosophy of mind in the last chapter of this book, a kind of project with which Kripke would hardly be sympathetic.

15 McKeown-Green (2002) offers several examples. Let me offer another. A certain undergraduate John Smith has been given the nickname 'Paris' by his girlfriend on the basis of a fancied resemblance to the actor who portrayed the Trojan prince in a certain B-movie, and has been given the nickname 'Paris' by his roommate in memory of certain adventures in the French capital over spring break. The resemblance to the actor is visible only to the eyes of love, and the roommate is unaware of it, while any details about French adventures have been discreetly kept from the girlfriend. Here we have a case where there seem to be two names 'Paris Smith' for the same person, despite identity of spelling and pronunciation *and bearer*. The distinctness of the names is indicated by the fact that if the girlfriend and the roommate wrote about Mr Smith to their common French pen-pal Pierre, the one would write 'Pâris Smith' and the other 'Paris Smith.' (The names of the Trojan prince and the French capital differ in French not only in spelling, by one circumflex accent, but also in pronunciation, since the final *s* is pronounced in one case but is silent in the other.) Yet if other students in their circle hear the girlfriend and the roommate speaking of 'Paris Smith,' to them it will seem that the two are using the same name, and indeed it seems that in the usage of these other students there *is* only one name, though there is not a single line of transmission leading back to a single initial introduction.

16 The situation is really very little different from that in Fielding's comic novel *Joseph Andrews*, where one of the characters constantly says things like 'That creature is a disgrace to our sect,' but is understood to mean 'That creature is a disgrace to our sex.'

2 Identity

1 There is a complication here, since if it isn't necessary that the Morning Star exists, as presumably it isn't, and if self-identity presupposes existence, as perhaps it does, then it isn't necessary that the Morning Star is self-identical. But most discussion in the literature focused on the example ignores the complication, which in any case can be avoided in other examples (such as (10) below).

2 It is said that Diogenes the Cynic came to Plato's Academy, held up a plucked chicken, and said, 'Behold Plato's man!' after which Plato's disciples added 'with broad, flat nails' to the definition.

3 Kripke's other conditions are that every distinguished term should designate some element of the domain we are quantifying over, that for every object in the domain over which we are quantifying a distinguished term designating it should be available, and that if t_1 and t_2 are two distinguished terms designating the same object, then for any context '__x__' the following should be true: 'It is necessary that ___t_1___if and only if it is necessary that ___t_2___.' If these conditions are met, we can 'reduce *de re* to *de dicto* modality' by taking 'It is necessary that ___x___' to be true of or satisfied by an object just in case 'It is necessary that ___t___' is true for some, or equivalently any, *distinguished* term t designating that object. And we can make sense of 'quantifying in' by taking 'There is an x such that it is necessary that ___x___' to be true just in case '___t___' is true for some *distinguished* term t. Such is the point that emerges over the course of several speeches of Kripke's in the post-colloquium-talk discussion. In this connection, it does not matter whether the distinguished terms are names or descriptions, so long as Kripke's conditions are assumed to be met. The difficulty lies in finding any such class of distinguished terms, so long as one is identifying necessity with analyticity. (Clearly 'Hesperus' and 'Phosphorus' cannot *both* be distinguished terms for Venus, and what reason could there be to prefer one over the other, or for that matter, 'Venus' over either?)

   Let me add that there is perhaps one very special domain where plausible candidates for distinguished terms may be available. That is the domain of the natural numbers, for which numerals may be suggested as distinguished terms. When we have different numerals for the same number, as with 'nineteen hundred forty-four' and '1944' and 'MCMXLIV,' the identities connecting them, such as 'MCMXLIV = 1944,' are arguably analytic. But this special case just underscores how difficult it is to find, for other domains of objects, any naturally privileged class of distinguished terms. Kripke himself has developed some very distinctive views about numbers and numerals (quite at variance with what I have just been suggesting), but as this material at present remains entirely unpublished, I will pass over it. Some information on Kripke's unpublished work in this area is available in (Steiner 2011).

4 The verbatim transcript of the audiotape shows that 'analytic' was the word actually used by Kripke in posing his question, and by Marcus in giving her answer, though the editing process has resulted in 'necessary' appearing in Kripke's question in the published version.

5 Marcus herself subsequently abandoned the dictionary view. Indeed, in the preface to the reprinting of (Marcus 1961) and (Marcus et al. 1962) in the collection (Marcus 1993), among other places, she in effect denied ever having held it. For she reported a recollection to the effect that by 'dictionary' she meant 'encyclopedia' and that she

was aware that an encyclopedia might have its facts wrong. She also suggested that her view was informed by the opinion of linguists that proper names are not 'lexical' items. Such reported recollections are part of a larger pattern of autobiographical reminiscences from the late Professor Marcus in her old age (from the middle 1980s onward) characterizing the views she held in her prime (in the early 1960s), or even her youth (in the middle 1940s), in a way that makes them almost indistinguishable from the views generally credited to Kripke and N&N. Given Kripke's presence at the Boston Colloquium, there can be no question of independent discovery here, so the tendency of such reminiscences is to insinuate that Kripke was either a knave (stealing Marcus's view) or a fool (walking off with it in a fit of absence of mind). But if Marcus really did hold the 'dictionary' view, there can have been only the most superficial, specious appearance of resemblance between any early view of hers and what is to be found in N&N.

Well, as for her meaning 'encyclopedia,' if one looks behind the heavily edited published version to the verbatim transcript of the audiotape, one finds that she said in so many words that she was talking about a book that would tell us when two words have the same meaning, and that she said in so many words that the reason she was mentioning it was to explain the sense in which 'Hesperus is Phosphorus' is analytic. Needless to say, no one explains the notion of analyticity in terms of what information or misinformation can be found in an encyclopedia that one knows might have its facts wrong. As for names not being 'lexical' items, we find her saying at a conference in Helsinki, the summer after the Boston colloquium, things very similar to the 'dictionary' remark, but this time using the word 'lexicon.' Thus in the paper (Marcus 1963) in the conference proceedings volume we read 'one doesn't consult the planets but the accompanying lexicon.' This paper she later rewrote as Marcus (1974), among other changes eliminating the quoted passage in the process, showing that she had become dissatisfied with it. But this was well after the publication of N&N. In short, Marcus's autobiographical reminiscences late in life about what she meant decades earlier – recollections that she clearly had not checked against contemporary documents, such as the verbatim transcript of the audiotape or her Helsinki paper as it stood prior to rewriting – are not reliable as records of historical fact. They may represent an instance of what psychologists who study memory call 'confusing hindsight with foresight.'

At any rate, that is the charitable interpretation. For an account of the whole sorry business that is just to Kripke and generous to Marcus, see (Neale 2001). For an account more concerned with justice than generosity, see (Burgess 1996), and compare (Burgess 1998).

6   The main difference between the linguists' 'dynamic' and the philosophers' 'metaphysical' modality is that the former includes *personalized* versions, talk of what *I* could do, *you* could do, *he* or *she* could do. The latter is generally not about me or you or him or her, but only about it, the 'it' that is the subject of the verb 'is' in 'it is the case that.' For the 'possibility' of modal logic when taken 'metaphysically' amounts to 'it could have been the case that,' and 'I could have done such-and-such' has to be construed as 'It could have been the case that I did such-and-such.'

7   This usage is comparable to that attributed by the documentary hypothesis to the biblical writer E, as explained to me once in conversation by Kripke himself. E uses 'El' or 'Elohim' for God up to the episode of Moses and the burning bush, where the name traditionally anglicized as 'Jehovah' was, according to E's account, revealed. The biblical writer J, by contrast, uses the latter name from the beginning, and represents the patriarchs as using it long before Moses.

     Augustus's wife, Livia, was by posthumous adoption in his will given the name 'Julia Augusta.' Tacitus, in mentioning her in his account of the reign of her son Tiberius, uses the latter name, while Suetonius continues to call her 'Livia.' The difference between Tacitus and Suetonius is a sort of mirror image of the difference between E and J.

8   The observations in this paragraph are relevant to the disagreements between Kripke and the late David Lewis over modal predicate logic that are alluded to in N&N; but that is an issue that cannot be pursued without getting into technicalities. On the Ludovician approach, formulations about what my 'counterpart' *is* doing in another world systematically replace ordinary formulations about what I myself *might have done*.

9   Doubts about cross-world identification were part of the reason Quine could not accept Kripke's mathematical work, his model theory for modal logic to be described in Appendix A, as by itself clarifying *de re* modality enough to make modal predicate logic acceptable. 'There is something such that it is necessary that *it* has such-and-such a property' becomes on Kripke's model theory 'There is something such that in every possible world it has such-and-such a property.' Quine is concerned about how we identify 'it' from world to world.

10   Indeed, the proof of (2) in Kripke (1971), deducing it from (1), comes more from a passing remark in Quine (1953), to which the result is credited in Kripke (1959a), than from Marcus (1947).

11   Or at least, for the Kripke of N&N; as we will see in Chapter 4, in the wake of (Kripke 1979) it is rather hard to say just what Kripke now thinks about the Homer case.

12   See (Soames, 2002, chapter 2) for a fuller discussion than there will be space to give here, including a fuller statement of some key details

of the Kripkean position than can be found in Kripke's own published works, and including also references to works of Michael Dummett, Jason Stanley, and others in which some of the best-known objections and some of the best-known replies originated.

13 A variation on this strategy, found in Wehmeier (2005), would insist (i) that the pertinent description must be written out with an explicit verb in the indicative mood, and (ii) that the name can only be replaced by the description *with the verb still in the indicative mood.* Requirement (i) obliges us to replace typical descriptions like 'the hemlock-drinking philosopher' or 'the bearer of the name "Plato"' by versions like 'the philosopher who *drank* hemlock' and 'the one who *bore* the name "Plato"' that show overt verbs. Requirement (ii) then has much the same effect as the 'actually' strategy, since the indicative always pertains to how things actually are rather than how they would or might have been under these or those counterfactual circumstances. Inserting 'actually' with the 'regimented' understanding indicated is an artificial way of accomplishing what is naturally accomplished by using the indicative mood. It is perhaps no accident that the theorist most associated with this strategy of defense, Kai Wehmeier, is a native speaker of German, because the distinction between indicative and subjunctive is much more clearly marked in German than in English, where subjunctive and indicative forms are often indistinguishable, especially when speaking of the past. For instance, where English has only 'had' for both indicative and subjunctive, German contrasts 'hatte' with 'hätte': a difference only of an Umlaut, though that does make a difference to pronunciation. For clarity, we might in writing use an Umlaut in English, too, to mark the subjunctive, without letting it affect pronunciation. Then the proposal is that 'Under certain circumstances it would have been the case that Socrates drank no hemlock' might become 'Under certain circumstances it would have been the case that the philosopher who drank hemlock dränk no hemlock.' Similarly, 'Under certain circumstances it would have been the case that Plato bore the name "Aristocles"' might become 'Under certain circumstances it would have been the case that the one who bore the name "Plato" böre the name "Aristocles."'

14 A variation on this strategy adopts or adapts the notion that a description (or cluster) does not 'give the meaning' but only 'determines the reference' of a proper name. This is a notion already alluded to earlier as developed even before N&N, without perhaps having this application specifically in mind. When we say 'Socrates need not have drunk the hemlock,' on this view, we are saying of a certain person that *he* need not have drunk the hemlock. The role of the description, 'the philosopher who drank the hemlock' (or the cluster consisting of this and other descriptions such as 'the teacher

of Plato' and more) is merely to determine which individual that is. It is as if we said, 'Consider the philosopher who drank the hemlock (and taught Plato and so on). *He* need not have drunk it.' The effect is much the same as on the wide-scope strategy, though there is no dependence on Russell's or any other specific theory of descriptions.

15   I was first convinced of the ephemerality of a priori contingencies while conversing with Michaelis Michael, rather than while reading Kripke, whom I don't know to have explicitly acknowledged the point.

16   The Neptune example is apparently in some respects fictionalized, but the meter example is certainly fictionalized in respects that are quite important. What the international convention prevailing from 1889 to 1960 actually specified was that the meter was to be, not the length of the X-shaped platinum-iridium alloy bar in question, but the distance between two scratches on it. More importantly, there was no mention of any time t_0; rather, the specification was that the distance was to be measured at the melting point of ice, or 0°C, it being implicitly assumed to be a law of nature that the distance at that temperature would not vary over time.

Further, some of what Kripke says leaves it somewhat unclear whether 'fixing the reference' here is a merely transitory status, or is supposed to be something more long term. One might even suspect that it may perhaps be something long term for experts but not for the general public. For on the one hand, the International Bureau of Weights and Measures, responsible for preserving the bar at is laboratories in Sèvres, was an important official organization for the scientific community, and industry as well, and experts were well aware of its role. On the other hand, neither the introduction of the bar standard for scientific and industrial purposes in 1889, to replace the earlier one based on the circumference of the earth, nor its abandonment in 1960, in favor of one based on the speed of light, registered in lay consciousness to any great degree, even in countries where the metric system was in daily use. But in Kripke (1986), a follow-up note to N&N, it is made clear that on Kripke's view experts have no special linguistic authority.

17   See Donnellan (1979) and Evans (1982) for two forms of dissent or deviation from Kripke on the contingent a priori.

3 Necessity

1   Whether the marble could over the years be taken away bit by bit and be replaced by concrete, until all the marble was in the British Museum or some German bank vault, and only concrete was left

atop the Acropolis, without the Parthenon thereby ceasing to exist, is not directly at issue, but only its *original* composition. Kripke's own example is the wooden table before him as he lectures, which he claims could not have been made originally of anything but wood. Kripke also hints it may be essential to this object that it was originally *table*. But this seems questionable unless qualified somehow. For suppose the company manufacturing the table had gone bankrupt before the table was assembled, and had given away its unused materials to its employees. And suppose one of these, the employee who in the actual world assembled the table, became an amateur sculptor, and took exactly the same pieces of wood from which the actual table was made, and attached them with exactly the same hardware and adhesives, in exactly the same positions relative to each other, to create a sculpture *Four Towers Rising from a Plain*, which was bought by a collector and donated to the Princeton art museum. And suppose that by some mistake, instead of being placed in the sculpture gallery, it ended up being placed on the stage in the museum auditorium, where philosophy lectures are often given, but upside down, with the result that it came to be used as a table for speakers. Can one claim that because the hypothetical sculpture would not have been originally made as a table, it would not have been the same artifact as the actual table formed from the same pieces in the same way by the same person?

2   For some of the discussion that has ensued in the secondary literature about the notion of 'rigidity' as it applies to 'general terms,' and for samples of divergent views, see the relevant section in Linsky (2011), and the treatments by Soames, Salmon, and others summarized there; compare also Gomez Torrente (2006).

3   Though there are likely to be many distracting features in any given example, the case of 'water' is perhaps worse than most. In what seems to be its primary use, 'water' is more like 'graphite' or 'diamond,' the word for a certain physical phase of a substance, rather than 'carbon,' a word for a substance itself. That is to say, the use of 'water' for the liquid phase seems more basic than the use that covers ice and water vapor also. Linus Pauling, for instance, in his widely read introductory college chemistry text, makes a point of using the uncommon expression 'water substance' rather than the mere 'water' when it is the substance rather than the liquid phase that he means. There is also the complication, with gold as well as water, that the word may be applied where there are many impurities, dissolved or suspended substances with water, alloyed metals with gold, though there are special terms with additional epithets for some of these, such as 'saltwater' and '14 carat gold.' One must look past distractions inviting quibbles to catch the spirit of Kripke's discussion.

4 Kripke's discussion of the gold example contains hints (especially in footnote 66) toward an account of colors and more generally of what early modern philosophers called 'secondary qualities.' But the bulk of Kripke's work in this area remains unpublished, and cannot be addressed here. Some information on Kripke's unpublished work in this area is available in Gomez-Torrente (2011), which contains an account of the notion of a 'prejudice,' in a certain distinctive sense, that plays a large role in Kripke's later thinking, and not just about the issues discussed in the present chapter. Though it is in connection with the 'gold' example that N&N touches tangentially on the issue of color, Gomez-Torrente's account presents Kripke's treatment of color as more closely related to his treatment of heat or light (to be discussed later in this chapter).

5 Since Kripke often mentions fool's gold, it should be noted that he never says it is a metal, and it isn't. But the substance *called* 'yellow metal' (also called 'Muntz metal') is indeed yellow and metallic and not gold, being an alloy of 60 percent copper and 40 percent zinc, with a trace of iron.

6 The case of 'Sannikov Island' or 'Sannikov Land' in the Arctic Ocean, which was according to some a mirage, may be a case, though some say there was a real low-lying sandbar subsequently submerged through erosion, while others consider the whole episode a hoax.

7 Putnam's example of jade, which has turned out to consist of two different kinds of stone, jadite and nephrite, has become a stock example in subsequent discussions.

8 Putnam's interest is mainly in arguing that the the *meaning* of 'water' is not something internal to the speaker, but depends on external matters, and notably on whether the speaker lives on our earth, surrounded by H_2O, or on twin earth, surrounded by XYZ. This issue of internalism *vs* externalism about meaning is not one that much concerns Kripke. Moreover, (Kripke 1986) shows a quite cool attitude toward some of Putnam's ideas about the *social* character of meaning.

9 By the way, it is probably no accident that he chose the tiger, the Princeton mascot, as his example, just as he had earlier used such Princeton personalities as Einstein and Gödel.

10 Corresponding to the natural kind terms 'horse' and 'swine' we have natural substance terms 'horseflesh' and 'pork.' If we introduce analogous terms 'placozooplasm' and 'trichoplacoplasm,' we seem to obtain a counterexample to any principle stating that identity statements involving natural substance terms are necessary if true. For it seems that 'placozooplasm is the same stuff as trichoplacoplasm,' is contingent rather than necessary.

Part of what is involved may be a certain difference in nature between common names and scientific names. Linguistic competence with the common names 'maple' and 'sugar maple' certainly does not require familiarity with such notions of scientific botany as genus and species, but at most familiarity with an intuitive, pre-scientific notion of kind. By contrast, it seems that linguistic competence with any bit of Linnean binomial nomenclature such as '*Acer saccharum*' requires the semantic knowledge that the term as a whole is the name of a species, while its first component is the name of the genus to which that species belongs, just as it requires the orthographic knowledge that the first but not the second term is to be capitalized, and that both are normally to be italicized. If this is so, then though '*Acer*' and '*Acer saccharum*' apply to exactly the same plants as 'maple' and 'sugar maple,' respectively, the pairs of terms are not synonymous.

Nor do the scientific or even the common names after all absolutely entirely lack descriptive sense or connotation, since it is presumably, even on Kripke's view, part of the meaning of 'maple' or 'sugar maple' that it names a kind of thing, and part of the meaning of '*Acer*' that it names a genus, and part of the meaning of '*Acer saccharum*' that it names a species. The fact (if it is one) that it is part of the meaning of 'placozoon' that is applies to all and only the members of a certain phylum, and part of the meaning of 'trichoplax' that it applies to all and only the members of a certain genus may go some way toward explaining the asymmetry that 'Trichoplaxes are placozoa' is necessary while 'Placozoa are trichoplaxes' is contingent, that the former is something like a law of nature (or even perhaps something like a definition), while the latter is merely a fact of natural history.

11 It might be questioned whether even calculation by hand, which at intermediate steps often involves, as commentators from Whitehead onwards have remarked, *not thinking about the meanings of the symbols one is manipulating, but only about their shapes*, really gives a priori knowledge.

12 For example, let p and q be unrelated necessary a posteriori statements, say 'water is H_2O' and 'tigers are mammals,' and let r be any old ordinary empirical and contingent statement, and let A be the compound 'Either p or else both q and r.' Then it can fairly easily be seen that for all we could have known a priori, A might have been necessary, impossible, or contingent (and in the last case, either true or false). Indeed, for all we can know a priori, p might be true and hence necessary, making A necessary, or p might be false and hence impossible; in the latter case, q might be false and hence impossible, making A impossible, or q might be true, hence necessary; in the latter case, A is contingent, and has the same truth value as r.

13 The problematic kind of modality is 'alethic' or 'dynamic' or 'metaphysical,' since the importance of making deontic and epistemic distinctions seem obvious.

4 Belief

1   Sentences like 'I love you' do not express propositions; only their
    utterances do. What proposition an utterance of the sentence
    expresses depends not only on the meaning of the sentence, but on
    certain features of the circumstances of utterance, beginning with
    who is speaking to whom. If Romeo utters the sentence to Juliet, the
    proposition expressed is that he loves her. If Juliet utters it to Romeo,
    the proposition expressed is rather that she loves him. The phenom-
    enon of context-dependence forces one to distinguish the 'meaning'
    of the sentence from the 'meaning' of utterances thereof, or in the
    terminology of David Kaplan, to distinguish the *character* of the
    sentence from the *content* of an utterance. These subtleties will be
    ignored here, as not affecting the examples at issue.

2   Ordinary usage of 'asserts' and 'believes' and 'proposition' certainly
    encourages these sorts of views; 'asserting that p' and 'asserting the
    proposition that p' are virtually interchangeable, as are 'believing
    that p' and 'believing the proposition that p.' Philosophers and lin-
    guists have been quick to point out, however, that this does *not* work
    with many other verbs such as 'know' or 'discover' or 'fear.' In
    particular, knowing that something is the case is not a matter of
    being acquainted with a certain proposition. Many theorists do,
    however, describe knowing that p as standing in the 'knowledge
    relation' to the proposition that p. Here the expression 'knowledge
    relation' is a terms of art. The only definition of it is that it is the
    relation that holds between a person and the proposition that p when
    the person knows that p.

3   A stock example is due to Quine. The painter Giorgio Barbarelli was
    called 'Barbarelli' because that was his family name, and was called
    'Giorgione' or 'Big George' because he was big. On anyone's theory,
    'Giorgione was so called because of his size' is true, while 'Barbarelli
    was so called because of his size' is false, despite the principle of
    substitutivity. These sentences are in some sense contractions of
    'Giorgione was called "Giorgione" because of his size' and 'Barbarelli
    was called "Barbarelli" because of his size. In the uncontracted ver-
    sions we see first a use of a name, then a mention of the same name.
    Substitutivity does not apply to mentions, but only to uses. Note that
    'Barbarelli was called "Giorgione" because of his size' is true, and
    'Giorgione was called "Barbarelli" because of his size' is false.

4   In this they contrast sharply with a group called 'two-dimensional-
    ists,' who while they may profess verbal agreement with Kripke on
    several points, fundamentally reject Kripke's whole conception of the
    relation of 'metaphysical' to epistemological notions. But the issues
    here are too large to be taken account of in the present study. A
    summary statement of direct reference theory's areas of agreement
    and disagreement with Kripke can be found in Soames (2011). A

classic reply, Kripkean in spirit, to the two-dimensionalism an be found in Byrne and Pryor (2004). An extend critique, from a direct reference theory perspective, to the two-dimensionalism of David Chalmers, Frank Jackson, and others, is to be found in Soames (2005).

5   City names are unique among French nouns in that, apart from 'Paris' and 'Rome' and a small class of further exceptions (not including 'Londres'), they have no fixed grammatical genders; there may even be a tendency to use the masculine in speech and the feminine in writing for the same city. Kripke writes 'jolie,' taking 'Londres' to be feminine, and this is not incorrect; but neither would it have been incorrect for him to take 'Londres' to be masculine, and write 'joli'; and though 'beau' and 'belle' may be more usual for cities than 'joli' and 'jolie,' either 'beau' or 'belle' would do with 'Londres.' For what it is worth, in a Google fight the masculine 'le Londres victorien' beats the feminine 'la Londres victorienne' by about 40K hits to 4K, despite the fact that the feminine can generally be justified with a city-name N by construing it as elliptical for 'la ville de N' ('the city of N,' wherein 'ville' for 'city' is feminine).

6   There is a slight asymmetry, in that one of Pierre's two languages is the very language in which we are conducting our discussion, while the other is not. This can be avoided by sending Pierre to Munich rather than London. The example can be so arranged that Pierre will assent to 'La Bavière est belle' and dissent from 'Bayern ist schön,' and we will have to use both translation and disquotation to get to each of the conclusions that Pierre believes Bavaria is beautiful and that Pierre believes Bavaria is not beautiful.

The Pierre example is like the Vietnamese example except that so long as Pierre sticks to French or to English, he makes no statement comparable to 'Saigon is more attractive than Ho Chi Minh City' or 'Ho Chi Minh City is less attractive than Saigon.' However, if Pierre lapses into Franglais, we may find him saying 'Londres est beaucoup plus pretty than London,' or 'London is much less jolie que Londres,' even while saying 'Aucune ville n'est prettier than itself' and 'No city is moins jolie qu'elle-même.'

7   But important or not, it should be acknowledged that it *is* a fact. I myself, for instance, for a long time didn't realize that Leuven, where they brew Stella Artois, and Louvain, where the University library was torched during World War I, are the same place.

8   Though indeed those metalinguistic theorists who are linguists are likely to point out that in ordinary usage one writes 'the place called London' or 'They named the town in Ontario London' *without* quotation marks, rather that 'the place called "London"' or 'They named the town in Ontario "London."' A linguist might further question whether the insertion of quotation marks, which philosophers regard as a 'correction' of the 'sloppiness' of ordinary language, may not perhaps be a *hyper*correction, or learned error.

9   There remains the Kripkean objection that no theory just about
    proper names is capable of clearing up the problems in this area,
    because exactly analogous problems can arise with natural-kind
    terms and others. One reason biologists insist on Linnean binomial
    nomenclature is that the same common name is often used for unre-
    lated organisms. Thus in (at least some dialects of) English, 'mango'
    may be used for the bell pepper (a cultivar group of *Capsicum
    annuum*) as well as for the tropic fruit (from the tree *Mangifera indica*),
    and 'mandrake' may be used for the humble may apple (*Podophyl-
    lum peltatum*) or its fruit as well as for the storied psychoactive plant
    (*Mandragora officianarum*). If there are genuine cases of ambiguity of
    this kind, there can be cases where a natural-kind term is mistakenly
    believed to be ambiguous. For instance, someone who has never
    seen trees of the genus *Sassafras* but only their leaves may believe
    that there are three kinds of trees called 'sassafras,' one with one-
    lobed, one with two-lobed, and one with three-lobed leaves. Such
    facts can be used to construct Paderewski-type examples not involv-
    ing proper names. The same kind of confusion can occur with
    natural-substance terms ('sassafras wood,' for instance).

10 It is the Locke Lectures that I had before me when writing the first
    draft of the present section, as I waited with mounting impatience
    for the appearance of the oft-advertised, oft-postponed appearance
    of Kripke (2011).

11 The distinction here can perhaps be illustrated even more vividly
    than with 'Sherlock Holmes' by the case of 'Mickey Mouse': On the
    one hand, no rodent is capable of human-like speech in a voice
    however squeaky; on the other hand, there is a piece of 'intellectual
    property' so valuable that every time it is about to pass into the
    public domain lobbyists for the Disney Corporation go to work and
    get American copyright law changed. Only a very young child
    would *seriously* use 'Mickey Mouse' in the first way, as a name for a
    supposed talking rodent, though troops storytellers have *pretended*
    to do so. Troops of lawyers run up many billable hours using 'Mickey
    Mouse' in the second way.

12 Salmon (2011a) suggests a neat solution that follows Kripke a con-
    siderable distance before diverging from him.

13 If only we had comparable access to Kripke's views on metaphysics!
    But material from his legendary seminars on color and on existence
    through time and 'temporal parts' remains unavailable at the
    time of this writing. On Kripke's unpublished work on the
    latter topic there is not even any information available in Berger
    (2011a).

14 The paper is noteworthy for introducing Kripke's notion of a 'toy
    duck case': A parent and child are in a store looking at rubber bath
    toys. The child asks, 'Is that a goose?' The parent replies, 'No, that's
    a duck.' The parent has said nothing wrong, but one should not infer

that some ducks are made of rubber, that there are two senses of 'duck,' or anything of the sort.

15 For the *cognoscenti*, the main problem is that of the 'hierarchy of indirect senses,' and Donald Davidson's claim that a language with such a hierarchy would be unlearnable.

16 For the *cognoscenti*, the problem is that in *PM* descriptions formed using the iota-operator are supposed to be eliminable, but when one goes to eliminate them, one may encounter 'hydras,' cases where eliminating one description just introduces another.

17 Still less do I want, in the body of the text, to get into 'On Two Paradoxes of Knowledge' (Kripke 2011b). That paper should, however, at least be mentioned in a footnote, though it stands apart by being directly concerned with knowledge and epistemology itself, more than with the question of *attributions* of knowledge or belief. 'Two Paradoxes' presents Kripke's views on puzzles, one old one and one new one of his own invention, in each case hinting at larger lessons.

One of the two puzzles is the well-known surprise examination paradox: A teacher tells the class there will be an examination on one of the next three days, and that up to the time of the exam it will be a surprise which. The students reason that it cannot be the last day, for after two days have gone by without an exam, there will be no surprise. Once the last day has been ruled out, they by similar reasoning rule out the second day and then the first, and conclude the teacher's announcement cannot be true. They are then very surprised when the second day comes and the exam is held. Kripke surprises us, too, by finding something quite new to say about this much-discussed example, and by indicating connections between this apparent mere trifle and substantial issues.

The other puzzle is the dogmatism paradox, novel when Kripke first spoke on it, but now familiar to epistemologists from second-hand accounts: If I know that p, then it is true that p, and if it is true that p, any evidence suggesting otherwise is misleading; to prevent anyone's being misled, if I take myself to know that p, I should not look at any evidence to the contrary, and should do what I can to prevent others from doing so, too. Clearly this line of thought does, when not so baldly put, exercise a certain influence, as with the scholastics who, according to a letter of Galileo to Kepler, refused to look through Galileo's telescope. It is of practical importance to recognize that the reasoning is faulty, and of theoretical interest to try to pin down just why.

5 Rules

1 The fact that the Wittgenstein book came out a full decade after N&N accounts for my treatment of it appearing so late in this book. Despite

the order of publication, however, Kripke in the front matter to his two books dates the main ideas in *Wittgenstein on Rules* to 1963–63, while dating the main ideas in N&N to 1963–1964. The early date for the Wittgenstein material is confirmed by a colleague of the present writer who was at Harvard at the time and made notes of Kripke's interpretation in the margins of his copy of Wittgenstein's *Investigations*. One consequence of the long delay in publication of the Wittgenstein material is that the book contains not only Kripke's basic interpretation, but also responses to objections thereto encountered in many discussions in the nineteen sixties and seventies. In his preface Kripke thanks quite a number of people in connection with such discussions. By contrast, in his work on naming and necessity, and on the two topics I am leaving for the appendices here, modal models and truth, there are few if any whom he feels a need to thank for direct influence.

On the other hand, in those other cases there are quite a few acknowledgments of philosophers or logicians who, though they did not directly influence Kripke's own work, are to be recognized either as precursors arriving at partial results in the same ultimate direction, or as independent workers arriving at overlapping conclusions. Under this heading come the citations of Donnellan and Putnam in N&N, to which I have already alluded, and of quite a number of writers (Jónsson and Tarski, Kanger, Hintikka, and Martin and Woodruff) in connection with the technical work. By contrast, in the Wittgenstein book Kripke contents himself with a blanket acknowledgment that (i) in the two decades between his arrival at his interpretation and his publication of it, a number of commentators have put forward not unrelated views, and (ii) while presumably some of these were influenced by second-hand accounts of Kripke's interpretation, presumably others of them were independent. Any attempt to name names would doubtless have resulted in an incomplete list, thus giving offense to those omitted, and it would have been infeasible to establish conclusively, and unseemly to discuss speculatively, which other writers were influenced by second-hand accounts of Kripke's work and which were operating entirely independently.

If there have been few complaints from other authors who, like Kripke, have wished to shift the emphasis in Wittgenstein studies toward examination of rule following, and whom Kripke might have mentioned but did not mention by name, I suspect that it is because most of them would prefer to emphasize differences rather than similarities between their interpretations and Kripke's (as is surely the case with the most distinguished interpreters in this class, notably Crispin Wright and John McDowell). The only clear expression of unhappiness at lack of a specific mention by name that I know of comes from Robert Fogelin, in the long footnote 10, page 241, 'amounting to a brief appendix' added to the second edition (1987) of his Wittgenstein. Though this makes for rather unpleasant reading in places, in the end even Fogelin emphasizes differences rather than similarities, though he tends to underestimate the former and overestimate the latter. The main similarity is that Fogelin also makes a comparison with Hume, though it is not quite the same comparison.

2 I recall being told, when Kripke's book first came out, by a person then very close to him and in a position to know, that he planned to wait until the problem had sunk in before offering his own solution. Three decades or so later, we are still waiting for that solution, though indeed it may be that the problem has not yet sunk in as much as it should have by now. If that is so, it is probably the diversion of so much of the discussion surrounding Kripke's work from philosophical to exegetical issues that is chiefly to blame. I am not aware of any version of Kripke's solution even in the various materials circulating in pirated versions among philosophers and students of philosophy, and at the time of this writing no relevant publication has been announced as forthcoming.

3 'Lewis Carroll' is the name under which Charles Lutwidge Dodgson published not only the *Alice* books but also most of his contributions to logic. The title of the work to be discussed is an allusion to Zeno's famous paradox, according to which the swift runner Achilles cannot beat even the slowest tortoise in a race, if he gives the animal a head start, since by the time Achilles reaches the tortoise's starting point, the tortoise will have advanced to a further point, and by the time Achilles reaches that further point, the tortoise will have advance to a yet further point, and so on. As Zeno's example is part of an argument for the impossibility of physical motion, so Carroll's seems an argument for the impossibility of logical motion, so to speak.

Berger (2011b) reports that Kripke in a Princeton seminar on Wittgenstein in the nineteen seventies began with Carroll and Quine's appropriation of Carroll rather as I am doing here. I did not know this when I was writing the first draft of the present chapter, but I am not surprised, since I had inferred from conversations that Kripke had a higher opinion of the closing passages of Quine (1936) than of most other works of that famous philosophical opponent of modal logic. In his Wittgenstein book, however, though Kripke cites other, later work of Quine and of his colleague Nelson Goodman, he does not go into the Carroll–Quine background.

4 Hume has been a favorite writer of Kripke's since his teenage years. Kripke has recently given (2011d) an interesting account of his reaction on first reading, as a high school student in Omaha, one of the most famous passages in Hume's *Treatise of Human Nature*, where he calls into question Descartes' notion of the self.

The comparison of Wittgenstein with Hume startles many, since Hume was a thinker for whose genius (and I fear, even for whose prose style) Wittgenstein had absolutely no appreciation whatsoever. Moreover, Wittgenstein seems to have been one of those by no means rare philosophers for whom the word 'skepticism' conjures up an image, not of a humanistic tradition graced by such figures as Cicero and Montaigne, but rather of a scarecrow held up by Descartes in the first of his Meditations. To take 'skepticism' and 'therapy' to be contrasting approaches is to forget that for Sextus and other ancient skeptics, skepticism was itself a form of what we would call psychotherapy, whose aim is to achieve ataraxia, or imperturbability, by learning to stop wondering and worrying about unanswerable questions.

5   From this point on, 'Wittgenstein' in the text always means 'Wittgenstein according to Kripke.' I would like to but in all honesty cannot quite say that 'Hume' henceforth means 'Hume according to Kripke,' since with Hume I am admittedly extrapolating.

6   Many versions of the *Enquiry* are available in print and online, but the section division is the same in all. The same is true of Kant's *Prolegomena to Any Future Metaphysics*, from which I will be paraphrasing below.

7   As for where these labels come from, the two sections of Hume's discussion of induction are entitled 'Sceptical Doubts concerning the Operations of the Understanding' and 'Sceptical Solution of these Doubts.' An important break in the Wittgenstein material occurs at §201, where the word 'paradox' appears (albeit in reference not so much to what is on Kripke's account the negative phase of the argument, as to the first and most important of three subphases of that phase). Kripke actually uses, like Hume, the Latinized spelling 'sceptical' rather than the now more common 'skeptical' that I am using.

8   Kripke goes overboard at the beginning of chapter 3 of his book, for instance. See Byrne (1996) for a warning against misinterpreting Kripke's real intentions on the strength of such overdramatized passages, and for citation of some Kripke critics, notably Paul Boghossian, whom Byrne seems to take to have made something like this mistake.

9   The latter sense is the one at work throughout Hume's companion *Enquiry*, the *Enquiry Concerning the Principles of Morals*.

10 That evaluation is pursued in Hume's *Dialogues Concerning Natural Religion*, along lines faintly adumbrated in §XI of the *Enquiry*.

11 The problem about other minds is just this: How does one know there *are* any? How do I know that you have one? How do you know that I do? The aim of any interpreter of Wittgenstein on this topic who wishes to have him coming out saying something sensible and on the right track, must be to save him from being some kind of behaviorist, and above all from being committed to anything like the

absurdities in the unintentionally comical book *Dreaming* by his disciple Norman Malcolm, who claims it is a 'conceptual confusion' to offer hypotheses about when during sleep dreaming occurs. I will not express an opinion about how well Kripke succeeds in such a task.

12 Through most of his exposition Kripke emphasizes the case of a *new* addition problem not previously anticipated, and the failure of anything that may previously have been said about addition to determine what is the right answer to the new question. This makes it look as if finiteness considerations are involved in the argument in the following way: There are infinitely many addition problems, and we can have considered only finitely many of them in advance, so there must be ones we have *not* considered in advance.

But in a footnote (his note number 34), Kripke in effect remarks that once one really gets into the spirit of the thing one will see that even if the specific problem '68 + 57' has been previously considered, and even if the answer '125' has been previously given, and even indeed if the explicit instruction, 'If this question is ever asked again, give the same answer,' has been given, yet still and even so a skeptic could raise doubts, when the question comes up again: doubts about what is meant by, or what is the right interpretation of, 'the same.' The real role of finiteness considerations in the argument lies elsewhere, in the rejection as absurd of the notion of an infinite regress of interpretations. Remarks of Mario Gomez-Torrente and Mark Steiner have in different ways convinced me of the need to emphasize Kripke's footnote about these matters.

13 Kripke passes up at this point the opportunity to quote one of the most famous passages in all Hume, about the impossibility of deriving 'ought' from 'is.' I do recall once asking Kripke decades ago about this omission, but for some reason there was not time for him to give a full reply, and I do not trust the accuracy of such recollection as I retain of his partial reply.

14 Kripke quotes at one point from a very famous passage in Wittgenstein, a bit outside the range of material that is officially his central concern. Jones is disposed to give the answer that seems right to him, but as Wittgenstein says (in context, of a somewhat different situation, in §258), 'One would like to say: whatever is going to seem right...is right. And that only means that here we can't talk about "right".'

15 Kripke also says it may be in a sense irrefutable. It has something like the character Hume attributes to Berkeley's arguments against the existence of matter, of admitting no refutation but producing no conviction. Kripke also says that 'if it is taken in an appropriate way Wittgenstein may even accept it,' but I take it that by this Kripke means no more than that Wittgenstein would agree that it *is* a fact that Jones means *plus* by 'plus,' if this assertion is taken in a Ramsey-

style deflated or pleonastic way, and not in a *Tractatus*-style inflated or metaphysical way.

16   Kripke's discussion tends to emphasize assertability conditions rather than applications, though he does acknowledge both. The emphasis on assertability in connection with the proposed new theory of meaning, coupled with his use of 'truth-conditional' in preference to 'fact-picturing' as a label for the rejected old theory of meaning, will tend to remind many readers among professional philosophers and students of philosophy of the 'truth conditions *vs* assertability conditions' or 'Davidson *vs* Dummett' debate that was so prominent in philosophy of language a couple of decades back, around the time Kripke's book appeared. But despite many passages on assertability *vs* truth, it is clear enough from other passages that it is anything but Kripke's intention to turn Ludwig Wittgenstein into Michael Dummett. Above all, the statement that Jones means *plus* by 'plus' is on Kripke's interpretation emphatically not a picture of the fact that Jones has internalized certain assertability conditions, any more than it is a picture of the fact that Jones has internalized certain truth conditions.

17   Mark Steiner has remarked in conversation that for the famous historical Wittgenstein questions about reinforcement and deterrence would have had a special relevance, after his experiences as an elementary school teacher in rewarding Austrian village children for doing their sums right, or much more often, punishing them for doing their sums wrong.

18   Crusoe was once the subject of a debate between the Wittgenstein disciple Rush Rhees and the Wittgenstein critic A. J. Ayer. His case is also, we are told by those who have seen them, a topic taken up by Wittgenstein himself in MS notes toward the *Investigations* that did not find their way into the final version. And Kripke, too, briefly remarks on it (footnotes 84 and 85, page 110, and the accompanying text).
      We easily imagine Crusoe introducing new words into his idiolect for new plants and animals he encounters on his island. We can imagine him seeing seagrapes (*Coccoloba uvifera*) for the first time and calling them 'amblongusses.' But a hasty reading of Kripke on Wittgenstein might suggest a commitment to the claim that, being no longer a member of any speech community, Crusoe cannot mean seagrape by 'amblongus,' and indeed cannot mean anything by anything. Kripke is at some pains to warn that this would be a misreading, though his account of what is supposed to be the correct reading is cryptically brief. If the account that has been given in this chapter is along the right lines, it would appear that the real question for Kripke and his Wittgenstein must be this: What role can the language-game move of asserting such a sentence as 'Crusoe means seagrape by "amblongus"' – or perhaps better, a sentence of which

the quoted one is a subordinate clause – play in our form of life, given that we live in total isolation from Crusoe, and he from us? The answer briefly hinted at by Kripke to such questions – not that he specifically considers my particular formulation as just given – is that taking Crusoe into our community in imagination is involved.

19   While the interpretation of Kripke on Wittgenstein is not nearly as controversial as the interpretation of Wittgenstein himself – few questions in philosophy or history of philosophy are – it is by no means without controversies of its own. For a recent example of how far, given the materials available in print, even sympathetic commentators can differ in their perspectives, compare Steiner (2011) with Wilson (2011).

6 Mind

1   Berger (2011a) contains two invaluable additions to the secondary literature. Shoemaker (2011), on Kripke's anti-physicalism, not only presents relevant views of Kripke's from N&N and elsewhere, but also describes and evaluates any number of responses in the literature. Buechner (2011) discusses Kripke's anti-functionalism in the light of a good deal of unpublished material in which Kripke expands on the key footnote in his Wittgenstein book.

2   The science here may be dubious or out-of-date. My own knowledge is not extensive, but I have been told that C-fibers have more to do with aches than with acute pains. The details don't matter for philosophical purposes.

3   There is said to be a village in the north of Sweden where 40 percent of the population exhibits the dangerous condition of *congenital analgesia*, or inability to feel pain. If wounded, they do not know it until someone tells them, or they notice blood dripping. It may be that to such persons all 'pain' can mean is exhibiting a certain behavioral syndrome they have noticed in about 60 percent of their neighbors. But for anyone who has had the experience of feeling pain, it is very unlikely that anything but that kind of experience would be associated with the word 'pain' as its meaning.

4   For readers new to these topics, the online Stoljar (2009) and Levin (2010) may be consulted for more extensive discussion, from a more sympathetic point of view than mine.

5   One might think that there would be less occasion to want a machine calculating such a function h, but it should be recalled that in the mathematical theory of games the best strategy for a player is often one that includes a random element, so that what the player is going to do cannot always be predicted by the opponent; and hence a function like h might conceivably have some use.

6 If a record of their creator's intentions had not survived, it might be hard to guess what function some of Pascal's machines were designed to calculate. For some of them were set up to do bookkeeping or surveying calculations using obsolete units of money or of length (12 *deniers* to the *sol*, 20 *sols* to the *livre*, or 12 *lignes* to the *pouce*, 12 *pouces* to the *pied*, 6 *pieds* to the *toise*). In the case of the brain, however, it is not that the design is hard to identify, but rather that there simply is no design.

7 Perhaps for many *philosophically unambitious* scientific applications of the simile or metaphor likening the brain to a computer, speaking of program states can be regarded as issuing promissory notes, to the effect that, as our knowledge of the anatomy and physiology of the brain improves, *some* way of construing the brain as an approximate concrete realization of an ideal abstract machine will be found, such that the claims the cognitive scientist is making today will turn out to be true relative to that construal. What the cognitive scientist is doing may then be not all that much different from what Mendel was doing in speaking about 'factors' determining heredity, before anyone knew where to look for an approximate physical realization of the ideal Mendelian model – an approximate physical realization we have since discovered in stretches of DNA. The cognitive scientist's claims, under such a proposal, would then amount to this, that the neuronal correlate of this or that mental state is the physical realization of such-and-such program states *now being posited*, under some appropriate construal *yet to be discovered* of the brain as an approximate realization of the program. It may well be that more than one construal turns out to be possible, but so long as at least one is, the promissory notes can be paid off, and the scientist does not have to declare intellectual bankruptcy.

8 Pain *can* be present, and felt, *though we are not bothered by it*. Certain drugs can produce this effect, and I have experienced it myself. But that is not what is at issue.

9 The full range of writers he has in mind is not made explicit, but I suspect they must include a certain well-known materialist who published a big book with the title *Consciousness Explained*, which many have remarked might more accurately have been entitled *Consciousness Denied*.

Appendix A Models

1 The main subtlety is that one must say, for each of the one-place predicate letters F and G and H, which are the objects that satisfy these predicates at a world w, *even in the case of objects that are not in the domain assigned to w*, and similarly for many-place predicate letters. So it is, in fact, something a little more than a classical model

that one is attaching to each world. This procedure is perhaps most easily made intuitive sense of when applied to temporal rather than modal logic. There the 'possible worlds' are simply *times*, and one world is 'possible relative to' another if it is *later than that other*. The result is that the box and diamond mean something like 'is always going to be' and 'is sometime going to be.' Now if the predicate letter F stands for, say, 'is famous,' of course some things are famous at time t that no longer exist at time t, so the requirement is intuitively not unreasonable that one must specify for every object that is in the domain at any s, and not just those objects that are in the domain at t itself, whether or not it satisfies F at t.

2   In Kripke (1963) there is an semi-intuitive explanation of why Kripke's choice from column (A) is superior to earlier ones but it would take us too deeply into technicalities for me to try to explain it here.

3   As is mentioned in Quine (1986), the present writer in the early 1970s found a similar lacuna in Quine's own adaptation of his axiomatic system to the logic of the empty domain; again it is something Quine would surely have caught himself if he had written out the details of his proposal for publication.

4   There has been some controversy over this matter, amounting at certain times and in certain circles, especially in Scandinavia, to something approaching an organized campaign to have Kripke models renamed. In particular, talk of 'possible worlds semantics' rather than 'Kripke models' has sometimes been, on the part of some who engage in it, a deliberate way of avoiding linking Kripke's name with his models.

5   Goldblatt tells the story in some detail, with references. McKinsey's paper connects modal logics with what are known as Boolean algebras, the Jónsson–Tarski paper connects Boolean algebras with frames; the former paper makes no mention of frames, and the latter no mention of modal logic. Kripke's own comments on this matter tend to emphasize Jónsson and overlook McKinsey. I suspect this is because the McKinsey–Tarski–Lindenbaum result is one of those things that seems obvious *once pointed out*, while this is far from being the case with the Jónsson–Tarski result.

   The principle of natural selection also has this character of seeming obvious once pointed out. Huxley, on hearing of Darwin's theory, is reported to have said, 'How extremely stupid of me not to have thought of that!' though of course it is not that Huxley was stupid, but rather that Darwin was a genius. Perhaps Kripke ought to give McKinsey more credit, especially since more of his own discoveries than perhaps he realizes have this character of seeming obvious once pointed out. That may be part of the reason, alongside his habitual exasperating tardiness about publication, that he has become involved in so many priority disputes. Too many of his contemporaries, lacking Huxley's degree of self-understanding and/or Huxley's degree of integrity, instead of saying, 'I could kick myself for not having seen that; I was so close but missed it!' have instead responded to Kripke's discoveries by saying, 'Hey, I thought of that first!'

6   In particular, the two types of issues are mixed together in a way that makes them almost impossible to separate in Hintikka (1982), a strange – to use no stronger word – paper that has been more influential than it ought to have been.

7   It may be mentioned that Kripke takes back in the addenda (part (a)) of N&N some things he said in passing by way of heuristic motivation in Kripke (1963), giving another indication that he still had not arrived at his mature view when engaged in his technical work.

8   These are the closing words of (Kripke 1976).

Appendix B Truth

1   Philosophers have also debated whether truth is primarily a property of certain linguistic expressions, sentences, or the thoughts these express, propositions. But perhaps not too much is at stake in this debate. For if we take the notion of truth for sentences as primary, we get a derivative notion of truth for propositions: A proposition is true if and only if a sentence expressing it is true. Inversely, if we take the notion of truth for propositions as primary, we get a derivative notion of truth for sentences: A sentence is true if and only if the proposition it expresses is true. The writers with whom I will be concerned in this chapter mainly treat the truth predicate 'is true' as applying primarily to sentences, and I will follow suit.

Now in general a sentence type, or repeatable pattern of utterance, does not have a fixed truth value: 'I love you' may be true or may be false, depending on who is speaking to whom (and when). So strictly speaking it is only sentence tokens, or individual utterances, that the truth predicate applies to. But like the writers with whom I will be concerned (Tarski and Kripke), I will generally ignore problems created by elements such as the pronouns 'I' and 'you' (and the present tense of the verb with its tacit connection to the moment of utterance) that create variation in truth value from token to token of the same type.

2   There are actually two types of 'liars': An *untruth teller* says of itself that it is not true, while a *falsehood-teller* says of itself that it is false, understood as meaning that its negation is true. The example (2) is an untruth teller, as will be all the 'liars' in this chapter.

3   The example (9) is generally attributed to Steve Yablo, and Yablo (1993) is the first explicit version known to me, though such infinite

Notes to pages 160–168

Notes to pages 160–168 201

regresses were key to some of Kripke's unpublished technical results not to be covered here, as reconstructed Burgess (1987).

4 As for how the T-schema is formulated, Tarski allows that the means of mentioning expressions of the object language need not be by quotation, but might be by spelling out or by some other kind of 'structural description.'

5 In what follows, in order avoid a build-up of (different kinds of) quotation marks, I will allow expressions of the object language to designate themselves, as is often done in discussions of this kind.

6 The treatment of quantification is more difficult than the version given here when one does *not* have in the language, for each element of the domain over which one is quantifying, a term of the language having that element as its value, in the way that in the present example we have a numeral for each positive integer. This is where the detour through the auxiliary notion of satisfaction, alluded to in Appendix A, is required.

7 We also need a clause specifying what happens if the value of t is *not* the code number of a sentence of L_0. Presumable $T_0 t$ and $F_0 t$ should both count as false in this case. We could eliminate the need for this clause by using a revised code numbering, less easily described than the one that has been indicated, in which *every* positive integer is the code number of a sentence of L_0.

8 What the sentence A_1 *literally* says is that there exists a positive integer z such that (i) z satisfies a certain condition $B(z)$ that is *arithmetical* in the sense of not involving the truth or falsehood predicates, and (ii) $\sim T_0 z$, where the arithmetical condition $B(z)$ is demonstrably fulfilled by just one number, the code number of A_1 itself. The 'diagonal construction' used to produce A_1 is one of the highlights of the usual proof of the Gödel incompleteness theorems. What Gödel uses the diagonal construction for is to obtain a sentence in effect saying of itself not that it is not *true* but that it is not *provable* in a specified axiomatic system. He then shows this sentence is indeed not provable in the specified axiomatic system, and is therefore a truth not provable in that system, showing the system to be 'incomplete.' Gödel shows that the 'syntactic' property of provability *is* expressible in the language itself, while Tarski shows that the 'semantic' property of truth *is not*. It follows that truth is not the same as provability in the specified axiomatic system, and this *whatever* axiomatic system may have been specified. Among the important contributions of Kripke to logic that are not being covered in this book is a new method of proving Gödel's theorems, along rather different lines.

9 Eventually one gets after $\omega < \omega \cdot 2 < \omega \cdot 3 < \ldots$ a limit $\omega \cdot \omega$ or ω^2, and after $\omega < \omega^2 < \omega^3 < \ldots$ a limit ω^ω, and that's just the beginning. Among the important contributions of Kripke to logic that are not being covered in this book is a theory of computations on such ordinals,

the theory of 'recursion on transfinite ordinals' barely alluded to at the beginning of this appendix.

10   It is a much bigger ordinal than any I have mentioned, including ω^ω in the previous note.

11   Note, however, that T-introduction only tells us that if we are warranted in *categorically asserting* that *p*, then we are warranted in *concluding* that it is true that *p*. It does not tell us that if we merely *assume hypothetically* that *p*, then we are warranted in taking it to *follow* under that hypothesis that it is true that *p*. The difference is subtle, but important. In any derivation of the liar paradox, at least one of T-introduction or T-elimination must be used hypothetically and not just categorically. Kripke's results imply that no contradiction will be forthcoming if they are only used categorically.

12   Kripke's construction, though on a purely technical level it is just one ingenious, philosophically interesting application of a general result about inductive definitions or ordinal computations as developed in mathematical work of Kripke and his successors, is without precursors on the philosophical side. Martin and Woodruff (1975) do obtain a fixed point, but is a *maximal* rather than a *minimal* one, obtained by a 'top down' argument invoking the axiom of choice rather than by a 'bottom up' inductive definition.

Actually, what I have roughly described would be more precisely termed the minimal fixed point on the Kleene strong trivalent scheme. The italicized phrase refers to the particular rules for assigning truth values to negations, junctions, and quantifications, set out as clauses (2)–(4) three sections back. Kripke considers also variations proceeding in different ways, especially the Frege weak trivalent scheme and the Van Fraassen supervaluational scheme.

13   What *A* literally *is*, is a sentence $\exists z(B(z)$ & $\sim Tz)$ where *B* is arithmetical, and where *B*(n) is true if and only if $n = a$. No matter how we begin the construction, at the first step all arithmetical sentences get their usual truth values, so all *B*(n) for $n \neq a$ will be made false. If at the start we put *a* into the extension of T, then at the first step Ta will be made true, and then $\sim$Ta will have to be counted false under our rules for negation. So every conjunction *B*(n) & $\sim$Tn will have to be counted false under our rules for negation, whether *n* is *a* or some other number. So $\exists z(B(z)$ & $\sim Tz)$ will have to be counted false under our rules for existential quantification. So its code number *a*, which we began by putting in the extension of T, will now have to be put in the *anti*-extension of T as well. If at the start we instead put *a* into the anti-extension of T, similar reasoning shows we will soon have to put it into the extension of T.

14   The italicized principle allows us to use T-introduction and T-elimination categorically, but not hypothetically, in the sense explained in an earlier note. Since one is not in a position to assert

(or deny) Goldbach's conjecture, having these rules available for categorical use is not going to be any help in getting to (2).

15 As the contributor of an article (Burgess 2011b) to the anthology (Berger 2011a), I have enjoyed more authorized access to unpublished Kripke materials on the topic of truth than on any other subject, but still there is nothing in anything I have seen that seriously addresses questions like (1).

Bibliography

Works by Saul Kripke

(1959a) 'A Completeness Theorem in Modal Logic,' *Journal of Symbolic Logic* 24: 1–14.

(1959b) 'Semantical Analysis of Modal Logic' (abstract), *Journal of Symbolic Logic* 24: 323–324.

(1963) 'Semantical Considerations on Modal Logic,' *Acta Philosophica Fennica* 16: 83–94.

(1971) 'Identity and Necessity,' in Milton K. Munitz (ed.), *Identity and Individuation*, New York: New York University Press, 161–191, reprinted in (2011a), 1–26.

(1972) 'Naming and Necessity: Lectures Given to the Princeton University Philosophy Colloquium,' in Gilbert Harman and Donald Davidson (eds), *Semantics of Natural Language*, Dordrecht: Reidel, 253–355 and (Addenda) 763–769.

(1975) 'Outline of a Theory of Truth,' *Journal of Philosophy* 72: 690–716, reprinted in (2011a), 75–98.

(1976) 'Is There a Problem about Substitutional Quantification?' in Gareth Evans and John McDowell (eds), *Truth and Meaning*, Oxford: Oxford University Press, 324–419.

(1977) 'Speaker's Reference and Semantic Reference,' in Peter A. French, Theodore E. Uehling, and Howard K. Wettstein (eds), *Studies in the Philosophy of Language*, Minneapolis: University of Minnesota Press, 255–276, reprinted in (2011a), 99–124.

(1979) 'A Puzzle about Belief,' in Avishai Margalit (ed.), *Meaning and Use*, Dordrecht: Reidel, 239–283, reprinted in (2011a), 125–161.

(1980) *Naming and Necessity*, Cambridge: Harvard University Press [reprinting with a new preface of (1972)].

(1982) *Wittgenstein on Rules and Private Language: An Elementary Exposition*, Cambridge: Harvard University Press.

(1986) 'A Problem in the Theory of Reference: the Linguistic Division of Labor and the Social Character of Naming,' in *Philosophy and Culture: Proceedings of the XVIIth World Congress of Philosophy*, Montréal: Éditions du Beffroi / Éditions Montmorency, 241–247.

(2005) 'Russell's Notion of Scope,' *Mind* 114: 1005–1037, reprinted in (2011a), 225–253.

(2008) 'Frege's Theory of Sense and Reference: Some Exegetical Notes,' *Theoria* 74: 181–218, reprinted in (2011a), 254–291.

(2011a) *Philosophical Troubles: Collected Papers, vol. 1*, Oxford: Oxford University Press.

(2011b) 'On Two Paradoxes of Knowledge,' in (2011a), 27–51.

(2011c) 'Vacuous Names and Fictional Entities,' in (2011a), 52–74.

(2011d) 'The First Person,' in (2011a), 292–321.

(2011e) 'Unrestricted Exportation and Some Morals for the Philosophy of Language,' in (2011a), 322–350.

Works by Others

Berger, Alan (2002) *Terms and Truth*, Cambridge: MIT Press.

—— (ed.) (2011a) *Saul Kripke*, Cambridge: Cambridge University Press.

—— (2011b) 'Kripke on the Incoherency of Adopting a Logic,' in Berger (2011a), 177–207.

Buechner, Jeff (2011) 'Not Even Computing Machines Can Follow Rules: Kripke's Critique of Functionalism,' in Berger (2011a), 343–367.

Burgess, Alexis G. and John P. Burgess (2011) *Truth*, Princeton: Princeton University Press.

Burgess, John P. (1987) 'The Truth Is Never Simple,' *Journal of Symbolic Logic* 51: 663–681.

—— (1996) 'Marcus, Kripke, and Names,' *Philsoophical Studies* 84: 1–47.

—— (1998) '*Quinus ab Omni Nævo Vindicatus*,' in Ali A. Kazmi (ed.), *Meaning and Reference: Canadian Journal of Philosophy Supplement* 23: 25–65.

—— (2005) 'Translating Names,' *Analysis* 65: 196–204.

—— (2006) 'Saul Kripke: Naming and Necessity,' in J. Shand (ed.) *Central Works of Philosophy*, vol. 5, Chesham: Acumen, 166–186.

—— (2009) *Philosophical Logic*, Princeton: Princeton University Press.

—— (2011a) 'The Logic of Necessity,' in Leon Horsten and Richard Pettigrew (eds), *The Continuum Companion to Philosophical Logic*, London: Continuum, 299–323.

—— (2011b) 'Kripke Models,' in Berger (2011a), 119–140.

—— (2011c) 'Kripke on Truth,' in Berger (2011a), 141–159.

Byrne, Alex (1996) 'On Misinterpreting Kripke's Wittgenstein,' *Philosophy and Phenomenological Research* 56: 339–343.

Byrne, Alex and James Pryor (2004) 'Bad Intensions,' in Manuel García-Carpintero and Joseph Macià, *Two-Dimensional Semantics*, Oxford: Oxford University Press, 38–54.

Carnap, Rudolf (1947) *Meaning and Necessity: A Study in Semantics and Modal Logic*, Chicago: University of Chicago Press.

Carroll, Lewis (1895) 'What the Tortoise Said to Achilles,' *Mind* 4: 278–280.

Church, Alonzo (1950) Review of Fitch (1949), *Journal of Symbolic Logic* 15: 63.

Copeland, B. J. (2002) 'The Genesis of Possible Worlds Semantics,' *Journal of Philosophical Logic* 31: 99–137.

Donnellan, Keith (1966) 'Reference and Definite Descriptions,' *Philosophical Review* 75: 281–304.

—— (1970) 'Proper Names and Identifying Descriptions,' *Synthese* 21: 335–358.

—— (1979) 'The Contingent a Priori and Rigid Designators,' in Peter A. French, Theodore E. Uehling, and Howard K. Wettstein (eds), *Contemporary Perspectives in the Philosophy of Language*, Minneapolis: University of Minnesota Press, 12–27.

Evans, Gareth (1973) 'The Causal Theory of Names,' *Aristotelian Society Supplement* 47: 187–208.

—— (1982) *The Varieties of Reference* (ed. John McDowell), Oxford: Oxford University Press.

Fine, Kit (1983), 'The Permutation Principle in Quantificational Logic,' *Journal of Philosophical Logic* 12: 33–37.

Fitch, Frederic (1949) 'The Problem of the Morning Star and the Evening Star,' *Philosophy of Science* 16: 137–141.

—— (1950) 'Attribute and Class,' in M. Farber (ed.), *Philosophic Thought in France and the United States*, Buffalo: University of Buffalo Press, 640–647.

Fogelin, Robert J. (1987) *Wittgenstein*, 2nd. ed., London: Routledge.

Føllesdal, Dagfinn (2004) *Referential Opacity and Modal Logic*, London: Routledge.

Frege, Gottlob (1956) 'The Thought: A Logical Inquiry,' trans. Anonymous, *Mind* 65: 289–311.

—— (1967) *Begriffsschrift*: A Formula Language, Modeled upon that of Arithmetic, for Pure Thought, trans. Stefan Bauer-Mengelburg, in Jean van Heijenoort (ed.) *From Frege to Gödel: A Source Book of Mathematical Logic, 1879–1931*, Cambridge: Harvard University Press, 1–82.

—— (1970) (trans. and ed. Peter Geach and Max Black), *Translations from the Philosophical Writings of Gottlob Frege*, Oxford: Basil Blackwell.

Geach, Peter (1969) 'The Perils of Pauline,' *Review of Metaphysics* 23: 287–300.

Goldblatt, Robert (2005) 'Mathematical Modal Logic: A View of its Evolution,' in Dov M. Gabbay and John Woods (eds) *Handbook of the History of Logic*, Amsterdam: Elsevier.

Gomez-Torrente, Mario (2006) 'Rigidity and Essentiality,' *Mind* 115: 227–260.

—— (2011) 'Kripke on Color Words and the Primary/Secondary Quality Distinction,' in Berger (2011a), 290–323.

Hintikka, Jaakko (1963) 'The Modes of Modality,' *Acta Philosophica Fennica* 16: 65–82.

—— (1982) 'Is Alethic Modal Logic Possible?' *Acta Philosophica Fennica* 35: 89–105.

Kanger, Stig (1957) *Provability in Logic*, Stockholm: Almqvist and Wiksell.

Kant, Immanuel (1929) *Critique of Pure Reason* (orig. 1781/87) trans. Norman Kemp-Smith, New York: St Martin's Press.

Kaplan, David (1968) 'Quantifying In,' *Synthese* 19: 178–214.

Kneale, William (1962) 'Modality de dicto and de re,' in Ernest Nagel, Patrick Suppes, and Alfred Tarski (eds), *Logic, Methodology and Philosophy of Science: Proceedings of the 1960 International Congress*, Stanford: Stanford University Press, 622–633.

Levin, Janet (2010) 'Functionalism,' *Stanford Encyclopedia of Philosophy*, http://plato.stanford.edu/archives/sum2010/entries/functionalism/.

Lewis, Clarence Irving and Cooper Harold Langford (1932) *Symbolic Logic*, New York: Century.

Linsky, Bernard (2011) 'Kripke on Proper and General Names,' in Berger (2011a), 17–48.

Marcus, Ruth Barcan (1946) 'A Functional Calculus of First Order Based on Strict Implication,' *Journal of Symbolic Logic* 11: 1–16.

—— (1947) 'The Identity of Individuals in a Strict Functional Calculus of Second Order,' *Journal of Symbolic Logic* 12: 12–15.

—— (1960) 'Extensionality,' *Mind* 69: 55–62.

—— (1961) 'Modalities and Intensional Languages,' *Synthese* 13: 303–322.

—— (1963) 'Attribute and Class in Extended Modal Systems,' *Acta Philosophical Fennica* 16: 123–136.

—— (1974) 'Classes, Collections, and Individuals,' *American Philosophical Quarterly* 11: 227–232.

—— (1993) *Modalities: Philosophical Essays*, Oxford: Oxford University Press.

Marcus, Ruth Barcan, Willard Van Orman Quine, et al. (1962) Discussion of Marcus (1961), *Synthese* 14: 132–143.

Martin, Robert L. and Peter W. Woodruff (1975) 'On Representing "True-in-L" in L,' *Philosophia* 5: 217–221.

Matushansky, Ora (2008) 'On the Linguistic Complexity of Proper Names,' *Linguistics and Philosophy* 21: 573–627.

McKeown-Green, Jonathan (2002) *The Primacy of Public Language*, dissertation, Princeton University.

Mill, John Stuart (1950) (ed. Ernest Nagel) *John Stuart Mill's Philosophy of Scientific Method*, New York: Hafner.

Neale, Stephen (2001) 'No Plagiarism Here!' *Times Literary Supplement*, February 9, 2011, 12–23.

Palmer, Frank R. (1986) *Mood and Modality*, 2nd ed., Cambridge: Cambridge University Press.

Prior, Arthur N. (1956) 'Modality and Quantification in S5,' *Journal of Symbolic Logic*, 21: 60–62.

—— (1963) 'Is the Concept of Referential Opacity Really Necessary?' *Acta Philosophical Fennica* 16: 189–199.

Putnam, Hilary (1973) 'Meaning and Reference,' *Journal of Philosophy* 19: 699–711.

Quine, Willard Van Orman (1936) 'Truth by Convention,' in O. H. Lee (ed.), *Philosophical Essays for A. N. Whitehead*, New York: Longmans, 90–124.

—— (1947) 'The Problem of Interpreting Modal Logic,' *Journal of Symbolic Logic* 12: 43–48.

—— (1953) 'Three Grades of Modal Involvement,' *Proceedings of the VIth International Congress of Philosophy*, Amsterdam: North Holland, 14: 65–81.

—— (1956) 'Quantifiers and Propositional Attitudes,' *Journal of Philosophy* 53: 177–187.

—— (1961), 'Reply to Professor Marcus,' *Synthese* 13: 323–330.

—— (1986) 'Autobiography,' in Lewis Edwin Hahn and Paul Arthur Schilpp (eds) *The Philosophy of W. V. Quine* (Library of Living Philosophers, vol. XVIII), LaSalle: Open Court, 1–46.

Richard, Mark (2011) 'Kripke's Puzzle about Belief,' in Berger (2011a), 211–234.

Russell, Bertrand (1985) (ed. David Pears) *The Philosophy of Logical Atomism*, LaSalle: Open Court.

Salmon, Nathan (1981) *Reference and Essence*, Princeton: Princeton University Press.

—— (1986) *Frege's Puzzle*, 2nd. ed., Atacadero: Ridgeview.

—— (2011a) 'Fiction, Myth, and Reality,' in Berger (2011a), 49–77.

—— (2011b) 'A Note on Kripke's Puzzle about Belief,' in Berger (2011a), 235–252.

Searle, John (1958) 'Proper Names,' *Mind* 67: 166–173.

—— (1967) 'Proper Names and Descriptions,' in Paul Weiss (ed.) *Encyclopedia of Philosophy*, New York: MacMillan, 487–491.

Shoemaker, Sydney (2011) 'Kripke and Cartesianism,' in Berger (2011a), 327–342.

Smullyan, Arthur (1947) Review of Quine (1947), *Journal of Symbolic Logic* 12: 139–141.

Soames, Scott (1991) *Understanding Truth*, Oxford: Oxford University Press.

—— (2002) *Beyond Rigidity: The Unfinished Agenda of 'Naming and Necessity,'* Oxford: Oxford University Press.

—— (2003) *Philosophical Analysis in the Twentieth Century*, (vol. 1 *The Dawn of Analysis* and vol. 2 *The Age of Meaning*), Princeton: Princeton University Press.

—— (2005), *Reference and Description: The Case against Two-Dimensionalism*, Princeton: Princeton University Press.

—— (2011) 'Kripke on Epistemic and Metaphysical Possibility: Two Routes to the Necessary A Posteriori,' in Berger (2011a), 78–99.

Stoljar, Daniel (2009) 'Physicalism,' *Stanford Encyclopedia of Philosophy*, http://plato.stanford.edu/archives/fall2009/entries/physicalism/.

Strawson, Peter F. (1959) *Individuals*, London: Methuen.

Tarski, Alfred (1935) 'Der Wahrheitsbegriff in den formalisierten Sprachen,' *Studia Philosophica* 1: 261–405; trans. 'The Concept of Truth in Formalized Languages,' in Tarski (1956), 152–278.

—— (1956) (ed. J. H. Woodger) *Logic, Semantics, Metamathematics: Papers from 1923 to 1938*, Oxford: Clarendon Press.

Van Inwagen, Peter (1977) 'Creatures of Fiction,' *American Philosophical Quarterly*, 14: 299–308.

Wehmeier, Kai (2005) 'Modality, Mood, and Descriptions,' in Reinhard Kahle (ed.) *Intensionality: An Interdisciplinary Discussion*, Wellesley: A. K. Peters, 187–216.

Wilson, George (2011) 'On the Skepticism about Rule-Following in Kripke's Version of Wittgenstein,' in Berger (2011a), 253–289.

Wittgenstein, Ludwig (1921/1922) *Tractatus Logico-Philosophicus*, trans. C. K. Ogden, London: Kegan Paul.

—— (1953) *Philosophical Investigations*, trans. G. E. M. Anscombe, New York: MacMillan.

Yablo, Stephen (1993) 'Paradox without Self-Reference,' *Analysis* 53: 251–252.

Ziff, Paul (1960) *Semantic Analysis*, Ithaca: Cornell University Press.

Index

Index   219